W9-CNY-030

COMPUTER SIMULATION OF PERSONALITY

Frontier of Psychological Theory

EDITED BY

SILVAN S. TOMKINS
Princeton University

and

SAMUEL MESSICK
Educational Testing Service

COMPUTER SIMULATION OF PERSONALITY

Frontier of Psychological Theory

John Wiley and Sons, Inc.
New York • London

LIBRARY OF CONGRESS CATALOGUE CARD NUMBER: *62-22072*

PRINTED IN THE UNITED STATES OF AMERICA

PREFACE

This book consists of the papers and the formal discussions of these papers presented at a conference on computer simulation and personality theory held at Educational Testing Service and Princeton University in June 1962.

It was our purpose in holding this conference, first, to accelerate the dissemination of information concerning computer simulation among investigators in the field of personality. To this end, the majority of the conference participants were personality theorists whose knowledge of the computer was minimal but who nonetheless welcomed an opportunity to become acquainted with recent developments in the computer field. It is a tribute to the resiliency and the catholicity of interest of investigators already otherwise deeply committed in the field of personality, that almost all of those invited responded with enthusiasm and devoted the better part of a week to expose themselves to a new field which might, or might not, prove profitable for them.

Second, we hoped to achieve some evaluation of the potential of computer simulation for the field of personality. We thought that the optimal strategy here would be the confrontation of that relatively small group whose expertise embraces both fields by that much larger group whose competence lies in personality theory and investigation. We envisioned this meeting not as a computer conference per se but rather as an opportunity for personality investigators to assess and evaluate the potential of the computer for their field and perhaps for them to extend a tender shoot into new soil.

The vitality and excitement of the conference depended not only upon the speakers and their formal discussants but also upon the skillful direction of the chairmen:

Robert R. Holt, New York University
John L. Kennedy, Princeton University
Robert Leeper, University of Oregon and
Benjamin B. Wolman, Albert Einstein College of Medicine,

and upon the spontaneous and enthusiastic interchanges between all of these and the other invited participants:

Irving Alexander, National Institute of Mental Health
Harold Basowitz, National Institute of Mental Health
Arthur Couch, Harvard University
Edward Engel, College of Medicine, State University of New York, Syracuse
Howard Hoffman, Pennsylvania State University
James C. Lingoes, University of Michigan
Perry London, University of Illinois
Walter S. Neff, New York University and
Warren T. Norman, University of Michigan,

as well as upon the members of the Research Division of Educational Testing Service and of the Psychology Department of Princeton University.

In our effort to publish the proceedings quickly to capitalize upon the timeliness of the remarks, we unfortunately omitted from this volume a few of the formal discussions presented at the conference. This was necessitated by such contingencies as prior commitments to travel abroad or to teach summer sessions at other universities which prevented some of the discussants from preparing their comments for publication before the book went to press.

We are indebted to Educational Testing Service and to the Psychology Department of Princeton University for their joint, generous sponsorship of this conference. We are especially indebted to William W. Turnbull of Educational Testing Service for his encouraging support and suggestions in the initiation of the conference. We also wish to acknowledge support from a training grant by the National Institute of Mental Health (Grant No. 2M-9453) which assisted in financing the proceedings. We would also like to thank the Center for Advanced Study in the Behavioral Sciences for providing office space and facilities for the editors. We are grateful to Mrs. Sally Matlack of Educational Testing Service for her invaluable help in arranging and scheduling the conference and to both Mrs. Matlack and Mrs. Ann King for their assistance in the preparation of this volume.

Silvan S. Tomkins
Samuel Messick

Center for Advanced Study in the
Behavioral Sciences, 1962.

CONTENTS

PART III: COGNITION AND AFFECT

PART IV: RÉSUMÉ

PROGRAM

PRINCETON, N.J. JUNE 13-15, 1962

Computer Simulation:

Frontier of Personality Theory

WEDNESDAY, JUNE 13

Introduction and General Problems

9:00 A.M. - 12:00

Chairman: SAMUEL MESSICK
Educational Testing Service

SILVAN S. TOMKINS
Princeton University

"Simulation of Personality: The Interrelationships Between Affect, Memory, Thinking, Perception, and Action."

Discussants:

DONALD W. MACKINNON
Institute of Personality Assessment and Research, University of California, Berkeley.

ERNEST R. HILGARD
Stanford University

2:00 - 4:30 P.M.

Chairman: ROBERT LEEPER
University of Oregon

WALTER R. REITMAN
Carnegie Institute of Technology

"Personality As a Problem-Solving Coalition."

Discussants:

DOUGLAS N. JACKSON
Pennsylvania State University

MILTON J. ROSENBERG
Ohio State University

THURSDAY, JUNE 14

Psychoanalytic Theory

9:00 A.M. - 12:00

Chairman: JOHN L. KENNEDY
Princeton University

GERALD S. BLUM
University of Michigan

"Programming People to Simulate Machines."

Discussants:

JACK BLOCK
University of California, Berkeley

JOSEPH H. HANDLON
Stanford University Medical School

2:00 - 4:30 P.M.

Chairman: ROBERT R. HOLT
New York University

KENNETH M. COLBY
Center for Advanced Study in the Behavioral Sciences

"Simulation of a Neurotic Process."

Discussants:

O. HOBART MOWRER
University of Illinois

JEROME L. SINGER
Institute for Psychological Research, Teachers College, Columbia University

FRIDAY, JUNE 15

Cognition and Affect

9:00 A.M. - 12:30 P.M.

Chairman: BENJAMIN B. WOLMAN
Albert Einstein College of Medicine

JOHN C. LOEHLIN
University of Nebraska
"A Computer Program That Simulates Personality."

Discussants:

WAYNE H. HOLTZMAN
University of Texas

GEORGE A. KELLY
Ohio State University

LEONARD UHR
Mental Health Research Institute, University of Michigan
"The Development of Perception and Language: Simulated Models."

Discussants:

JEROME KAGAN
Fels Research Institute, Yellow Springs, Ohio

WILLIAM KESSEN
Yale University

2:30 - 5:00 P.M.

Chairman: SILVAN S. TOMKINS
Princeton University

ROBERT P. ABELSON
Yale University
"Cognition and Affect: Simulation of Rationalization."

Discussants:

DAVID L. ROSENHAN
University of Pennsylvania

MICHAEL A. WALLACH
Massachusetts Institute of Technology

Resumé:

SAMUEL MESSICK
Educational Testing Service

PART I

INTRODUCTION AND GENERAL PROBLEMS

1

SILVAN S. TOMKINS
Princeton University

Simulation of Personality: The Interrelationships Between Affect, Memory, Thinking, Perception, and Action

Many years ago, in the late 1930's, I was seized with the fantasy of a machine, fearfully and wonderfully made in the image of man. He was to be no less human than auto-mated, so I called him the humanomaton. Could one design a truly humanoid machine? This would either expose the ignorance or reveal the self-consciousness of his creator or both.

Such an exercise can be as exciting as it is instructive if it is undertaken in the spirit of play. At the worst it is a harmless conceit. But excitement and the delight of play are not the only affects evoked by such a fantasy, and it would be well at the outset of a conference on computer simulation to recognize the full spectrum of human responses to the idea of man creating a machine in his own image.

The machine itself, apart from the machina ad hominem, has evoked every variety of human response. It has seemed benign as well as malignant, as often an object of indifference as an object of pride, the servant of man and sometimes his master, stupid or clever, dynamic as well as static. There have been as many images of the machine as of the gods. It is because the machine lends itself to such idealization that the relation between man and machine becomes electric when man takes himself as a model for a machine to be built in his own image.

Feelings towards the machine, already somewhat heated, become incandescent when man himself is to be explicitly exteriorized in a machine. Those who can love and worship only a machine, because they are as alienated from themselves as they are from others, regard the simulation of the human being as fully as absurd and repellent as they would putting feathers on a jet plane in order to simulate a bird. For these individuals the power and beauty of the machine would only be desecrated by modelling it after its creator. For these, man attains his highest reach in and through the machine, whose competence exceeds the intelligence of man as a steam shovel exceeds the muscular power of a human being, they suppose. The machine is also preferred by many of those who have been given an ineradicable sense of their own unworthiness as well as by those who are alienated from their own feelings and from rewarding affective interaction with others. The comparison between man and the machine is for them an invidious one, to the disadvantage of man, and so to them also the idea of simulation is entirely unappealing.

A second ground for a rejection of simulation is the assumption of the machine's inherent inferiority rather than its superiority. For these, the machine is necessarily a senseless, thoughtless, feelingless, unconscious, mechanical servant of man, which it is absurd to dignify with even the possibility of intelligence, let alone personality. For these, the comparison is also an invidious one, but to the disadvantage of the machine rather than to the disadvantage of man. For some, this rejection is based on alienation of the individual from that part of nature which is impersonal. Just as some love the machine because they may not love man, so there are some who may love only man, and who hate and fear the machine because they may not love anything which will not respond in kind. Still others exaggerate its superiority over man—because of an ineradicable sense of their own unworthiness. In this latter case, the self is elevated not by identification with a superior but by exaggerated differentiation from whatever seems inferior.

The same essential dynamic generates a third ground for the rejection of computer simulation of the human being. Here the concern is lest man be degraded not by too close identification with an inferior mechanism, but by domination, enslavement, or, at the least, invidious comparison with a superior entity with which man cannot compete. In contrast to those who reject simulation because man is assuredly no model worthy of simulation, these reject simulation because they love man and wish to protect him from an unequal and unfair competition. The comparison is invidious but regrettable. Rather than pride in the externalization of man's intelligence in the machine, they are concerned lest the image of man be irreparably tarnished by the machine's superiority. The individual who is truly prejudiced against the machine in favor of man will often oscillate between the contradictory prejudices that the simulation of man by the machine will degrade man by virtue of the inferiority of the machine, but also that the machine may subdue and enslave man. When both of these arguments are affirmed by the same person it is likely that the threshold for shame and invidious comparison is low and diffuse.

The fourth ground for the rejection of computer simulation of man is as old as Judaism and Christianity. Building a machine in the image of man is a pretentious aspiration and not without the dangers which first attended the loss of innocence.

Neither the Old nor the New Testaments are indifferent to overweening pride. To eat of the fruit of the tree of knowledge is to aspire to God's omniscience, to invoke His wrath and to be thrust out of the Garden of Eden, to work thenceforth by the sweat of one's brow. The Devil has always been a projection of a projection—God in Man, his childish guilty yearning after omniscience and omnipotence. Man wishes to be God, but he has never been altogether sure that God would have it so. The Angel with the flaming sword may yet appear at this conference enjoining us to study man as he exists here and now, by the sweat of our brow, and to leave unto God the things that are God's—the creation of man. There can be little doubt that the presumption which inspirits the idea of the computer simulation of man seems arrogant and vainglorious and therefore, to some, full of peril.

We may expect then that computer simulation will evoke not only delight and excitement, but also contempt and shame, anxiety and anger.

If one is to be at home with the computer one must regard human beings as worthy of simulation, and sufficiently worthy that there arises no invidious comparison with the machine to the disadvantage of man, nor invidious comparison with man to the disadvantage of the machine. He must not identify so closely with early models of computers that he becomes ashamed because he created them in his own image. He must in short neither derogate nor idealize himself or the computer. Finally, he must be a presumptuous risk-taker, bold and perhaps arrogant.

Computer simulation has attracted and will continue to attract strange bedfellows—psychoanalysts, Pavlovians, psychometricians, clinical psychologists, philosophers, engineers, mathematicians. One should forget neither that they are strange nor that they are bedfellows. They are strange bedfellows not only because they come from different fields, but even when they come from the same field they may be attracted to the computer for very different reasons. The computer offers not only much promise but also many different promises.

It enables one to deal with organized complexity, and so it recommends itself to all who object to the varieties of impoverishment of science which have been recommended in the name of method, cleanliness, rigor, and empiricism. It is a complexity amplifier as the microscope was a space amplifier. Its increment of transformability of concepts is of the same order of magnitude as that of arabic numerals over Roman numerals.

Like any good method it is conceptually neutral. It has no hidden built-in biases nor constraints. It does not favor one type of theory over another, nor one aspect of personality over another, and so it will lend itself to the preservation of the competition of ideas which is the lifeblood of science.

It places a premium on creative, constructive thought. The computer is not only neutral, it is deaf, dumb and inert, a tabula rasa whose passivity cries out for the activity of the programmer. Contrary to methods such as projective techniques and factor analysis, such inertness of the computer will serve to inhibit malignant data growth which is uninformed by prior ideation.

It places a premium on clarity. The computer is sufficiently concrete minded, sufficiently moronic, so that the theorist must be meticulous, certain and detailed in how he instructs the computer, whose favorite response seems to be "huh?"

Finally, it is a method par excellence of testing ideas—a psychic wind tunnel in which the overly pretentious, the flimsy, the unbalanced, the clumsy, airy abstractions of the personality theorist can be subjected to stresses of any desired degree of severity.

This combination of characteristics makes the computer a method of extraordinary promise. Not only will it permit the exploration of organized complexity, of the personality structure within, in a social field of equally complex structure, both of which may be simulated to change over time, but it demands conjointly creativity, clarity, and confirmation through test. Finally, by being conceptually neutral it both permits and encourages extreme partisanship and competition between alternative theories and theorists.

This is the promise of computer simulation. Can the promise be subverted? It can, it is, and it will be again unless we take the idea of simulation literally. Many years ago Zipf (1949) described a phenomenon which must be resisted if we are to maximize the yield of this method. This was the tendency of jobs to be adapted to tools, rather than adapting tools to jobs. If one has a hammer one tends to look for nails, and if one has a computer with a storage capacity, but no feelings, one is more likely to concern oneself with remembering and with problem solving than with loving and hating.

The central problem for computer simulation of personality is what shall we try to simulate? Consider the problem in other domains. A ship model need not be the same size as the ship it simulates so long as the relative spatial relationships are preserved. A model airplane to be useful for aerodynamic engineering does not need to have the same color as a real airplane. For many purposes we must distinguish sharply those characteristics which are essential for simulation from those which are trivial, either for theory or for practice. But if the color and size of a model are trivial characteristics of a ship or an airplane, they need not be for the simulation of a human being. Possessing a dark skin or being 8 or 4 feet tall can and does make a great deal of difference for the Negro, for a giant or a Pygmy. Should our computer be equipped with eyes, ears and nose? Should he be astigmatic and require a correction? Should he have pain receptors? Should he get hungry and thirsty? Should he be bright or dull, more or less active or phlegmatic? Should he require sleep? Should he need the company of other computers? Should he be distractible? Should he be able to move in space and at what speed? Should he get tired, out of breath? Should his physical condition vary? Should he be mortal? In short how much of a human being should he be if we are to take the idea of simulation seriously?

The problem is a serious one, but also something of a pseudo-problem, because simulation per se should not be the primary criterion for evaluating a computer model. One does not require that a personality theory account for all personality phenomena so long as its power is sufficient to account for some, with sufficient economy of assumption. Similarly, computer simulation must be judged not by its resemblance to human beings, but by its conjoint economy, explanatory, and predictive power.

A computer simulation of personality, then, should include and exclude the same parameters as any other general theory of personality. It is a language and a method whereby a theory can be expressed, as mathematics is a language and a method of expressing theory. This method, like mathematics, can never provide more than the medium for the expression and testing of the basic theory of any domain. It is a vehicle for, and not a substitute for, ideas of the nature of personality.

Let us turn then to our topic proper—the nature of the human being. How should a computer be built and how programmed if it is to bear a reasonable resemblance to the critical characteristics of a human being? We will present the general outlines of a model of the human being which was constructed with one eye on the human being and the other on the automata. This may be the best way to bring neither image into focus and the resultant may please neither personality theorists nor automata specialists. It is in no sense a complete blueprint for the construction of a humanomaton, nor a specific program which might be standard equipment for such a creature. I have thought it appropriate to pay much more attention to the human being than to the problem of the design of automata, but I have also tried to look at the human being through the eyes of an engineer whose job it was to duplicate the mechanism.

We conceive of the human being as governed by a set of mechanisms which are from moment to moment not only in competition with each other, but are also relatively independent of each other, as well as somewhat dependent on each other. Such organized programs as are inherited govern at best only small sectors, in fits and starts. The whole human being seems at the outset more fearfully than wonderfully made. Indeed, were it not for the concern of his parents, the neonate would not be viable. It is difficult to exaggerate his incompetence.

An infant may cry because he has gas, and stop crying after he has been burped, without awareness of cause, or control of it, without awareness of the possibility of remedial action, without taking such action or even awareness of what the critical action was which relieved both his pain and his crying.

How then should one devise the humanomaton? He must, first of all, be equipped to function with much less certainty than our present automata. He would require a relatively helpless infancy followed by a growing competence through his childhood and adolescence. In short, he would require time in which to learn to learn through making errors and correcting them. This much is clear and is one of the reasons for the limitations of our present automata. Their creators seem temperamentally unsuited to create and nurture mechanisms which begin in helplessness, confusion, and error. The automaton designer is an overprotective, overdemanding parent who is too pleased with precocity in his creations. As soon as he has been able to translate a human achievement into steel, tape, and electricity, he is delighted with the performance of his brain child. Such precocity essentially guarantees a low ceiling to the learning ability of his automaton, despite the magnitude of information incorporated in its design and performance. A more patient designer would suffer through the painful steps which are required to nurture the learning capacities of the machine.

But a critical feature entirely absent today must be introduced. The automaton must be motivated. It must be equipped with a drive signal system which tells it when it is running out of cards, oil, and electricity, and it must be motivated to store energy as it now stores information. It must also be motivated to reproduce itself. Türing, being a logician, understandably limited the problem of self-reproduction to asexual techniques, but if we are interested in the problem of human simulation, the race of automata must be perpetuated not only by knowledge but by passion. Further, the humanomaton must have pain receptors which defend its integrity from overzealous investigators who would run it too long and too continuously. This is not to say that there is a "rule" in its program that it is to shut off after so many hours of continuous use. Rather, the humanomaton must be equipped with receptors which are activated by a variety of noxious conditions, which in turn produce messages possessing priority over the ongoing program and which will prompt both programmed (reflex) responses to the pain and, more general, instrumental responses if the former should not succeed in turning off the pain messages.

The possession of such a drive system, however, would not per se radically increase the complexity of this automaton over contemporary models. A lively concern for its own integrity and reproduction is after all characteristic of the simplest forms of life.

What more than the primary drives for alternating current and IBM cards is called for if he is to be a humanomaton and not just another automaton? At this point we must know what humans want. If we turn to the history of this inquiry, we find that the philosopher, the theologian, the artist, and the jurist precede the psychologist by centuries and that, until recently, the psychologist's view of the nature of human motivation departed in no essential way from the conception of the philosophers or of Everyman. From Plato through Freud man has been conceived to be motivated by his biological "drives." The clarity and urgency of the state of hunger provided the basic paradigm that captured the imagination of all theorists. Protests against this paradigm have been perennial, but none of its competitors have had its hardiness.

We will argue that there is a radical error in this argument for the primacy and urgency of drives as motives. Consider the need for air. One has only, it would seem, to interrupt momentarily the inspiration of air by cupping one's hand over the mouth and nostrils of anyone to create immediately the most urgent gasping for breath. And yet what we are primarily observing is not the drive for air, but the rapidly mounting panic which is ordinarily recruited as an amplifier of a drive signal whose strength we misidentify with the concomitant affect. That the drive signal itself is not necessarily either strong or urgent unless appropriately amplified can be seen if we examine the consequences of anoxic deprivation at 35,000 feet when pilots in the last war refused to wear their oxygen masks. Rather than panic, it was euphoria which was activated by the more gradual anoxic deprivation and some of these men died with a smile on their lips.

Consider next that most imperious, not to be denied, most primary of drives—sex. The tumescent sexual organ is the site of sexual pleasure but not of excitement. One is excited and breathes hard in the chest, the oesophagus, the face, and in the nose and nostrils. Sexual pleasure is ordinarily as amplified by excitement as anoxia is amplified by panic. The sexual drive is, however, notoriously vulnerable to attenuation if the affect of excitement is inhibited or if sexuality recruits fear or shame or anger rather than excitement. The central role of affect in human sexuality is revealed by those types of disturbance in which the sex drive per se is unimpaired, and there is sexual pleasure, but no satisfaction either because of a decrement in the affect of excitement, by repeated intercourse with the same person, or a decrement in the affect of enjoyment because of hostility or shame in the interpersonal relationship. Inappropriate affect not only can rob sexual pleasure of the necessary amplification, but it can also readily interfere sufficiently with the sex drive itself so that there is impotence or frigidity.

The relationship which we have postulated between the drive system and the affect system must also be postulated between both of these and the nonspecific amplifying systems, such as the reticular formation. This and other amplifier circuits serve both motivational and nonmotivational systems. The words activation and arousal have tended to confound the distinction between the added intensity from amplification of any kind of message, as, for example, of neural transmissions over the visual pathways, and the added intensity from affective responses per se.

Amplification is the preferable, more generic term. The terms activation and arousal should be abandoned because of their affective connotations. We need a term which will describe equally well the increase or decrease in gain for any and every kind of message or structure.

If the drives have insufficient strength as motives without concurrent amplification by the affects and the nonspecific amplifiers, they nonetheless play a critical role as sources of information—vital information without which the human being could not live. The basic nature of this information is of time, of place, and of response—where and when to do what when the body does not know how to otherwise help itself. When the drive signal is activated it tells a very specific story—that the "problem" is in the mouth in the case of hunger, farther back in the throat in thirst, in the finger or wherever we have hurt ourselves in the case of pain, in the nose and throat and chest if it is an oxygen drive, in the urethra if it is the urination drive, at the anal sphincter if it is the defecation drive. In learning experiments we have been concerned primarily with the drive as a motivator of instrumental learning, assuming that the animal knew how to consummate the drive when he found the reward. He does know how, but for a very special reason—this information has been built into the site of consummation so the probability of finding the correct consummatory response is very high.

Let us suppose that the hunger drive were rewired to be localized in the palm of the hand or the urethra. In the former case the individual would first open and close his hand to relieve his hunger. When this did not work he might reach for a wide variety of "objects" as possible satisfiers, cupping and rubbing his hand over this potential food. If the signals were delivered to the urethra, he might first release the urethra and urinate to relieve his hunger. If this did not relieve it, he might use his hands to find objects which might be put inside the urethra. This brings us to the second informational characteristic of the drive signal system, in reference to the consummatory response. A large safety factor has been included in this design. Not only does it tell us where we must concern ourselves, but also when we must start and stop consummatory activity. We become hungry long before our tissues are in an emergency state of deficit and we stop eating, due to satiety, long before the tissue deficit has been remedied. Such specificity of information of time and place of the drive system, critical though it is for the viability of the human being, is, nevertheless, a limitation on its general significance for the human being.

It is the affects rather than the drives which are the primary human motives. First, the affects constitute the primary motivational system not only because the drives necessarily require amplification from the affects, but because the affects are sufficient motivators in the absence of drives. One may be sexually excited. Indeed, one must be excited to enjoy the sexual drive, but one need not be sexually aroused to be excited. One can be excited about anything under the sun. Second, in contrast to the specificity of the space-time information of the drive system, the affect system has those more general properties which permit it to assume a central position in the motivation of man. Thus, the affect system has generality of time rather than the rhythmic specificity of the drive system. Because the drive system is essentially a transport system, taking material in and out of the body, it must impose its specific temporal rhythms. But the affect system is under no such constraint. One can be anxious for just a moment or for half an hour, or for a day, or for a month, or for a year, or a decade, or a lifetime, or never, or only occasionally now though much more frequently some time ago, in childhood, but not as an adult, or conversely. The affect system permits generality not only of time, but of intensity. I can feel strongly about this and weakly about that. It also permits generality of density of affect investment. I can feel strongly about something for a little while, or less intensely for a longer while, or very intensely all my life. Thus, affects are capable of both insatiability and finickiness as well as extreme lability.

Feedback and affect are two distinct mechanisms which may operate independent of each other. The infant passively enjoys or suffers the experience of his own affective responses long before he is capable of employing a feedback mechanism in instrumental behavior. He does not know "why" he is crying, that it might be stopped, or how to stop it. Even many years later he will sometimes experience passively, without knowledge of why or thought of remedial action, deep and intense objectless despair. Without initial awareness that there might be a specific cause that turns affect on and a specific condition which might turn it off, there is only a remote probability of using his primitive capacities to search for and find these causal conditions. The affect system will remain independent of the feedback system until the infant discovers that something can be done about such vital matters. Even after he has made this discovery it will be some time before he has achieved any degree of control over the appearance and disappearance of his affective responses. Indeed, most human beings never attain great precision of control of their affects. The individual may or may not correctly identify the "cause" of his fear or joy and may or may not learn to reduce his fear, or maintain or recapture his joy.

We have stressed the ambiguity and blindness of this primary motivational system to accentuate what we take to be the necessary price which must be paid by any system which is to spend its major energies in a sea of risk, learning by making errors. The achievement of cognitive power and precision requires a motivational system no less plastic. Cognitive strides are limited by the motives which urge them. Cognitive error can be made only by one capable of committing motivational error, i.e., being wrong about his own wishes—their causes and outcomes.

The creation of a humanomaton would require an affect system. What does this mean in terms of a specific program? There must be built into such a machine a number of responses which have self-rewarding and self-punishing characteristics. This means that these responses are inherently acceptable or inherently unacceptable. These are essentially aesthetic characteristics of the affective responses—and in one sense no further reducible. Just as the experience of redness could not be further described to a color-blind man, so the particular qualities of excitement, joy, fear, sadness, shame, and anger cannot be further described if one is missing the necessary effector and receptor apparatus. This is not to say that the physical properties of the stimuli and the receptors cannot be further analyzed. This analysis is without limit. It is rather the phenomenological quality which, we are urging, has intrinsic rewarding or punishing characteristics. If and when the humanomaton learns English, we would require a spontaneous reaction to joy or excitement of the sort "I like this," and to fear and shame and distress, "Whatever this is, I don't care for it." We cannot define this quality in terms of the instrumental behavioral responses to it, since it is the gap between these responses and instrumental responses which is necessary if the affective response is to function like a human motivational response. There must be introduced into the machine a critical gap between the conditions which instigate the self-rewarding or self-punishing responses, which maintain them, which turn them off, and the "knowledge" of these conditions, and the further response to the knowledge of these conditions. The machine intially would know only that it liked some of its own responses and disliked some of its own responses but not that they might be turned on, or off, and not how to turn them on, or off, or up, or down in intensity. The circuitry of combined central assemblies and storage would be so constructed that there was a high probability that these responses would slowly become the target of the assemblies operating on the feedback principle. The humanomaton then would begin to examine ways and means of maximizing its own self-rewarding responses and minimizing its own self-punishing responses. The designer of the machine could bias it in any set of directions he chose by the circuitry which activated, maintained and reduced these built-in, self-rewarding, and self-punishing responses. He could interest the machine in its own self-preservation if, whenever a threat to the integrity of the machine impinged on its receptors, the self-punishing responses were activated. He could interest the machine in learning something of the structure of its environment by connecting a self-rewarding response to an optimal rate of change of information transmitted over its nervous system and a self-punishing response to any rate of change outside of the positive spectrum, defining the optimal rate of change as that for which the machine at that time had optimal scanning, transformation, and storage mechanisms.

He could interest such a machine in other machines like itself by connecting special self-rewarding responses, such as the smile, to the reception of messages which indicated the presence of machines like himself.

Such automata would be much more interesting than our present computers, but they would also have certain disadvantages. They would be capable of not computing for the designer for long periods of time when other computers were sending to them, when they were afraid of overly severe fluctuations in their sources of electricity, and when having tried unsuccessfully to solve then insoluble problems, they became depressed, or manic with overweening false confidence. They would, in short, represent not the disembodied intelligence of an auxiliary brain, but a mechanical intelligence intimately wed to the automaton's own complex purposes. The fragmentation and amplification of man's capacities by automata has been the rule—the microscope was a visual amplifier, the radio a speech and hearing amplifier, the steam shovel a muscle power amplifier, and the computer an intelligence amplifier. The next and the final development of simulation would be an integrated humanomaton—with lenses and ears, with powered arms and legs, with a complex feedback circuitry powered by a generalizing intelligence obeying equally general motives having the characteristics of human affects. Societies of such automata would reproduce and care for the young automata. How friendly or hostile to man they might become would depend on the design of the relative thresholds of these two affects and the conditions under which their circuitry was activated.

If the affects are our primary motives, what are they and where are they? Affects are sets of muscle and glandular responses located in the face and also widely distributed through the body, which generate sensory feedback which is either inherently "acceptable" or "unacceptable." These organized sets of responses are triggered at subcortical centers where specific "programs" for each distinct affect are stored. These programs are innately endowed and have been genetically inherited. They are capable, when activated, of simultaneously capturing such widely distributed organs as the face, the heart, and the endocrines and imposing on them a specific pattern of correlated responses. One does not learn to be afraid, or to cry, or to startle, any more than one learns to feel pain or to gasp for air.

Most contemporary investigators have pursued the inner bodily responses, after the James-Lange theory focused attention on their significance. Important as these undoubtedly are, we regard them as of secondary importance to the expression of emotion through the face. We regard the relationship between the face and the viscera as analogous to that between the fingers and forearm, upper arm, shoulders, and body. The fingers do not "express" what is in the forearm, or shoulder, or trunk. They rather lead than follow the movements in these organs to which they are an extension. Just as the fingers respond both more rapidly and with more precision and complexity than the grosser and slower moving arm to which it is attached, so the face expresses affect, both to others and to the self via feedback, which it more rapid and more complex than any stimulation of which the slower moving visceral organs are capable. There is, further, a division of labor between the face and the inner organs of affective expression similar to that between the fingers and the arm. It is the very gross and slower moving characteristic of the inner organ system which provides the counterpoint for the melody expressed by the facial solo. In short, affect is primarily facial behavior. Secondarily it is bodily behavior, outer skeletal and inner visceral behavior. When we become aware of these facial and/or visceral responses we are aware of our affects. We may respond with these affects, however, without becoming aware of the feedback from them. Finally, we learn to generate, from memory, images of these same responses which we can become aware of with or without repetition of facial, skeletal, or visceral responses.

The centrality of the face in affective experience may be seen in the relationship between the hand and the face. The hand acts as if the face is the site of feeling. Thus, when one is tired or sleepy, the hand commonly either nurtures the face, in trying to hold it up to remain awake, or attempts conter-active therapy by rubbing the forehead and eyes as if to wipe away the fatigue or sleepiness. In shame, the hand is often used as an additional screen over the eyes behind which the face may be further hidden from view. In aggression which is turned against the self, the hand may be used to hurt one's own face by slapping it. Children sometimes claw their face with their fingernails. In surprise, the hand is commonly clapped to the cheek or over the forehead. The head or chin or cheek may be scratched when one is uncertain. In great joy, the hand is commonly placed on the forehead or cheek, particularly when there is an element of surprise in the joy. In distress, one hand is frequently placed over the eyes and forehead, and in extreme shock both hands cup the face and hold it up while it is weeping.

The significance of the face in interpersonal relations cannot be exaggerated. It is not only a communication center for the sending and receiving of information of all kinds, but because it is the organ of affect, expression, and communication, it necessarily is brought under strict social control. There are universal taboos on looking too directly into the eyes of the other because of the likelihood of affect contagion, as well as escalation, because of the unwillingness to express affect promiscuously, and because of concern lest others achieve control through knowledge of one's otherwise private feelings. Man is primarily a voyeuristic animal not only because vision is his most informative sense but because the shared interocular interaction is the most intimate relationship possible between human beings, since there is in this way complete mutuality between two selves each of which simultaneously is aware of the self and the other. Indeed the intimacy of sexual intercourse is ordinarily attenuated, lest it become too intimate, by being performed in the dark. In the psychoanalytic myth, too, the crime of the son is voyeuristic in the primal scene, and Oedipus is punished, in kind, in blindness.

If the affects are primarily facial responses—what are the major affects? We have distinguished eight innate affects. The positive affects are, first, interest or excitement, with eyebrows down, stare fixed or tracking an object. Second, enjoyment or joy, the smiling response. Third, surprise or startle, with eyebrows raised and eyeblink. The negative affects are, first, distress or anguish, the crying response. Second, fear or terror, with eyes frozen open in fixed stare or moving away from the dreaded object to the side, and with skin pale, cold, sweating, trembling, and hair erect. Third, shame or humiliation, with eyes and head lowered. Fourth, contempt or disgust with the upper lip raised in a sneer. Fifth, anger or rage, with a frown, clenched jaw and red face.

If these are innately patterned responses, are there also innate activators of each affect? Inasmuch as we have argued that the affect system is the primary motivational system, it becomes critical to provide a theory of the innate activators of the affect system. We do not believe that the specific "releaser" theory provides an adequate account of the innate basis of affect activation in human beings, despite its persuasiveness in accounting for some imprinting phenomena among birds and fishes. The affect system in man is activated by a variety of innate activators, such as drive signals and other affects as well as external activators. The most economical assumption upon which to proceed is to look for communalities among these varieties of innate alternative activators of each affect. We have done this and we believe it is possible to account for the major phenomena with a few relatively simple assumptions about the general characteristics of the stimuli which innately activate affect.

We would account for the differences in affect activation by three general variants of a single principle—the density of neural firing or stimulation. By density we mean the number of neural firings per unit time. Our theory posits three discrete classes of activators of affect, each of which further amplifies the sources which activate them. These are stimulation increase, stimulation level, and stimulation decrease. Thus, there are guaranteed three distinct classes of motives—affects about stimulation which is on the increase, stimulation which maintains a steady level of density, and stimulation which is on the decrease. With respect to density of neural firing or stimulation, then, the human being is equipped for affective arousal for every major contingency. If internal or external sources of neural firing suddenly increase, he will startle, or become afraid or become interested depending on the suddenness of increase of stimulation. If internal or external sources of neural firing reach and maintain a high, constant level of stimulation, he will respond with anger or distress, depending on the level of stimulation. If internal or external sources of neural firing suddenly decrease, he will laugh or smile with enjoyment depending on the suddenness of decrease of stimulation. The general advantage of affective arousal to such a broad spectrum of levels and changes of level of neural firing is to make the individual care about quite different states of affairs in different ways. It should be noted that according to our views there are both positive and negative affects (startle, fear, interest) activated by stimulation increase, but that only negative affects are activated by a continuing unrelieved level of stimulation (distress, anger), and only positive affects are activated by stimulation decrease (laughter, joy). This latter, in our theory, is the only remnant of the tension reduction theory of reinforcement. Stimulation increase may, in our view, be punishing or rewarding depending on whether it is a more or less steep gradient and therefore activates fear or interest. A constantly maintained high level of neural stimulation is invariably punishing inasmuch as it activates the cry of distress or anger, depending on how high above optimal levels of stimulation the particular density of neural firing is. A suddenly reduced density of stimulation is invariably rewarding, whether, it should be noted, the stimulation which is reduced is itself positive or negative in quality. Stated another way, such a set of mechanisms guarantees sensitivity to whatever is new, to whatever continues for any extended period of time, and to whatever is ceasing to happen, in that order. In Figure 1 we have graphically represented this theory.

Let us consider first startle, fear, and interest. These differ, with respect to activation, only in the rate at which stimulation or neural firing increases.

Startle appears to be activated by a critical rate of increase in the density of neural firing. The difference between startle (or surprise in its weaker form) and interest is a difference in the steepness of the gradient of stimulation. The same stimulus therefore may evoke surprise or interest, depending on the steepness of the rise of stimulation (which in turn depends on numerous factors, prominent among which is the degree of unexpectedness). Thus, a gun shot will evoke startle rather than interest. An unexpected tap on the shoulder by someone who is not seen will also evoke startle rather than interest. In the case of the gun shot, the suddenness of increase of stimulation was primarily in the auditory stimulus itself.

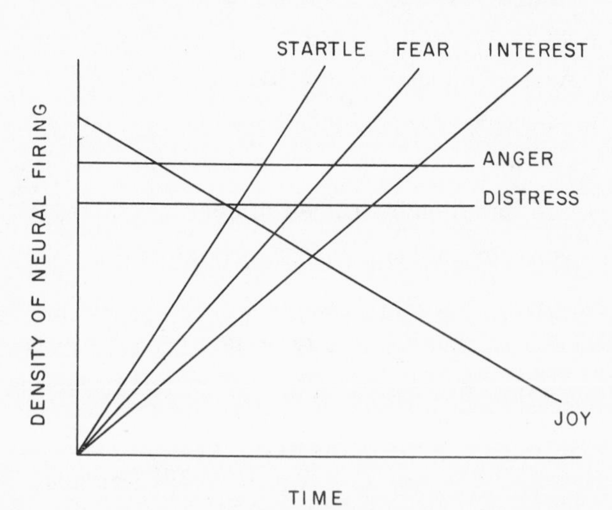

Figure 1. Graphical Representation of a Theory of Innate Activators of Affect.

In the tap on the shoulder the suddenness of this stimulus might have been sufficient, but the over-all density of stimulation was so low as to have been insufficient to become conscious in the competition between messages for transformation into reports. We assume that such a weak stimulus must recruit information from memory, which has a steep rate of increase of neural firing to activate a sequence of further, more rapid retrievals which summate to activate startle.

The affect of interest may itself also activate startle rather than the converse. The "double take" is such a case. Here the individual first responds with weak and brief interest in looking at an object, but this interest is sufficient to activate further retrieval from memory which itself produces a sudden enough change in stimulation to evoke further interest. This interest combined with the ongoing retrieval of further information now provides a sufficiently steeper increase of stimulation to startle the individual and then to support further interest and a second look at the object.

If startle, fear, and interest differ with respect to activation only in the rate at which stimulation or neural firing increases, then we can account for the unstable equilibria which there seems to be between them. First, it would illuminate the familiar sequence of startle, fear, interest. The same object which first startles quickly passes over into fear, and this somewhat less quickly is transformed into interest or excitement. Lorenz (1952) has reported the characteristic lability of fear and excitement in the raven who, on first encountering anything new, flies up to an elevated perch and stares at the object for hours, after which he gradually approaches the object, still showing considerable fear. As he comes closer, he hops sideways with wings poised for immediate flight. Finally, he strikes one blow at the object and flies right back to his perch. This sequence is repeated until eventually he loses interest in it. Harlow and Zimmerman (1959) have also noted the alternation between escape from, and exploration of, the feared object when the model mother is present. The infant monkey alternates between clinging to the mother and when the fear has somewhat abated, exploring the object, and then returning to the mother.

In comparison with startle and fear, the affect of distress appears to be based not on an increase of density of stimulation, but rather on an absolute level of density of stimulation or neural firing. Thus pain characteristically produces crying in the infant. The suddenness of pain is not the critical feature of the activation of distress. Either sudden or prolonged pain is equally capable of activating distress. Thus, a sudden stab of pain elicits a sudden scream of distress, and prolonged pain ordinarily produces prolonged crying. In contrast to fear, it is the total quantity or density of stimulation over time which further increases the density of stimulation through crying. It is the quantity rather than the quality of stimulation which appears to be critical. The cry and moan of excessive sexual pleasure in intercourse is an example of stimulation which is predominantly pleasurable, nonetheless evoking a cry of distress. If distress is activated by a general continuing level of nonoptimal neural stimulation, then we can account for the fact that such a variety of stimuli, from both internal and external sources, can produce the cry of distress in the infant and the muted distress response in the adult. These range from the low level pain of fatigue, hunger, cold, wetness, loud sounds, overly bright lights, to the cry itself as a further stimulus.

This theory would also account for some of the observed differences in types of affect which specific drives recruit as amplifiers. Thus, according to our view the sudden interruption of the air supply activates fear, whereas hunger drive characteristically first activates interest, because the former produces a more dense and steeper gradient of stimulation. As the hunger drive signals gradually increase to a higher and higher level of neural stimulation, interest changes to distress, but not to fear. We should expect on the basis of our theory that variations in metabolic rate between different animals should move the hunger drive between an extreme of steepness of gradient of stimulation, in the case of animals with very high metabolic rate who must eat often to survive, to an extreme of low level stimulation from the hunger drive signal, with a very gradual gradient of neural firing. For some animals, then, hunger would have effects similar to the interruption of the air supply and activate fear, and for others, with a very low metabolic rate, hunger would rarely activate any affect and then only distress, as the level of neural stimulation gradually rose with deprivation.

Further, the characteristic differences between hunger and air on the one hand, and the sex drive, on the other, would also be a consequence of differences in gradients and levels of neural firing. In man, sexual stimulation is often enough sudden and peaked in arousal to activate excitement, but not so steep a gradient as to activate fear, as in the interruption of the air supply.

Another affect which is activated by the absolute density level of stimulation is anger. It is our assumption that anger is activated by a higher density level of stimulation than is distress. Hence, if a source of stimulation, say pain, is adequate to activate distress and both of these continue unrelieved for any period of time, the combination of stimulation from pain and distress may reach the level necessary to activate anger. This is also why frustration may lead to anger. Further, either distress alone or pain alone might be sufficiently dense to activate anger. Thus, a slap on the face is likely to arouse anger because of the very high density of receptors on the surface of the face. In contrast, a stab of pain elsewhere in the body may lack both the requisite density and the duration to activate more than a cry of distress. This principle would also account for the irritability produced by continuous loud noise, which would tend to recruit widespread muscle contraction which, added to the distress affect, could raise the density of stimulation to that necessary for anger.

Finally, in contrast to stimulation increase and stimulation level, there are also affects which operate on the principle of stimulation reduction. The smile of joy and laughter are the primary examples of such a mechanism. The relatively steep reduction of pain or excitement or distress or anger will produce the smile of joy (which represents relief in the case of pain and distress), the smile of triumph in the case of anger, and the smile of familiarity in the case of the sudden reduction of excitement.

The smile of joy to the sudden reduction of stimulation accounts for two very disparate phenomena. On the one hand, it would account for the incremental reward of the sudden cessation of any negative stimulation, such as pain, distress, fear, shame, or aggression. On the other hand, it would account for the very different phenomenon of the enjoyment of the familiar.

If we assume that any unknown but familiar stimulus will first produce interest, with a sudden increase in neural firing from the feedback of this affective response, and then an equally sudden reduction of this stimulation when the familiar stimulus (e.g., the face) is recognized as familiar, then this latter will in our theory activate the smile of joy and so reward the individual for re-establishing contact with a familiar object, personal or impersonal.

This would account for the smiling of the child to the mother, since she moves in and out of view often enough to evoke first excitement by her unexpectedness, and then provokes the smile when the excitement is suddenly reduced because she is recognized. It would also account for Piaget's (1952) observation that his children sometimes smiled at their toys when they were unexpectedly uncovered.

The same type of mechanism, we believe, operates in the affect of shame, except that stimulation reduction is incomplete compared with joy and appears to be restricted to the reduction of positive affects themselves rather than to the reduction of any kind of stimulation. Hence, any barrier to exploration—whether because one is suddenly looked at by one who is strange, or because one wishes to look at or commune with another person but suddenly cannot because he is strange—which involves an interruption and incomplete reduction of interest or smiling will activate the lowering of the head and eyes in shame, and thereby reduce further exploration powered either by excitement or joy.

The biological utility of affects with sharply peaked profiles, such as startle, fear, and excitement to aspects of the environment which themselves may be highly variable, and the more continuous arousal of distress and aggression by aspects of the inner or outer world which continue to overstimulate the individual, as in constant pain, is evident. No less useful is the decreased probability of becoming aware of affects, such as joy, which are activated by reduction of stimulation, whenever these are in competition either with continuing overstimulation or suddenly rising stimulation which may signify danger or novelty and either startle, frighten, or interest the individual. The joy response is a luxury response when it competes with pain or danger or novelty, and the general relationship between the principle of selection of messages for the central assembly and the principles of the three major types of affect activation guarantee that it is the most vulnerable to exclusion in competition for consciousness.

Let us turn now to some of the general features of information flow and processing characteristic of the human being as he receives, transmits, and transforms information. At the terminal of the brain there are receiving stations whose function it is to duplicate those aspects of the world duplicated first at the sensory receptors and then duplicated again all along the sensory nerves.

At this receiving station there is a type of duplication which is unique in nature. Transmitted messages are here further transformed by an as yet unknown process we will call _transmuting_—which changes an unconscious message into a _report_. We will define a report as any message in _conscious_ form. It is our belief that the afferent sensory information is not directly transformed into a conscious report. What is consciously perceived is _imagery_. The world we perceive is a dream we learn to have from a script we have not written. It is neither our capricious construction nor a gift we inherit without work. Before any sensory message becomes conscious it must be matched by a centrally innervated feedback mechanism. This is a central efferent process which attempts to duplicate the set of afferent messages at the central receiving station. The individual must learn this skill of matching the constantly changing input as one learns any skill. It is this skill which eventually supports the dream and the hallucination, in which central sending produces the conscious image in the absence of afferent support. Why postulate what appears to be a redundant mechanism? Why not assume that what has been carefully transmitted to the central receiving station is directly transformed into conscious form? Instead of putting the mirror to nature we are suggesting a Kantian strategy, putting the mirror to the mirror. Is this not to compound error? Certainly the postulation of a feedback mechanism, which will have to learn to mimic what in a sense the eye does naturally, would at first blush appear perverse. But the possibility of error is the inherent price of any mechanism capable of learning. If we are to be able to learn perceptually, we will have to invoke a mechanism capable of learning errors as well as correcting its errors. But, it will be objected, we do not need to learn perceptually. Why may we not use our perceptual system as a mirror put to nature, by means of which we learn what else we need to know to achieve our purposes? Should learning not be restricted to the nonperceptual functions?

There are many reasons why the human being requires a feedback matching mechanism under central control. First, as a receiver of information, he is at the intersect of an overabundance of sensory bombardment. There is an embarrassment of riches, which paradoxically renders him vulnerable to confusion and information impoverishment. The individual must somehow select information to emphasize one sensory channel over another and focus on limited aspects of the incoming information within that channel.

The simplest case of overabundance is the binocular information received from the two eyes. We see one world, though we receive two worlds. This is the clearest instance of the perceptual feedback system in operation, since it is the clarity of the perceptual report which appears to govern the organization of the perceptual information. Thus, if the disparity of the two images is increased beyond a critical point, there is commonly a suppression of the information from one eye.

Second, there is not enough information in the overabundant sensory bombardment. The world changes over time and so, therefore, does the information it transmits. At any one moment in time the same transmitted information is a subset of a pool of messages which has in fact varied from one receiver to another. The pool of alternatives relevant for the identification of any discrete message includes the messages which have been sent in the past and which may be sent in the future. This is in varying degrees idiosyncratic to each recipient. As this set grows and as it is organized and used in the interpretation of new incoming information, the latter increases in the amount of information it carries. By means of memory and the conceptual organization of memories, what is now being duplicated in the immediate present by the sensory system can be ordered in varying ways with what that same sensory system duplicated a moment ago, a week ago, or for the entire past history of that individual. It is not our intention to put the subjective into opposition to the objective nature of the perceptual information. Our interest is rather in the amplification of information which becomes possible through the use of a matching feedback mechanism which can be sensitive to more than one source of information. Perceptual skill is based on such a mechanism, which can select from the flow of sensory messages those redundancies that have occurred before, as well as higher order trends across time which, in a real sense, cannot be represented at any one moment of sensory transmission.

Before going on with the final argument for the postulation of an additional intervening duplicating mechanism, let us examine briefly our theory of memory.

By an as yet unknown process some aspects of every conscious report are duplicated in more permanent form. Not all the information which bombards the senses is permanently recorded. Rather, we think, it is that information which in the competition for consciousness has succeeded in being transmuted that is more permanently duplicated. An equally critical type of duplication is that of information retrieval. Permanently preserved information would be of little utility unless it could be duplicated at some future time as a report, or as a preconscious "guide" to future perception, decision, and action. We have distinguished sharply the storage process, as automatic and unlearned, from the retrieval process which we think is learned. Both are duplicating processes, but one is governed by a built-in, unconscious mechanism and the other by a conscious feedback mechanism.

The reasons which prompted us to postulate two independent but close-coupled mechanisms with respect to sensory information are also relevant with respect to stored information. There is, on the one hand, an overabundance of stored information which would overwhelm consciousness if it were the direct recipient of all such stored past experiences, and, at the same time, there is insufficient information across time and across separately stored items. Sequential phenomena, trends, and the variety of higher order organizations of his past experience which the individual must achieve require a centrally controlled feedback mechanism, one which can match the stored information but is not so closely coupled that its matching is limited to the passive reporting of either one isolated memory trace at a time or to the Babel which would occur if all of the stored information were suddenly to become conscious. The inner eye, whether the recipient of information from the outside or from the inside, is postulated to be active and to employ feedback circuitry. Relating the past to the present is possible because these two skills are based on a shared mechanism which can turn equally well outward to the senses and inward to memory and thought.

Our final argument for the postulation of a centrally controlled feedback reporting mechanism rests upon the fact that the human being, as we conceive him, has purposes which he achieves through the feedback principle. His purpose is a centrally emitted blueprint which we shall call the Image. Although sensory data becomes conscious as imagery and memorial data must be translated into imagery, and both of these kinds of imagery are the consequence of a mechanism which employs the feedback principle, there is, nonetheless, a sharp distinction we wish to draw between the operation of imagery in sensory and memorial matching and the Image as the blueprint for the primary feedback mechanism. In sensory and memorial matching the model is given by the world as it exists now in the form of sensory information, and as it existed once before in the form of memorial information. In the Image the individual is projecting a possibility which he hopes to realize or duplicate and that must precede and govern his behavior if he is to achieve it. But how can a human being do what he intends?

Messages are continually transmitted to muscles and glands, but it is only the afferent messages from these areas which are transmuted into reports. If consciousness is limited to afferent reports, how then does the peripheral efferent system come under control? We propose that this is achieved by a _translation_ process. We conceive of the efferent and autonomic system as the space in between a dart thrower and his illuminated target, in an otherwise dark room. One can learn to throw a dart to hit a target in a dark room without ever knowing what the trajectory of the dart might be, so long as one knew how it felt just before the dart was thrown and where the dart landed. The trajectory described by the dart would and could never become conscious, but the effects of the trajectory could be systematically translated into the preceding conditions in such a fashion that, for such and such a feel before throwing, one could be reasonably certain that the visual report, after the trajectory, would be the desired report. We conceive of the efferent messages as the dart trajectory, controlled by the afferent reports which precede and follow the efferent messages. We have called this a translation because there are two different languages involved, the motor and the sensory. One must here learn to translate a desired future sensory report into the appropriate motor trajectories. In addition to a process of translation, however, a further step is necessary. In the beginning of dart throwing the translation is after the fact; i.e., such and such a feel led to such a distance off the target. Eventually the desired report must come before the translation and guide the process, or else one would not be able to repeat any performance, good or bad. Therefore, we conceive of the total afferent-efferent chain as follows: The desired future report, the Image, must be transmitted to an afferent terminal and at the same time translated into a peripheral efferent message. The message which initiated the translation is the same message which must come back if the whole process is to be monitored. The monitoring process is, however, not a comparison between the first message and the feedback, but between the first report and the feedback after it has been transmuted into a report. In other words, the individual can be aware only of his own reports, whether they are constructions from memory, or his constructions guided by an external source. Such a state of affairs would appear possible. Is there any evidence that such a guiding Image does indeed exist? On the basis of this theory we successfully predicted the conditions under which the Image would be revealed—namely, if we were to interfere with the masking feedback in the case of over-learned motor skills such as speaking and writing. To speak a word, we are supposing that one must first transmit this word to the auditory center and shortly thereafter transmit a translation of this word into those tongue movements which will produce the sound waves which will provide the feedback identical to the initial message.

This feedback need not be identical so long as it is equivalent. Thus, some individuals transmit visual messages while speaking, rather than auditory messages. We have exposed this chain by interfering with ordinary speech. If one speaks very softly, moving the lips but not allowing the sound to reach an audible level, one will then "hear" the internal speech which precedes and monitors the feedback. Under these conditions some individuals emit a visual message. The same process can be shown to underlie motor performance—by closing the eyes and drawing a square in the air or writing one's name in the air. One will then "see" the square or one's name. The visual messages, which constitute the Images which are translated into motor messages, become conscious. So much for how, in general, an Image comes to control and monitor the feedback process. If our view of this is correct, then this is the fourth most critical reason why we must postulate a central sending mechanism to match the message from the receiving mechanism.

So much for imagery and the Image, and the arguments—perceptual, memorial, and motoric—which appear to require central constructive activity if the sensory bombardment and the memory traces are to be optimally utilized and aims translated into action. Let us now examine more closely the central executive agency.

We conceive of a central executive assembly, made up of parts that enter and leave this ever-changing administrative organization, which continues to control the remainder of the system by means of a fluctuating membership.

The term central assembly refers to a mechanism involving consciousness. Messages in the nervous system may or may not become conscious. If they become conscious we call them reports, and the mechanism which transforms messages into conscious form we refer to as the transmuting mechanism. It is our view that the components, or sub-systems, of the nervous system, which are functionally joined with the transmuting mechanism, vary from moment to moment as determined by the set of sub-systems which were functionally joined to the transmuting mechanism in the previous moment, by the transmuted information contained in those previously joined sub-systems, and by the nature of the messages within the sub-systems which are competing at the moment for the limited channel capacity of consciousness. The transmuting mechanism plus all those components of the nervous system which are functionally joined to it at a given moment in time we refer to as the incompletely overlapping central assembly. By this term we mean that the components of differing central assemblies, at different moments in time, will in part be the same and in part be different. Similarly, the set of messages in any component of the central assembly may be in part the same and in part different at differing moments in time. The central assembly may, however, be entirely disassembled and cleared at any moment, for example, by the activation of the startle response, which has the characteristics of an emergency mechanism in a communication system which interrupts ongoing activity with a special announcement. This response produces such sudden and widespread bombardment of sensory feedback that the central assembly is disorganized and reorganized as a conscious experience of startle. It serves the function of orienting the individual to unusual information which he had neglected, or to unusually intense stimulation whether expected or unexpected.

This experience is neither expected, wanted, nor controlled. It is the consequence of a mechanism which is antagonistic to the normal functioning of a feedback system.

Invasions of purposeful central assemblies are, of course, not limited to the startle response. Messages from memory or sensory sources can activate distress, anxiety, or shame, which in turn may disassemble ongoing purposive activity. All central assemblies involve consciousness, but only when there is some aim to be realized, an attempt to achieve this aim, and reports of how close this aim is to realization, is a central assembly operating on feedback principles. The gain in information from the interaction of relatively independent parts is like the gain in information from a set of elements when they are combined according to the rules of a language. The ultimate combinations of affect with the receptor, analyzer, storage, and effector systems produces a much more complex set of combinations than could have been built either into the affect system alone, or into any predetermined program. It should be noted, however, that the central assembly is at best an untidy aggregate. It has none of the orderliness of our present-day programs. It is perpetually vulnerable to interference, drift, and disassembly, and even when it enjoys freedom from interference one will characteristically find that it is more like an information stew than it is like a program. Some dimly felt pressure from the seat of the pants mingles democratically with a suddenly remembered appointment and a fleeting glimpse of an interesting face of a passerby. This is not the stuff of hierarchical organization, nor indeed necessarily of any organization. As nature is said to abhor a vacuum, so psychologists have been loathe to look entropy full in the face.

Let us now examine more closely the role of two cognitive mechanisms, memory and thought, whereby the central assemblies are increasingly subordinated to endopsychic control.

The human being employs two radically different strategies in the processing of information. In one, the strategy of memorizing, the aim is to create a unique object. In the other, the conceptual strategy, the aim is to create, ideally, an infinite set of objects. In terms of class membership, memory aims at the construction of a class with a single member or at least to minimize the number of members of a class, whereas the conceptual strategy ideally aims at maximizing the number of members of a class. We have distinguished sharply the storage process, as automatic and unlearned, from the retrieval process which we think is learned. Both are duplicating processes, but one is governed by a built-in unconscious mechanism, the other by a conscious feedback mechanism. The individual may not choose what he is to store or not store, but he may choose to "memorize" or not to memorize, i.e., to learn how to reproduce past experience, to retrieve information which has been permanently stored without reliance on sensory input.

We will examine as an example how an individual teaches himself to remember a telephone number. We conceive of this as a process of informational compression in which the individual produces more and more miniaturized copies of the original information. This he does by using the original to produce a more miniature copy, and then using this compressed copy to produce a still more miniaturized copy, which in turn is miniatured in a series which, for example, may begin 5 - - - 9 - - - 2 - - - 3 as it is first read from the telephone book, and then is speeded up in the first internal reproduction to 5 - - 9 - - 2 - - 3, which is then reverberated in immediate memory and further speeded up on the second internal reproduction to 5 - 9 - 2 - 3, which on the next repetition is said still more quickly as 5923, until finally it is so abbreviated that it is unconscious, but one knows that one knows it and can reproduce it from within. This miniaturization, however, involves more than simply speeding up the performance, since the sounds of the digits had to be clipped and abbreviated without destroying their essential message. Otherwise such a series of increasingly compressed equivalents might be like the blurred features of a person seen from an increasing distance. They would be of no use unless they were recognizable as compressions of the original model rather than equivalents of the just preceding miniature. It must be possible not only to recognize the original from the miniature, but also to reproduce the original exactly from the miniature. The compression relationship must be reversible and expandable. This is achieved in teaching oneself to remember by applying the inverse of the compression transformation—for example, using the operator "decreased speed" on the miniature, which had been produced from the original by the operator "increased speed." In this way one can learn to reverse what one has just done.

Miniaturization, however, involves, as we have said, more than speeded performance. In addition to increased speed, the sounds must be clipped without destroying their essential message. The relationship between the various parameters of any performance which is to be compressed is complex. In attempting to operate on one, it will often happen that other parameters will also be transformed unintentionally. Thus, in speeding up our handwriting, we may lose legibility. Increased speed may, however, improve a certain performance by so altering the relationships between the parts that it becomes easier to duplicate. This is the case in learning to ride a bicycle. It takes much more skill to ride a bicycle slowly and expertly than to ride it moderately fast.

The compression process reduces the density of reports to messages so that consciousness increasingly legislates itself out of representation, and the individual may become aware of the remembered telephone number for the first time only as he hears himself talk to the operator. Not only is information being stored in increasingly compressed form at different sites in the brain, but the individual is learning these addresses and where and how to find the stored information and reassemble it.

At this point we wish to introduce the concept of a name, which is commonly conceived to be a relatively unique symbol for something. We will define a "name" as any message, conscious or unconscious, which is capable of activating a particular trace at a particular address. We will assume that a "name" itself may or may not have an address and that this address itself may, therefore, have a "name."

The retrieval ability which is being learned under the conditions of miniaturizing just described consists, then, not only in the deposition of traces at specific addresses, but also in the central assembling of names for each address, and the storage of these names at still other addresses.

The relationship between early memories and later memories may be continuous or discontinuous. New learning may proceed by transformations on older memories or by the assembling of relatively new components which result in the deposition of relatively independent traces and names of traces. Accessibility of these traces will vary as a consequence of the relative continuity or discontinuity of learning and the stored traces resulting from learning. We will now present an experimental test of a derivative of the theory in which we were successful in the prediction of retrieval of early memories. The experiment was as follows: The subject is required to write his name very slowly, at a rate approximately three seconds per letter. Under these conditions the handwriting closely resembles that of childhood rather than his present handwriting, if he is now an adult. Long forgotten ways of forming letters are reproduced.

In the second experiment of this type a subject is asked to shout at the top of his voice the phrase "No, I won't!" Not all subjects are willing or able to do this, but most comply. The consequences are somewhat varied. On the faces of most adults the lower lip is protruded immediately after speaking, giving the appearance of a defiant, pouting child. Spontaneously emitted reports from many subjects indicate a re-experience of childish affect of distress and anger, with recollection of long-forgotten specific incidents in which such affect was evoked.

Let us now examine further that part of our theory of memory upon which these experiments were based. In the case of both handwriting and speech there are at least two aspects of both early and late performance which co-vary, so that early performance is characterized by one value of each parameter and the later performance by a different value of each parameter. In the case of handwriting, the early performance is slow, the late performance more rapid. The co-varying other parameter is, in fact, a set of parameters which produces the more regular script, or the more idiosyncratic adult signature. In the case of speech, the early performance is louder than the late performance. Pitch appears to be one of a set of co-varying other parameters. Since the early handwriting is slow and the late handwriting is fast, our particular instruction is effective in retrieving the only set of traces which are stored which have a program for guiding the slow movements of the hand in writing the name.

Such an instruction applied to speech does not work because speed in speech is variable, whether the speech is early or late. One has learned to speak both slowly and rapidly as a child and as an adult. The critical discontinuity in early and late speech is loudness or intensity of speech. While children speak at varying levels of intensity, the intensity is required to be much reduced in adulthood. The child's loud speech is under steady negative pressure from parents and teachers who insist that the child lower his voice. Eventually this produces an adult who rarely shouts. Because of this discontinuity, the instruction to shout at the top of the voice is effective in retrieving early speech whereas instruction to speak more slowly or more rapidly is not. It is, however, not effective for those who continue to shout as adults.

One of the most outstanding characteristics of these two sets of early and late performance is their almost complete segregation one from the other. The debate about primary versus recency and early versus late experience is a mistaken polarity since it appears that the nervous system is quite capable of supporting two independent sets of traces under certain conditions. Thus, given the specific conditions under which we learn early and late handwriting, two quite independent organizations may exist side by side with little interaction in either direction. Early memory here does not influence later memory, nor does later memory alter early memory. There is neither proactive nor retroactive interference. Each address has its own name, and each name has its own address. The subject continues to be unable to write as he wrote early at a rapid rate, nor does he appear to be able to write his adult signature slowly. The primary cause of the state of segregation of the two sets of traces and the skills they program is the number of transformations which would be necessary to build a set of bridges between one set of traces and the other set of traces. This is what we have defined as the "inter-name distance," the number of transformations upon a name which is necessary to enable the formation of a modified trace with a modified name.

Consider that each signature is guided by a set of conjoint messages which inform the fingers of the hand how to move from moment to moment to create the unique tracings which constitute the two signatures. Let us simplify the problem and represent the first set as composed of a series of three subsets of instructions, one of which, q, is a constant slow speed, another, x, is a set of instructions to proceed to a particular set of points with respect to an abscissa, and the third, y, is a set of instructions to proceed to a particular set of points with respect to the ordinate. The second set we may conceive as another program composed of q', which is a faster constant rate, and x' and y' analogous to x and y but systematically different. The subsets of x and y, and x' and y' are very numerous, and each individual instruction has one of two speed markers tightly linked to a particular xy or x'y' reading. The empirical correlations between the distinctive components of each signature are critical for how many information transformations will be required to learn the new skills q'xy and qx'y', i.e., to write a fast, childlike and a slow, adult signature. If a very small change in speed produces a large and inappropriate change in an x reading or a y reading or in both, and if a small change in an x reading produces a very large change in a y reading, then, conversely, a great deal of work will be required to build a series of bridges between qxy and q'x'y' and q'xy and qx'y'. If, on the other hand, one could change q half way to q' without disturbing the xy part of the program, and change q' half way to q without disturbing x'y', then with only a few more transformations one might achieve q'xy and qx'y', i.e., fast early writing and slow late writing. The number of intermediate transformations which will be necessary to achieve the new programs and their traces, the inter-name distance, will depend on how much distortion in early writing is caused by how much speed up, and how long it will take to learn to correct these distortions at each new intermediate speed. The number of such intermediate transformations that would be required to achieve handwriting skill which was free of speed effects would be a function of the strength of the correlation between all components of the set.

If the correlations between components of the distinctive sets are weak, then relatively simple transformations will bridge the small inter-name distance, and the intrusion of early memories will be short lived. If it were in fact easy to learn to write early handwriting rapidly and late handwriting slowly, the instructions we used would not provide a stable regressive phenomenon. Sometimes, for some subjects who shout "No, I won't! ", this does prove to be an unstable regressive phenomenon, just because it is readily transformed into a variant of adult speech and therefore no longer recovers early memories or affects. The introduction of negative affect into the distinctive, discontinuous behavior enormously complicates the inter-name distance. The very thought of using a specific parameter, such as very loud sounds, which was once relinquished under the threat of negative sanctions is itself often sufficient to reactivate the same negative affect. Every time the possibility of so behaving is imminent and negative affect is aroused, the segregation and discontinuity between the two types of speech is heightened. Under such conditions, the initiation of a set of transformations which would reduce this distinctiveness must contend not only with the potential inter-name distance, which would be there even if there were no anxiety to discourage the work of transformation, but in addition must be motivated to tolerate the punishing negative affect involved. This is involved in psychotherapy where there must be not only tolerance of the intrusive affect, but a wish to confront, master, and integrate these alien elements of the personality. If the wish for self knowledge and integration is not strong, the punishment during the confrontation necessary to reduce the inter-name distance will not be tolerated, even though it could be tolerated if the wish for integration were stronger.

Let us turn now to that other major strategy of information transformation—thinking. Thinking is a technique of dealing with classes of objects rather than with unique objects. Memory is organized to minimize class membership, and thinking is organized to maximize class membership.

If memory involves the recognition or reproduction of a whole from a part, the symbol involves the detection or generation of a critical, communal, non-unique part from the whole. What is an instance of the concept in the particular whole object is embedded in the object and is often hidden by other characteristics which may be more salient. The aim of thinking is to construct a class with a symbol, rather than a unique object with a name. The difference between a "name" and a "symbol" is a critical distinction within our theory of cognition.

The "symbol" is the neurological structure which enables the detection of the similarity between members of a class and an indefinite number of new instances of members of a class which may differ radically from previously identified members of the learned class.

We will define a "symbol" as any learned technique for maximizing the repetitions within a class, which is stored at a specific address. In memorizing, the non-unique characteristics of the object which are common to it and other objects are compressed; e.g., the speed and volume of speech is compressed in memorizing the telephone number, whereas what is selected for permanent storage is what is unique in the information. In contrast, when a set of objects is conceptualized or symbolized, it is just that aspect of a set of objects which they share in common that is detected, compressed, and miniaturized, and the other, relatively unique information about each object is disregarded. That which is unique in the object is preserved in one compression-expansion transformation, whereas that which is common in the object relative to other objects is preserved in the other set of transformations.

It should be noted that compression-expansion transformations are used both in memorizing and in concept formation. The major differences are, first, in whether it is the unique or the common features of the object which are compressed, and, second, in the scope of such transformations. Whereas the model to be compressed is given in memorizing and can be continually used to monitor the adequacy of retrieval, such is not the case in concept formation. Not only is it the non-unique aspect of the object which must first be detected and then compressed as a "symbol," which will enable the detection of other instances of class membership, but unlike memorizing this aspect is never immediately given in experience. The concept itself has first to be learned, and it is never certain that the concept has in fact been adequately understood until it has been detected in objects other than the original object.

If a computer program were stored at a specific address within the computer it would constitute an instance of a "symbol." A symbol therefore may have a name, but a name need not be the name of a symbol, since it can also be the name of a specific memory.

Whereas we could give a somewhat detailed account of the process of memorizing as a set of compression-expansion transformations, no such general paradigm exists for thinking because of the great increase in degrees of freedom in thinking. Because a symbol is a stored, learned technique of maximizing the repetitions within a class, it is a continually unfinished business, with the properties of an open rather than a closed system. Whether the next object will be coordinated to one symbol or another will depend in part on the competition between symbols and the monopolistic power of one symbol over another, as well as on the nature of the object. Because of the competition between symbols and between symbols and unique objects, they characteristically grow stronger or weaker. Every new encounter with the same object as well as with new objects has within it the potentiality of destroying the symbol which was once achieved in commerce with it.

The limitation of channel capacity in both perception and action requires constant analysis and resynthesis to enable the human being to enlarge his ability to deal with increasing amounts of information. This process is like a grasping hand which compresses the material it touches until it is such a size that it can be held in the hand and permit yet another object to be grasped and compressed and this operation to be repeated cumulatively. This is the same technique employed in science. Phenomena which appear to be discrete or laws which are about different domains are painfully and slowly reformulated until they become special cases of a more general and simpler theory or law. The general trend of these compressions through analyses and resyntheses is to maximize the number of repetitions in all domains, since once a domain has been conceptualized the application of the same rules will handle further instances with a reduced claim on the channel capacity. The individual does not constantly increase the complexity of his performance but rather transforms complex information into simpler information, which is to say he maximizes the number of repetitions within the information he processes. Just as a single concept maximizes class membership by maximizing the number of repetitions of instances of a concept, so a theory or set of concepts maximizes the number of repetitions in its domain by minimizing the number of separate concepts within the theory. Simplification of concepts within a larger theory may be achieved either with an increase or a decrease of power. The former is ordinarily defined as integration, the latter as de-differentiation. In the early stages of learning it is often necessary to produce oversimplified caricatures of conceptual organization as a base for later differentiation and integration. It is possible to produce such simpler structures by stressing the later more differentiated structures.

We have been able to study the structure of complex symbolic organization by placing skilled motor performances under speed stress. Just as we were able to recover early memories through modification of the speed of handwriting, so if one radically increases the speed of writing one can expose the component symbols which together constitute the program for writing. We assume that within any complex organization there are symbols or classes which vary in their generality or specificity. The more general subclasses are those which have the greater number of repetitions or class members. If one places the entire organization under stress, these more general classes should be less vulnerable to disorganization by stress than the more specific classes which have a smaller number of repetitions, or class membership.

This is a special case of what we have called the principle of conservation of information. It is our assumption that when information is transformed, either in the direction of information gain or in the opposite direction of information loss, then whatever information loss may be involved is minimized. More specifically, this implies that when subsets of any set of concepts which together constitute a theory are transformed, it will be that subset which contains the smallest class membership which will be transformed. In de-differentiation under stress, therefore, it will be the most specific class of instructions within a program which will be lost, and the more general class should now replace it and thereby increase its class membership. We will now present an experiment by which we tested this hypothesis.

We required subjects to print as quickly as they could a series of letter N's, so: NNNNNNNNNNNN . If we examine the components of the set of messages which must guide this series of responses, it would be as follows: Up Down Up (down, but off the paper) Up Down Up (down, off the paper) Up Down Up (down, off the paper) Up Down Up. This describes approximately the production of the first four letters. The stroke down which is off the paper would look as follows if the pencil were not lifted from the paper: MW . Since the down stroke which is drawn in the air is similar to the other down strokes in some respects, but different in others, it is organized as a residual class of greater specificity than the more general class of UP DOWN UP, which contains two successive alternations (from up to down and down to up). This class, when the N's are drawn ten times, contains 20 alternations as opposed to ten strokes in the air between the letters.

The complete description of the component directions of even the simplest motor performance is a formidable problem. Consider that the drawing of each of the straight lines is not necessarily a ballistic response, but may have to be repeated as the line gets longer. Consider also that the length of two of the lines which go in the same direction is also equal, thus making a correlated repetition in contrast to the diagonal line which is longer as well as unrepeated in direction. Consider also that the size of the angle of the two uprights is repeated, and the size of the first angle of the diagonal is not. The temporal rhythm tends also to be repeated more within the letter than between letters, aided by the correlated repetitions of length and direction plus the repeated direction alternation with the pencil continuing on the surface of the paper. In contrast the space between letters lifts the pencil from this surface, often changes the speed, changes the length of the line as well as the angle from the top of the letter to the beginning of the next letter. Any change in rhythm is the focal point for intrusion effects, since this is where the instructions to simply repeat must be supplemented by either new or additional instructions. Under stress therefore we should expect the more specific class of messages to be more disturbed than the more general class, which has the greater number of repetitions. This disturbance should be reflected in an increase in the number of repetitions of the classes of components which already have the most repetitions relative to the residual, more specific classes of components. Such experimentally produced errors should be reflected in an increase in the number of repetitions. These are errors which may have occurred earlier in the learning process before the finer differentiations between classes were achieved, or new errors due to new stresses not encountered in the original learning.

In the case of the repeated N's, one way of increasing the number of repetitions would be to add a down stroke either to the end of the letter, or to the beginning of the letter. Either addition would increase the repetitions by an Up-Down-Up-Down repetition instead of an Up-Down-Up asymmetry. These two possibilities are the principal errors produced. The more common one is to introduce the additional down stroke at the beginning of each letter as follows:

Less commonly, the additional stroke is added to the end of the letter as follows:

In this case as soon as the error is detected it is corrected and the line is rarely completed. The more common error, in contrast, is frequently not detected at all. This is possible in part because the additional line may be drawn so close to the beginning stroke that it appears only as a thickening of the line.

These experiments were derived from our principle of conservation of information, which stated that any transformation of information will tend to conserve information by transforming those subsets whose change represents the smallest information loss for the total set. This is another way of saying that the aim of symbolic organization is to maximize class membership and minimize the number of classes.

A humanomaton, then, must have at least these degrees of freedom: the freedom to care in a variety of ways about a variety of objects for a variety of different times and durations; the freedom to match from within what was first encountered outside the skin; the freedom to construct from within a replica of a unique object; and, finally, the freedom to construct a class of which the object is no more than a special case. These are the freedoms inherent in affect, imagery, memory and thinking.

2

DONALD W. MacKINNON
University of California, Berkeley

Discussion:
Simulation of Cognition and Innate Affects or Simulation of Personality

The freshness and scope of Dr. Tomkins' intriguing fantasy of a computer simulated personality, one which he chooses to call a humanomaton, sets the stage for some unfettered and original thinking about the possibilities of the marriage of computer simulation to personality theory.

The several attitudes he describes, both positive and negative, toward the purposes of this conference are attitudes which in one guise or another have been held toward almost all new theoretical and methodological extensions of the psychology of personality. In recent years, for example, I have repeatedly experienced negative attitudes toward my efforts to study the creative process and creative persons which are very similar to those described by Dr. Tomkins. But whatever the attitudes of lay persons and other psychologists may be, I venture to guess that of the several emotional reactions to the possibilities of computer simulation in the domain of personality ours are more apt to be delight and excitement rather than contempt and shame or anxiety and anger.

Early in his paper Dr. Tomkins raises what must certainly be a very crucial and basic question for our deliberations, the question as to whether we are to be concerned with the simulation of persons by computers or the testing of theories of personality by appropriate and relevant computer programs. I find Dr. Tomkins' answer to this question unclear. Though he explicitly states that "computer simulation must be judged not by its resemblance to human beings, but by its conjoint economy, explanatory and predictive power," he also tells us that the humanomaton must "be motivated to reproduce itself...if we are interested in the problem of human simulation the race of automata must be perpetuated not only by knowledge but by passion." Here, then, is a central issue about which we must become clear.

Having asserted that the humanomaton must be motivated, Dr. Tomkins quite properly addresses himself to the question as to what are the primary motives of men which must be simulated. They are, he argues, emotions rather than drives, for he is convinced that there is "a radical error in the argument for the primacy and urgency of drives as motives." Thus he stands with an increasing number of psychologists who on one ground or another reject one aspect or another of the concept of drive and the drive-reduction theory of motivation. His arguments are compelling, but it is doubtful that all motivational theorists will find his thesis acceptable. Dr. Tomkins reminds us that "from Plato to Freud man has been conceived to be motivated by his more biological 'drives'," and though this view has been repeatedly attacked, Dr. Tomkins recognizes that "none of its competitors have had its hardiness." I am sure, then, that he does not expect his view to be immediately and universally accepted, and we should remind ourselves that its merits and strengths have to be judged not only in relation to the claims of a drive-primacy paradigm, whether of Freud or of Hull, but also in relation to the behavior-primacy theory of Woodworth and the competence-primacy theory of White. What I am suggesting is that Dr. Tomkins has offered us one model, a fascinating and intriguing one, but clearly only one of many available for simulation.

One of the more intriguing and original aspects of Dr. Tomkins' affect-primacy theory is its assertion that affect is primarily facial behavior and only secondarily bodily behavior, outer skeletal and inner visceral behavior. The illustrations offered of the leading role of the face in the expression of emotions are both vivid and amusing, but whether these affective expressions are unlearned as Dr. Tomkins believes and as Darwin claimed in his 1873 book, _The expression of emotions in man and animals_, remains, I believe, a moot question.

It is perhaps unfair to criticize Dr. Tomkins' discussion of the emotions on the grounds that it is restricted to an explication of the emotions which he believes are innate. In such a pioneering and difficult field as that of computer simulation there is some merit in beginning with the simpler rather than the more complex phenomena. But personality by its very nature is complicated and complex, and the task which this conference has set for itself is the exploration of the possibilities of computer simulation of it. Since personality in all conceptual representations and theoretical formulations with which I am acquainted is largely an acquired or learned structure, we can hardly restrict ourselves to the simulation of innate affects if our simulation of personality is to be at all adequate.

Here, however, I would question very seriously whether the eight affects which Dr. Tomkins describes are, as he claims, innate. I find it difficult to believe that shame or humiliation is innately given rather than in large part learned and acquired as a result of interpersonal experience.

Whether shame or any other emotion is or is not innate, however, is less important both for Dr. Tomkins' theory and for our deliberations than is the adequacy of his explanations of the different qualities of emotion in terms of three general variants of a single principle—the density of neural firing or stimulation. The case for three distinct classes of activators of affect—stimulation which is on the increase, stimulation which maintains a steady level of density, and stimulation which is on the decrease—is convincingly made for six affects—startle, fear, interest, anger, distress, and joy. One is left to wonder, though, how adequate the single principle of density of neural firing or stimulation is for the explanation of more subtle and more complex emotions. I do not, for example, immediately see how such a principle can deal with anxiety, the emotion which according to Freud is the core affect in all psychoneuroses and which many observers see as the pervasively disturbing emotion of modern man. It is the peculiarity of anxiety that it is at once both positive and negative, it being that compounded emotion which one experiences when, unclear about where he stands and what the future holds for him, he simultaneously hopes for the best but fears the worst. The emotion of anxiety which arises when an individual is simultaneously moving in psychologically opposed directions poses serious difficulties, I believe, for Dr. Tomkins' principle of neural firing or stimulation.

Dr. Tomkins does not directly address himself to one of the most crucial problems in personality theory, namely the question as to whether the laws and principles of personality are identical with or different from the laws and principles of general psychology, but I would gather from his discussion that he sees no necessity for treating personality apart from the main body of psychological science. He offers, for example, paradigms for two types of cognitive process, memory and thinking, but none for the more generally recognized functions of personality—scheduling, decision-making, reality-testing, repression, sublimation, reaction formation, and the like. In illustrating the usefulness of his concept of the Image he discusses its role in a person's learning to hit the target in a game of darts played in the dark. It may well be that for purposes of clarity and simplicity in explicating the concept of the Image he chose the far simpler example of the neuro-muscular patterning of a motoric response in preference to the more complex case of a person's behavior being guided by his image of his ideal self. But for some, I am sure, the illustrations which Dr. Tomkins has given will raise questions as to whether the ground is being laid in this introductory paper for the simulation for cognitive processes or the simulation of personality.

If there are indeed those who feel that the level of aspiration for this conference has been lowered by Dr. Tomkins' exposition, I would remind them that we were bid to a meeting which was rather modestly described as one to consider Computer Simulation: Frontier of Personality Theory. The question as to how we may best make forays at this frontier into new territory is one of strategy. Instead of parachuting us deep into the domain of personality Dr. Tomkins has chosen to lead us more cautiously in a series of expeditions which may well serve best to secure for us ground upon which an effective computer simulation of personality theory may ultimately be achieved.

3

ERNEST R. HILGARD
Stanford University

Discussion:
The Simulation of Affects, Images, and Thoughts

The advantages of a computer as a humanoid machine are well stated, and because the other papers in this symposium bear also upon this general problem, I shall refrain from adding my comments.

Of considerable substantive interest is Dr. Tomkins' treatment of the relationship between affects and drives. I have elsewhere expressed my belief that in the standard drive-reduction theories of motivation this relationship is too simply conceived. Affects, such as fear and anxiety, enter into these theories as high-tension states to be relieved through their reduction in the course of goal-achievement. I have argued that affects enter not only as drives, but as concomitants of motivated activity (as in McDougall's view that there is pleasure in striving), and as goals of motivated activity, when, for example, one seeks an occasion for laughter or pleasure (see Hilgard, 1962, pp. 176-178). I have thus been prepared in my own thinking to retain the distinction between affects and drives, while noting their close relationship; I find it interesting, therefore, to examine the distinction as proposed by Dr. Tomkins, which is rather different from my own.

Let me summarize his position, with some remarks occasionally interspersed.

1. Affects, rather than drives, are the primary human motives. There are two main points here – first, that affects may motivate in the absence of drives and, second, that drives without amplification by affects are not effective motivators at all. Drives alone are merely sources of information as to where and when to do what – when there has been sufficient affective arousal.

2. Affects are muscular and glandular responses, generating feedback that is acceptable or unacceptable. Thus, affects are positive (acceptable, satisfying) or negative (unacceptable, annoying); their occasions and circumstances have to be learned. Dr. Tomkins gives great centrality to the responses of the face; the hand-face gestures very commonly serve as the interpersonal signs of affect. I find this proposal ingenious and inviting, but it seems to me to be a little too extreme.

If this affective feedback system is to be worked into the machine, there must be some sort of self-rewarding and self-punishing responses built into the computer so that it can take steps to maximize self-reward and minimize self-punishment. With this I am in agreement.

3. Innate activators arouse affect according to changes in the density of neural discharge. Here is another effort to distinguish among affects on the basis of quantity—a proposal that has appeared from time to time from Fechner to McClelland. Dr. Tomkins' version is as follows:

a. An increase in the density of discharge will provoke either positive or negative affect, depending upon the circumstances. It may lead to the negative affects of startle, fear, and terror or to the positive ones of interest and excitement. Thus, slight changes in rate of change may account for the admixture of fear and fascination, of thrill.

b. Prolongation of stimulation at a steady level invariably leads to negative affect, as in distress and anger.

c. Decrease in density of discharge always leads to positive affect, to enjoyment, smiling. This is the point of overlap with the drive-reduction theory of motivation or the Freudian theory of pleasure.

I am not prepared to accept or refute this analysis; it appears to be stated in a form that should permit empirical testing, provided some behavioral meaning can be given to density of neural firing ("neural firings per unit of time"). The theory can scarcely be that concretely physiological or neurological; if it is, some consideration has to be given to the distinction between mere _intensity_ of activity and affectivity. Possibly the intensity has to have some sort of locus, not now specified in the theory, unless it is to be measured in the face. The mixtures of affect produced by various gradients of increased stimulation seem to me particularly plausible.

Having come to this point, Dr. Tomkins turns a corner, drops all but minor consideration of affects, and considers information-processing and memory. He finds that images are centrally generated blueprints for controlling feedback, reminiscent of some of the discussion in Miller, Galanter, and Pribram (1960). The problems of information storage, of duplication, of retrieval are relevant ones, and they are certainly ones that computers can be used to represent. Here are introduced two experimental findings—the one about the characteristic facial expressions involved in saying "No, I won't," the other the nature of errors in writing a series of N's. One would only wish for more of this to see further how the discussion can move from its essay character to something subject to tangible test.

In fairness to Dr. Tomkins, it must be noted that he made a deliberate decision to write in the authoritative mode of one who knows the answers and not to clutter the text with the usual acknowledgments of sources of ideas or related conceptions that are more customary in scientific writing. It would have taken a great deal more space to deal with the arguments from other positions. Hence I do not conceive it to be my task to fill in the gaps that he knows he left. In relation to the objectives of the symposium, I believe these contributions stand out:

1. The introductory material on reasons for, and common objections to, the simulation of man by machine is a useful orientation.

2. The theory of affects in relation to drive (especially affects as amplifiers) and the quantitative theory of positive and negative affect are stated in terms that can be translated into form for empirical testing.

3. The general interpretation of information processing, memory, and thought is of a kind to be fitted into computer simulation concerned with cognitive processes.

4 WALTER R. REITMAN
Carnegie Institute of Technology

Personality As a Problem-Solving Coalition

Looking over my copy of the program for this conference, I suddenly found myself recalling an incident described by John Livingston Lowes (1927). The details are a bit fuzzy now, but the incident seems to have concerned a medieval geographer who had come across an account of a strange and wonderful but far-off land. The geographer duly recorded the details in his next map; but, wise perhaps in the enthusiasms of his colleagues, he also added a simple marginal note of his own—"believe it not."

Now, the word "frontier" in the title of this conference certainly seems a reasonable enough characterization of the present relation between computer simulation techniques and the study of personality. Yet as some of the grander images associated with the word came to mind, I could not help wondering how many of those coming across these proceedings (and

Financial support from the Carnegie Corporation of New York is gratefully acknowledged. The writer also is very much indebted to Professors Robert Leeper and Allen Newell for ideas and suggestions concerning the problems discussed here.

knowing the penchant of behavioral scientists for what someone once termed "dawn of discovery metaphor") would feel called upon to make similar annotation in the margins.

A substantial body of work utilizing computer models already exists, however, in several other psychological areas, and believers and non-believers alike may find some light shed upon the prospects for computer simulation of personality by an examination of some of these other efforts to apply computer modelling techniques to the study of psychological processes. Since Dr. Uhr's paper (Chapter 14) makes reference to the literature on simulation models in perception, the present discussion will be limited mainly to extrapolations from computer models of human problem-solving behavior—in particular, from the work of A. Newell, J. C. Shaw, H. A. Simon and their students and associates at the Carnegie Institute of Technology and the RAND Corporation (for a general discussion of these programs see Reitman, 1961).

We will make use of this work in two ways. In the first place, we will want to explore the possibilities for extending these models to include a broader range of personality processes. Problem-solving models, to be sure, cover a very limited number of the phenomena subsumed under the concept of personality. Nonetheless, as Dr. Tomkins has pointed out, to study personality is to study basic interrelations involving memory and thinking, and so it may well prove worthwhile for personality theorists to consider what might be accomplished by taking as a conceptual and methodological starting point in this area these existing computer simulation models of problem-solving behavior.

In the second place, since the first two sessions of this conference are intended to encourage exploration of some of the more general problems of computer simulation, we also may find it helpful to view work on problem-solving programs more broadly, in the light of the experience with these new techniques. In this connection, we will want to raise and consider questions concerning the kinds of structures and processes that can be represented in a computer program, and the kinds of problems and payoffs that may be expected by a theorist who wants to incorporate his hypotheses in a computer model. Any such over-all interpretation of this material is likely to prove subjective and fallible at many points, but it should serve to highlight some of the problems and possibilities which those who venture across this particular frontier are likely to encounter.

The General Problem Solver

For those less familiar with recent work on problem-solving programs, it may be helpful if we begin with a consideration of the General Problem Solver (Newell, Shaw & Simon, 1960), an excellent example of a highly sophisticated problem-solving program whose behavior has been compared systematically with that of human problem solvers (Newell & Simon, 1961). This program represents a deliberate attempt to devise a system which will handle a variety of kinds of problems. Its core consists of a basic executive and of heuristic methods for setting up, evaluating, and attempting goals. The long-range aim of its designers is to make this core of the program applicable to problems in any area which can be viewed as consisting of objects, operators for altering objects, features possessed by objects, and differences between objects.

The methods themselves, of course, are quite abstract and may be thought of as strategies, or plans for action, which are initiated by the executive. Each strategy consists of several units of behavior; as a unit is completed, control returns to the executive, which then evaluates the results. If progress has been made, in the sense that the current subproblem appears easier to solve than the original problem, the executive sets up a new attack on the subproblem. Thus, considerable behavioral flexibility is achieved by providing the executive with detailed, effectively continuous feedback concerning the consequences of the activities it has initiated, and by leaving it free after each of its acts to modify or adapt its plans in the light of this information.

Much of the power of the General Problem Solver depends upon an extremely important pair of characteristics. It is recursive, i.e., able to call upon itself to solve subproblems encountered in the course of a problem. Furthermore, this recursive capability is achieved by organizing problems in terms of goal structures—hierarchies whose elemental units are goals. Each of these goals is built up out of a series of common attributes, and it is this regularization of the total problem space which makes it possible for the basic core of problem-solving routines to work on problems wherever it finds them in the system. It is interesting to note that this same strategy of standardization within the problem space also enters as a significant factor in the success of a number of other important information processing models, e.g., Feigenbaum's (1961) model of discrimination learning and Lindsay's (1961) program for building information from the environment into cognitive maps.

Problem-Solving Models and Personality Processes

If we wish, we may view the General Problem Solver as one possible model of those aspects of cognitive activity which Rapaport[1] (1959, p. 71) termed "ordered veridical thought." As such, it is not immediately applicable to phenomena such as dreams, daydreams, or reveries, but it does constitute an explicit system of hypotheses about a subset of the processes and memory structures which enter into cognitive activity.

We may take the problem of intrapsychic communication as an example of the issues which such models raise for personality theory. An unprogrammed computer is passive and ignorant: it knows nothing and is capable of nothing. Thus, the theorist who wishes to assume some communication among the components of his psychic model must specify, either directly, or through the provision of appropriate learning and self-organizing capabilities, the manner and form in which information, commands, and requests at one level in the system are transmitted elsewhere. Nothing is available automatically until the appropriate storage and retrieval mechanisms, and the memory structures they serve, have been described in full on the theorist's code sheets. And as his system deals with its problems, generating new information and obsolescing old, it must have the means for learning, i.e., for adding new items to its memory, updating others, and disposing of still others. It

[1] While recognizing the wide differences which exist among personality theories, we are here, and in what follows, interested primarily in certain features which are quite generally characteristic of most analytic and non-analytic theories alike. Therefore, to avoid raising issues involving differences in language or emphasis which would be tangential to the questions considered here, we have by and large utilized Rapaport (1959) as a standardized reference throughout.

also must have, of course, processes enabling it to decide which items are which.

The theorist-programmer who deals with these problems may very well not be able to evaluate the consequences of his decisions until he has had some experience with his theory as a system of processes operating on the computer. Indeed, a principal reason for programming the theory is to provide just such experience with its implications. Only after he has had this kind of opportunity to explore the behavior of his system is he likely to be able to decide whether his intrapsychic communications are better thought of as terse Caesarean signals, or whether instead subsystems should be enabled to send and to interpret long-winded essays on local conditions to insure that no critical detail is missed, even though most of the information received turns out to be irrelevant. How much and what kind of information, for example, does the system need to keep from getting lost? And, on the other hand, how much complexity is assumed to be too much for the system, so that the theorist would want it and expect it to get lost when it passed that point?

Perhaps it seems far-fetched to characterize these kinds of questions as appropriate problems for the personality theorist. On the other hand, how otherwise is one to take account in a computer program of interrelationships such as those Dr. Tomkins has described in Chapter 1? A similar conclusion would seem to be implied for any theorist whose views are consistent with the position Rapaport (1959, pp. 83-84) takes in stating that:

> ...no behavior can be described as an id behavior, or an ego behavior, or a conscious behavior. These

> concepts all refer to specific aspects of behaviors and not to specific behaviors. Every behavior has conscious, unconscious, ego, id, superego, reality, etc., components...every behavioral phenomenon has perceptual, learning (memorial), conceptual (cognitive), motor, etc., components.

If we abstract the essence of this statement from the terminological mold in which it is cast, it seems likely that a great many personality theorists of widely differing persuasions would agree with it. Some of them still may judge it desirable as a tactical expedient to defer for a time consideration of the kinds of intrapsychic processes we have just discussed. But it is difficult to see how any theorist who agrees with the basic substance of Rapaport's position can avoid coming to grips with these questions in the long run. And it is just exactly here that the experience incorporated in sophisticated problem-solving models may be useful to the personality theorist who wishes to think about, represent, and program systems consisting of complex hierarchies of differentiated structures.

Possible Extensions of Problem-Solving Models to Personality

To explore the problems involved in extending problem-solving models to personality theory, we first must make explicit those aspects of personality theory which are not now represented in such models. We may do this by imagining for a moment what the "personality" of a General Problem Solver is like. Apart from the over-all lack of anything corresponding to affective processes, perhaps the most striking characteristics are the absence of conflict, of defenses against conflict, of wishful thinking, and, in general, of anything which might undermine the total unity of purpose such a system displays.

Compare this, for example, with the psychoanalytic conception of personality, with its emphasis on the dynamics of conflicting drives, drive discharge thresholds, countercathectic energy distributions controlling and defending against drive discharge, drive derivatives resulting from conflicts among opposing forces, and on the varied psychic manifestations of these phenomena—in short, on the instincts and their vicissitudes. Problem-solving models as now conceived simply make no use of such drive constructs. Energy is assumed to be available, and once such a system has begun to work at a problem, it will halt only when it can find no new possibilities to explore, or discovers that it lacks the information processing capacity with which to explore them.

There are two aspects of this basic difference in conceptualization between problem-solving models and personality theory which must be considered. The first has to do with the preference for information or energy concepts as basic. The second is a problem of system organization and involves dynamic and structural implications associated with the unitary character of problem-solving models, as compared with those which derive from the multiple drive conceptions of personality theory. Here it is not simply the difference between information and energy which concerns us, but also the consequences which follow from the postulation of distinct and perhaps conflicting needs and motives.

Energy vs. Information as Basic Concepts

Some of the structural and dynamic differences associated with the choice of information concepts rather than energy concepts as basic to problem-solving models may be seen by comparing the notion of a goal hierarchy as found in the General Problem Solver with the related idea of a motivational hierarchy. The General Problem Solver generates subgoals at every level in the course of its activity. The relation of any goal to its subgoal consists in the fact that attainment of a series of subgoals (i.e., solution of a set of subproblems set up in working on a higher-order problem) means attainment of the higher-order goal as well, regardless of the distance between the original goal and particular subgoals in the goal hierarchy. In psychoanalytic formulations, however, satisfaction of a derivative motive generally is considered to provide less and less satisfaction, for the antecedent motive as the derivative motive becomes increasingly distant from its antecedents. And, conversely, while motives may be partially satisfied, informational goals—in the General Problem Solver at least—are either attained in full or they are not attained at all.

The General Problem Solver in processing symbols is not attempting to discharge energy, but rather to construct a path between points in a problem space. Consequently, attainment of any full set of subgoals means in effect that the last link in the path has been found and that the work of path construction is complete. The motivational model also is concerned with path construction, of course, but it faces the added problems of energy utilization, transformation, and disposition as well, and must take into account energy configurations related to path capacity, path blockage, and so on.

It seems fair to assert that at the present time no single theoretical framework encompasses both the energetic and informational aspects of psychological activity in a wholly satisfactory fashion. Certainly, stimulating and imaginative efforts to bridge the gap between cognitive and drive concepts —D. O. Hebb's (1949, 1955) formulations, for example—are major steps in this direction. But it remains true that problem-solving models in effect avoid the issue by assuming energy availability and by working only with activities which can be dealt with solely in terms of the functioning of the cognitive apparatus. Psychoanalytic models, on the other hand, although they may assume some more or less neutral energies at the disposal of the ego, are obliged, at least in Rapaport's (1959, p. 96) judgment, to face the fact that "the problem of the energy supply of these apparatuses (when they are not triggered by drives) has so far not been satisfactorily solved." The main point to be emphasized here is that the preference for information concepts in problem-solving models clearly has no necessary relation to their formal status as computer programs. The issue is purely and basically psychological, and it seems reasonable to suggest that computer programs, by allowing us to compare the detailed behaviors implied by a variety of possible formulations, may prove useful in enabling us to make further headway in dealing with it.

Differences in Dynamic Organization

If we turn now to those organizational features comprising the second side of the basic difference between problem-solving models and personality theory referred to above, we find them to concern a fundamental question of initiation and control of activity. What is involved is the distinction between serial vs. parallel, or centralized vs. decentralized, decision making, although since the alternatives actually are much more complex, as we will see, these dichotomies are perhaps best regarded primarily as useful first approximations.

In dealing with this question, it is extremely important to differentiate between serial conceptualization and serial realization of computer models. Any model which runs on a present-day computer will be serially realized, because these computers can do only one thing at a time. But while many of these models, particularly in the area of perception or pattern recognition,[2] are conceived and executed as approximations to systems which may do many things at once, current problem-solving models are serial not only in realization, but also in conceptualization. That is, only one process may be active at any one time, and all activity is subordinated to a single hierarchy of control.

Such a formulation clearly conflicts with the underlying organizational assumptions inherent in most theories of personality, which allow for the possibility of several independently originated activities simultaneously under way. Psychoanalytic theories, for example, treat the id as a "congeries of drives (coexistent even if contradictory)" (Rapaport, 1959, p. 95). Psychic activity is considered to arise from a variety of sources —sensory stimulation, drive excitations, or, in the case of dreams, from preconscious day residues (Rapaport, 1959, p. 67)—with no explicit constraints, apparently, on the number of activities which simultaneously may be under way and exerting influence on cognitive processes. Even the ego, though it serves primarily as a many-sided control system regulating and

---

[2]See Uhr (1960, 1962) and White (1962) for discussions of these programs. Reitman (1962a) describes a very interesting parallel pattern recognition program, the work of the Soviet scientist M. M. Bongard.

channelling tensions from varying sources, is held by many to have some degree of independence and autonomy with respect to other personality components, and thus it constitutes still another set of loci from which activity may originate.

Such a decentralized system of parallel active agents poses a variety of possibilities for conflict, cooperation, and coordination which simply do not arise in a centralized decision-making system such as the General Problem-Solver. Here there never are any conflicts about ends, but only uncertainties as to means. There may be, of course, several alternate subgoals available at one time, from among which the executive must make a choice, and certain subgoals consequently may never be attempted. But such choices are not conceptualized as the outcomes of competitions among conflicting forces; rather they reflect centralized decisions made among alternatives in the light of their relative promise. The subgoals themselves have none of the characteristics of desires, cooperating and competing in their simultaneous striving for satisfaction. They are no more than alternate possibilities for action, passively awaiting and accepting the evaluations and decisions the controlling executive makes in the light of its over-all goal. Since no concept of distinct and potentially competing drives is involved, there is no sense in which the system, in achieving one goal, simultaneously may be said to be frustrating others. Rejected subgoals, unlike blocked and frustrated drives, have no dynamic implications for the future behavior of the system. They are simply there—action alternatives which might have been initiated, but never were.

Personality as a Problem-Solving Coalition

Given this basic discontinuity in underlying organization between current computer models of cognitive activity on the one hand and personality theory on the other, how is the theorist who wishes to use related computer simulation models in the study of personality to proceed? How might it be possible to design a parallel model which incorporated the information processing sophistication of a General Problem Solver? Certainly if our goal is the construction of comprehensive models of personality which include representations of the cognitive functions of the ego and yet are consistent with the assumption of fundamentally parallel personality structure, some such aspiration would seem to be required.

Part of the problem involved in such an attempt arises from the vagueness of the very concept of a parallel processing system itself. As we mentioned earlier, the serial vs. parallel or centralized vs. decentralized dichotomies are merely rough footholds in a very complex territory. For just as the assertion that a system is nonlinear tells us nothing about the ways in which it deviates from linearity, so the concept of a parallel system of itself implies nothing about the kind or extent of parallel activity, or about the constraints to which that activity is subject.

Nor is there very much experimental evidence available to guide us as we attempt to reduce to the specifics of computer programs the general concepts of personality as some kind of a parallel system. A number of investigators (for example, Broadbent, 1958, 1962; Miller, 1956) have made clear certain of the limitations such programs would have to reflect, by presenting some striking evidence demonstrating some of the things humans can not do. Within these limitations, however, there remains a large number of underlying organizational principles which might serve as bases for explanations of how humans achieve those performances of which they are capable.

Similarly, although we also have data from a number of investigations of the behavioral effects of experimentally induced parallel motivational activity (e.g., Atkinson & Reitman, 1956), these studies generally have been designed largely in terms of energy concepts, and so they too cast relatively little direct light on underlying principles of organization and control. Both of these lines of exploration quite likely could be expanded to provide experimental evidence regarding fully developed models of the organization of psychological activity. But such a prospect, however promising it seems, would appear to require much closer interaction between computer model building and experimental sophistication and imagination than is generally the case at the present time.

Lacking this sort of firm evidence regarding the underlying organization of psychological processes, some personality theorists may perhaps wish to examine what we do know about the structure and dynamics of certain parallel problem-solving systems which lie outside the domain of intrapsychic phenomena. The perceived relevance of this data will depend on the extent to which we are willing to go beyond our usual frames of reference and look at the problem of personality organization from a cybernetic or systems point of view.[3]

---

[3] For several different discussions of this point of view and its possible advantages, see Ashby (1956), Miller (1955), Reitman (1962b), Simon (1962), Wiener (1961), and Wiesner (1958).

Should we be willing to utilize such a framework, we may view problem solving and decision making as a process of resource allocation involving cycles of choices made over alternative information generating subsystems in the light of previous experience, current feedback, and over-all system goals. Thus, for example, the General Problem Solver, as it decides among the paths, methods, and subgoals available at some point in time, may be considered to be making decisions regarding allocation of the time and capacity resources of the system. A considerable amount of effort has been devoted to the study of such resource allocation decisions in larger parallel processing systems such as business firms and economic organizations generally (e.g., Whinston, 1962). The resulting data and theoretical formulations are of interest because of the relative ease with which coordination and control mechanisms in such systems may be observed, and also because the data are organized to reflect upon precisely the sorts of problems with which we are concerned.

With extension of problem-solving models to parallel systems as a goal, if we now utilize a resource allocation framework to examine the functional organization of, say, a business firm (see Dalton, 1959; Dill, Hilton, & Reitman, 1962; Simon, 1957), we find that the activities of subsystems in such an organization are mobilized and controlled by utilizing resources not simply to _permit_ subsystem contributions, as in the General Problem Solver, but also to _induce_ and _reward_ them. This observation suggests that problem-solving models might be extended to enable them to cope with personality dynamics by thinking of personality as a coalition of subsystems, with interdependent but by no means necessarily identical interests, operating within the constraints of a common organism and a common information processing apparatus.

In terms of such a framework, with each subsystem seeking to advance its own ends, individual activated goals no longer need have the unchallenged imperative force of executive mandates in the General Problem Solver. Instead, each could be viewed as imposing constraints, i.e., offering positive and negative inducements to the relevant information-processing components. Assuming, furthermore, certain limits upon the set of inducements at the command of any element in the coalition, such a formulation would seem to provide a possible bridge across the gap discussed earlier between information-oriented and drive-conceived theories of psychological activity. For example, one might arrange matters so that drives and environmental stimuli as well, originated independently, implied positive or negative outcomes associated with system activities, and perhaps also had direct effects upon the capabilities and mode of functioning of the cognitive apparatus.

The basic potential advantage of such an approach is that it encompasses both the active, parallel character of psychological needs and also the information-processing and problem-solving capabilities of the organism. But while we have tried to state it in a manner which is consistent with the programming methods now at our command, the particular formulation given here is in itself certainly not novel (cf. Hebb, 1955), nor does it immediately answer any of the questions we raised concerning the specific organization and the extent of parallel activity in humans. We have not attempted to specify, for example, whether memory structures activated by drives might themselves facilitate activation of other structures, as

Hebb (1949) suggests; or whether memory is to be thought of instead as wholly passive, as in the General Problem Solver, with parallel activity confined entirely to drives (and with such drives conceived of as implying changing patterns of potential reward values for the various goal possibilities up for consideration at particular times). Similarly, since we have left open the question of the inducements at the command of the control apparatus itself, such a formulation leaves open a full range of possibilities related to degree of integration of the control apparatus and its ability to withstand patterns of drive originated inducements which could bias the outcomes of information-processing activities in certain components, thus distorting the information available to the rest of the system.

Earlier, in discussing intrapsychic communication, we noted that the existence of an item somewhere in a system hardly insures that it will get to where it is needed in usable form, and we pointed out some of the questions about memory organization and the associated processes for recording and retrieving information which arise in designing problem-solving systems. If now we consider a system in which subsystems are able to do such things as induce concealment or refuse access to information which other subsystems require to achieve their aims, perhaps using defensive techniques analogous to those observed in multiperson systems (e.g., Dalton, 1959, especially Chapters 3 and 4), obviously the programming problems we face become extremely complex. All of these psychological possibilities have been discussed in the literature, however, and the over-all formulation of them considered here almost certainly could be specified for the computer in a form enabling at least some degree of exploration of their implications. In this sense, a conception of personality as a problem-solving coalition would seem to offer a framework at once broad enough to permit delineation and investigation of a variety of hypotheses concerning personality organization, and yet specific enough to be compatible with current problem-solving programs, thus enabling us to take full advantage of the programming experience and sophistication incorporated in serially conceived models such as the General Problem Solver.

Methodological Considerations

Having now completed our consideration of some of the ways in which current problem-solving programs might be extended to enable them to deal with a broader range of personality processes, we turn to a brief examination of some more general questions of computer simulation as they appear in the light of experience with problem-solving programs we now have.

The points to be made here deal with the limits of computer representation of psychological theories, with simplification and approximation as model building strategies, and with the role of computer models in the context of the set of theory building and theory testing methods available to psychology. The section concludes with brief discussions of appropriate aspiration levels for computer models of personality processes, and of some of the problems which communication about these models may involve.

Computer Models as Representations of Psychological Structures and Processes

Let us consider first the question of theory representation. What kinds of ideas may be specified in a computer program, and what kinds may not? In examining the uses one can make of the computer, we may think of it both as a memory system for storing information and also as a processing system for manipulating that information. Just as pencil and paper permit us both to store and also to manipulate representations of ideas, so it is with the computer; it serves both as a medium and as a tool.

The variety of computer models of problem-solving processes will bear witness to the fact that, in considering the potentialities of the computer as a medium, it is important to avoid imagining that we are dealing with something akin to a cupboard full of numbers. Perhaps computer memories are instead better thought of as having an organizational flexibility not very much different from that of a sheet of paper. Certainly the wide range of uses to which they have been put reflect something very close to this degree of flexibility.

Those who have employed computers for such computational assignments as analysis of variance, regression analysis, factor analysis, etc., are familiar with a memory organization which, in terms of our analogy, might be compared with graph paper, with each point on the paper having coordinates associated with it. But this is hardly the only way in which computer memory may be organized. One might equally well ignore the dividing lines and treat the memory as an approximation to a two-dimensional space, almost like a blank sheet of paper. White (1962), for example, describes a number of studies in which computer memories have been used to store representations of visual patterns. The distinction with respect to continuity between computer memory and paper is, after all, a relative one, since we might just as well consider paper as a two-dimensional array of units whose size is just below the resolving power of the human eye as defined by the two-dot limen.

Having said this, I certainly don't wish to pretend that such a use of computer memory is anything but inefficient and expensive, relative to other representational media holding the same information. On the other hand, there are certain structures we wish to represent, e.g., higher order abstract spaces, for which computer memory is very well suited. By contrast, as those who have rotated factor structures by hand will testify, the number of axes which may be represented simultaneously on a sheet of paper is extremely limited. And this is the whole point: the appropriate way in which to consider the advantages and limitations of a particular representation in a particular medium is relative to a particular use. Just as the absolute limitations of the sheet of paper as a medium in which to represent abstract spaces will for most other purposes be of no particular concern, so the limitations of a particular organization of computer memory need be of no consequence so long as we understand the advantages and disadvantages they imply relative to the particular use to which we wish to put the memory.

For those working with mathematical representations of psychological processes, this point must be perfectly obvious. I emphasize it only because computers, being new and having been used so far primarily as computational devices, sometimes are treated as if their organization were as restrictive as that of a desk calculator, particularly when it comes to serving as vehicles for psychological theory.

Before we can specify in just what ways a particular theory depends in any fundamental or critical sense on the advantages and limitations of the medium in which it is represented, we first must explore these limitations in detail, learn what constraints they imply, and then determine in the light of what we ideally would like to do whether a particular organization of a particular medium allows us to do it easily, with difficulty, only with certain simplifications, or perhaps not at all.

By the same token, just as we ought to avoid confusing the limitations of a particular memory organization with those of the underlying medium, so we will want to avoid unwarranted generalizations from the limitations of a particular model to putative characteristics of the memory organization in terms of which that model is defined. The fact that some problem-solving models, for example, lack semantic referents for symbols should not be taken to mean that information-processing systems cannot provide such internal semantic referents. There are in fact models which do (e.g., Gelernter, 1960; Lindsay, 1961). Similarly, the fact that the General Problem Solver is serially organized and lacks drive terms implies not that problem-solving models somehow are intrinsically unable to deal with multiple energy formulations, but only that having started off with information concepts, they so far have not _had_ to do so, and have not done so.

If we return now to the representational possibilities for psychology inherent in the particular organization of computer memory (Newell, 1961, 1962) used in most of the problem-solving programs to which we have referred, we find that items of information are tied together in memory in a manner analogous to writing them down on paper and then drawing interconnecting lines from one item to any others associated with it. The items themselves are treated as pure symbols, and may stand for anything at all—ideas, concepts, affects, or what have you—and they may be moved about or reconnected with one another at our convenience. Thus, this organization of computer memory is very well suited to the representation of psychological associations generally, since the only things that matter are the items themselves and the connections among them. The basic units such an organization of memory provides are themselves associative, for example, the list and the list structure. At a higher level, these basic units may be organized to provide more complex structural concepts such as Feigenbaum's (1961) discrimination net, Lindsay's (1961) cognitive map, and Newell, Shaw and Simon's (1960) goals and goal hierarchy. Similarly, the basic flexibility of the memory organization permits specification of a wide variety of types of processes, and these may be integrated into programs—tools for manipulating the information structures in memory—which may be as complex as we choose to make them.

Though our basic memory organization may permit a degree of flexibility and complexity of representation which verges on the heroic, there are times, particularly in beginning the exploration of a new area, when it may be wiser to be a live jackal than a dead lion. Or as McKeachie (1962) has put it, in speaking of a similar situation, sometimes it pays to think small. This is not an injunction to work at any particular level of psychological theory, but simply an attempt to point out that programs may be constructed in such a way as not to require completeness and full detail immediately. The advantage of information-processing models at this point, given some overall idea of the system you wish to deal with, is that they allow you to make any initial simplifications you choose, and yet at the same time to organize your work in such a way as to make possible the gradual removal of simplifications—the gradual filling in of the blank spaces, without necessarily requiring any reworking of what you already have done.

Consider as a hypothetical example how one might treat affect in a model which at least initially is focussed on some other intrapsychic phenomenon. We spoke of using a pure symbol as a representation for an affect. While this will allow one to do little more than associate affects with other psychological phenomena, for some purposes, at least initially, that may be enough. Later on, or should this turn out to be too severe a simplification, we may convert these symbols into independent variables, thus allowing the affect value associated with a phenomenon to generate consequences elsewhere in the system. Or, again, we might also choose to make affect a dependent variable, a function of changes in drive level, or perhaps in cognitive activity, as Hebb (1949) would suggest.

Each new complication will, of course, mean a longer running time on the computer, and may also add to the number of things we, as programmers, must worry about as well. Consequently, perhaps long before the capacity limits of the computer have been reached, we may decide that for our particular purpose we would prefer to accept certain simplifications so as to focus more effectively on the details of some other aspects of our problem. Given the flexibility of the computer, however, it is extremely difficult to conceive of a structure or process which could not be represented, at some cost and to some degree of approximation, and this is the reason for our emphasis here upon patterns of advantages and limitations relative to a particular memory organization and a particular intent, in preference to unconditional statements about what computers can or cannot do.

Possible Roles for Computer Models in Psychological Research

Accepting for the moment these general propositions regarding computer representations, and with reference to the total set of research methods available to the personality theorist, what roles are computer models peculiarly suited to? One possibility derives from the computer's ability to incorporate a system of hypotheses concerning the structure and functioning of a complex psychological system. Rapaport (1959, p. 131) in fact suggested that:

> ...structures play such a crucial role that as long as the propensities and changes of psychological structure cannot be expressed in the same dimensions as psychological processes, dimensional quantification is but a pious hope. In other words, the study of the process of psychological structure formation seems to be the prime prerequisite for progress toward dimensional quantification. We must establish how processes turn into structures, how a structure, once formed, changes, and how it gives rise to and influences processes.

We have to do here with basic issues involving the establishment and development of a complex interacting system over time—just the sort of thing we can study with relative ease and precision in terms of a computer model and the behaviors it emits as it is run. In general, the use of computer models in the formalization, objectification and analysis of systems of interlocking structures and processes should, as Rapaport implies, prove extremely useful as an antecedent to studies of behavior conceived of primarily in terms of the kinds of measures and measure interrelations now employed, by serving to provide precise hypotheses about a class of variables which such studies do not now seek to measure directly.

I may, perhaps, seem to be emphasizing this role of computer models as simply one component of a battery of psychological tools at the expense of the concept of "simulation"; if so, here is why. If "simulation" is used as a synonym for model, then of course the words are interchangeable. But while model usually refers to a representation of hypotheses concerning the variables underlying some phenomenon, the term simulation often seems to carry with it the suggestion that the performance of the model we have built in fact reproduces in some respects the behavior of the natural system. If this is the case, then to speak of simulation would imply that we have solved the relevant measurement problems with respect to the natural system. If this implication is intended, however, we must take care to determine and to communicate just exactly the sense in which the performances of the natural and artificial systems are similar, and, at least as important, in what respects they are not similar. To bring the point home with an extreme example, Mr. Robert Dupchak, a graduate student at Carnegie Tech, has written an ingenious computer program for a penny matching game. It records information about the pattern of its opponent's plays, attempts to outguess its opponent, and modifies its internal structure as a consequence of the results of its performance. Thus we might say that by some definitions, this program perceives, learns, and solves problems (making money, incidentally, as it goes). But this program consists of a total of seven operating instructions!

Mr. Dupchak, of course, makes no claim to having solved three of psychology's basic problems in seven instructions, and I have introduced his program here mainly because it brings out so clearly the basic problem we all face. If we are to avoid arid definitional disputes in connection with claimed simulations and instead make ourselves and our work understood, we must be careful to explain precisely what we have simulated, what we have not simulated, and most important of all, perhaps, just what is the importance of those aspects we have been concerned with in the context of the over-all psychological functioning of the organism and the over-all enterprise of psychological research.

Perhaps I might suggest a second reason for caution in focussing too literally on simulation in the second sense specified above. Without trying to guess at the success we are likely to achieve in efforts to reproduce in detail patterns of behavior of significance for personality theory, I wonder whether too strong an emphasis immediately on reproducing behavior may not in fact obscure one of the really basic virtues of computer models. As discussions by Chapanis (1961) and others make clear, until very recently most areas within psychology have had little experience with anything other than verbal models. Even when we used physical processes as analogues, the mechanics of manipulation remained verbal. Now, however, the computer offers us new vehicles for stating and exploring the implications of systems of psychological constructs. While I believe that in the long run we must strive for predictive tests of our models, in exactly the sense that experimental psychology now conceives of predictive tests, we ought not ignore the benefits to be derived from objectification and experimentation with the constructs themselves, even in those cases in which experimental verification of our formulations is not immediately feasible.

As George Kelly (Chapter 13) has pointed out, the fact that one gets out of a computer model, in some sense, just what one puts in is in many ways not a disadvantage but an advantage. There can never be an doubt but that the behavior the computer emits follows *necessarily* from our model. And if we are willing to equate this behavior with those organismic behaviors which concern us, then we know that our theory is *sufficient* to generate those behaviors.

It is in indicating these necessary and sufficient connections that computer models excel, as compared with either verbal models or direct experimental manipulations. With verbal models, it is practically impossible to be certain that one's conclusions follow from explicit assumptions only, and that they in no way depend upon "unprogrammed" assumptions which somehow or other may have entered unperceived into the course of the argument. With direct experimentation on living subjects, there is no way to separate a test of one's *theory* from the test of the environmental manipulations, measures, and *ceteris paribus* conditions which couple the theory via operational definitions to the real world. Only in a model expressed in a formal language—be it a mathematical or a computer language—is it possible to formulate, manipulate, and deduce the necessary consequences of one's theory *independent* of the operations which relate it to data.

Admittedly, the benefits of such investigations are limited. They do not provide either immediate empirical tests of theory or immediate solutions for the difficulties we face in measuring and quantifying personality processes. They do, however, offer a real opportunity, perhaps our first real opportunity, to provide public and objective representations of complex systems of intrapsychic processes, and to explore the properties of such systems. If it is true, as many have argued, that most tests of personality theory propositions, and in particular of propositions from psychoanalytic theory, have not cast much light on the validity of the theory because they have been tests of isolated relations, rather than of systems of relations as a whole, then the use of computer models to objectify such systems of propositions may be an invaluable and indispensable first step in devising experimental validations.

I should like very briefly to indicate three further points which arise in connection with this view of the uses of computer models in connection with personality theory. While it is helpful to write down a program which expresses formally a particular process or procedure even when we think we understand it quite well, the real power of the computer is realized only when we write down a set of processes whose interactions we do not understand, but wish to explore. It is quite common, for example, for students in a course on the uses of computer models to hunt out a psychological theory or problem more or less amenable to formalization in terms of a relatively fixed sequence of discriminations and operations, in part, perhaps, to insure having a program which runs by the end of the semester. This strategy does make for rapid development of skill and confidence in the use of computers and computer models, but it also probably underplays the potential of these models as devices for exploring systems of assumptions whose implications are not reasonably clear in advance.

My second point follows from the first and has to do with the fine art of collecting information concerning a system's capabilities—much as one might do with an experimental animal, to use an analogy Dr. Abelson once suggested. The problem involved is comparable to that which confronts the investigator who teaches one class using one technique and a second class using another, and then wishes to account for the differences he obtains. Since each technique consists of many aspects, a great deal of further experimentation will be required before he can say with any certainty just what accounts for what. Like a modern jet airplane, a computer model consists of a great many interacting components. True, malfunctioning of the jet is likely to be a great deal more catastrophic, but the same kind of analysis, exploration, and testing is required in both cases before we can be sure that we understand why what goes on goes on. Without this exploratory work, computer simulations are mainly demonstrative in nature, existence proofs testifying that a system which achieves certain kinds of results can, in fact, be built without, however, pinning down the details whereby the results are achieved.

My final point has to do with the communication problems those who build computer models will face, and it follows from the first two. What is the man who constructs a twenty thousand instruction system to say about it? Even a good static description of such a system is likely to run to well over a hundred pages (see, for example, the detailed description of a recent version of the General Problem Solver in Newell, 1962), and I know of no good way to communicate the dynamic details of such a system, i.e., how it works and what it does as it runs. This problem is sure to cause difficulties even with the best of intentions, and it is at least as much for this reason as for any other that I have stressed and would emphasize again the confusions which are likely to arise from unqualified use of the term "simulation" to describe incompletely specified resemblances between human behavior and the behavior of a complex model.

These caveats notwithstanding, experience with computer models of problem-solving behavior clearly suggests that computer models of personality processes are likely to make invaluable contributions to personality theory in a number of important directions, and, in particular, in these three:

(1) Since they provide a unique opportunity for concept objectification (for example, of such concepts as "goal hierarchy" or "cognitive map" as discussed above), they should contribute immeasurably to more adequate specification of problems and to the exploration of the implications of our concepts.

(2) Since they allow us to separate tests of the implications of a theory from the associated measurement problems, they provide what is probably our first real opportunity to explore our theories systematically in a manner which is at once objective and yet independent of variables defined statistically over many individuals.

(3) Finally, since they permit us to work in terms of processes and structures as well as attributes, they enable us to undertake analyses of the actual time

paths of those active, problem solving, pattern seeking behaviors which make up so much of the socially significant aspects of human life.

In other words, to return to the "dawn of discovery" metaphor with which we began, it would seem that we have good reason for high hopes as we cross this particular new frontier. This is not to imply that the three directions mentioned above should in any sense be taken as summaries or prescriptions with respect to the kinds of uses to which computer models may or should be put. As we have noted, the range of employments is extremely broad and not to be captured in a few sentences. Nor does it mean that everyone will find computer models to his liking or advantage. The importance of a consideration of possibilities relative to a particular purpose cannot be overemphasized. It means simply that we now have a new general purpose tool, that explorations with it so far have proven very promising, and that there is good reason to hope that explorations in the future will prove still more so.

5 DOUGLAS N. JACKSON
Pennsylvania State University

Discussion:

Strategic Problems in Research on Computer Models of Personality

Dr. Reitman (Chapter 4) has provided us with a balanced and lucid discussion of both some of the potentialities and some of the possible pitfalls in the development of computer models of personality. I found his explication of the similarities and the differences between problem-solving models and personality models particularly useful. When I first learned the title of his paper, I was set to argue at length the proposition that personality is something more than a chess player or other type of complex problem solver, but Reitman himself has done this so well and so thoroughly that it is hardly necessary for me to proffer additional comments on this theme. However, Reitman does not stop with a mere cataloguing of differences between personalities and problem solvers. He argues persuasively that personality theory might gain by considering its dynamics in terms of an amalgamation of parallel processes.

The author thanks Perry London for his careful reading of this discussion.

The author is on leave, 1962-63, at the Institute for the Study of Human Problems, Stanford University, on a Special Research Fellowship of the National Institute of Mental Health, U.S. Public Health Service.

While functioning within an organized system, each of these processes would have only partially common goals and each would seek to further its own ends. Constraints would be imposed not only by a common information processing apparatus but by the very hominoid quality of being able to "look ahead" to discover the implicit positive or negative outcomes in alternative system activities, with their resultant potential for altering the future mode of cognitive functioning of the organism. Reitman's grasp of the potentialities and the pitfalls involved in such an approach reflects, I believe, an intimate association with computer science as well as a scholarly appreciation of the personality theory he has chosen as illustrative, namely, latter-day psychoanalytic ego theory (Rapaport, 1959).

Reitman's enthusiasm for this "frontier" of research is so well tempered with scientific caution, and his arguments so well flavored with a close analysis of the ways in which existing problem-solving programs may depart from the proper form of a model of personality, that I should like to forego the usual discussant's prerogative of serving as a sort of super-ego which, on the one hand, notes that "while frontiers are fine, let's return to reality" and, on the other hand, makes carping remarks about details of the exposition. Reitman's analysis, being in the nature of an exploratory foray into essentially uncharted territory, indicates the general directions of potentially fruitful pathways, the general nature of a few traps to avoid, and some possible special advantages of computers in theory construction. Whether or not the specific details of this foray prove in time to be the most useful approaches, we should not venture to guess in the absence of extensive experience with this type of simulation. Rather I prefer to present some general remarks on two topics: (a) the strategy of simulation and the choice of a model; and (b) the problem of measurement and of individual differences.

The Choice of a Model

Reitman has admonished us, particularly in the exploratory phases of computer simulation of personality, to "think small" in the sense that one might be well advised to work with a program that is far from complete in all of its specifications and implications, rather than run a severe risk of failure in attempting to construct a complete model. Reitman is not explicitly arguing that any particular kind of theory or any particular level of abstraction will be necessarily more fruitful than others, although he repeatedly draws upon Rapaport (1959) for illustrative purposes.

I believe that the injunction to think small is at least as relevant to the abstraction level of the model and theory as it is to the informational completeness of the model. An abstract theory or model which has many oversimplifications of terms may indeed have very general implications, but its very lack of specificity and remote relation to possible data does not permit those implications to be adequately realized. Like the pantheistic god, or perhaps a general theory of behavior systems (cf. Borgatta, 1954; Buck, 1956), at some point meaning may be sacrificed for inclusiveness. The discovery of a general law of some particular class of phenomena is clearly a desirable goal of science. However, it is the present author's view that those who struggle to find completely general statements about personality are quite optimistic in view of the inherent complexity of the domain and the host of particular considerations operating at any given time. Indeed, complete generality of treatment of a domain as vast as behavior without specification of rules of correspondence or a clear delineation of referents might well result in an informational void (Buck, 1956). Given a choice between Reitman's two examples, penny matching or psychoanalytic ego theory, I believe that a more fruitful first step might be the development of a program for personality variables in penny matching than in the more grandiose alternative. Of course, a theory of the scope of psychoanalytic theory might be an ultimate goal, but here, as elsewhere, a useful antecedent to learning to run is learning to walk.

There is yet another reason for preferring a problem of not much more scope than a model of binary choice behavior over a general theory of motivation as a beginning in simulation research. Most of the processes that the psychoanalytic model purports to describe are intrapsychic, often with remote behavioral consequences which are difficult both to observe and to specify. The hope is that by developing and programming a model for intrapsychic processes we can then be in a position to follow, for example, an energy transformation as in the emergence of a repressed idea into consciousness, thereby understanding a process through simulation which in real life must be inferred from, at best, indirect observation. But on what basis do we conclude that our simulated process is the real "McCoy"? By what criterion do we conclude that this process and no other accounts for the emergence of this particular idea into consciousness? Is our whole output history of the computer on a particular program a good indication of the process? I doubt that events having remote observable consequences, such as those described by psychoanalytic ego theory, will be rendered more observable by looking at the behavior of a computer. Of course, if behavioral consequences of a given process were rather direct, an investigator might be quite well satisfied with a model which described the necessary and sufficient conditions for the behavior, even though it did not simulate underlying processes—but then no statement could be made about these processes. To be sure, one might seek to simulate the processes of a particular individual about whom a great deal of data has been accumulated regarding essentially intrapsychic processes, as Colby (Chapter 9) has so carefully done with the neurotic organization of beliefs of a single patient undergoing psychoanalysis. Beyond running the risk of developing a model peculiar to a single individual, one might rapidly encounter a paradox similar to Reitman's problem of one-hundred page program descriptions, namely the paradox of Tristram Shandy, who spent many years writing about the first days of his life (Sterne, 1962). As Reitman suggests, computer simulation allows complexity and flexibility of heroic proportions, but if the esthetic sense of the scientist is to be appeased, some inductive generalizations from models for single individuals would be needed, a requirement of which I am sure those developing such models are aware.

Individual Differences and the Problem of Measurement

Much of what I wish to say about measurement is implicit in the foregoing. As in any other type of model construction, there is the necessity at some point of returning to the bewildering diversity of sense impressions, to borrow Einstein's phrase, in order to establish that our model in some sense describes the real world, rather than being a purely formal system. In the case of the computer model, there is the necessity to establish the relevance of the model for describing personality or motivation as it actually occurs. Reitman notes that computer models allow one to explore the implications of a theory independently of measurement operations, by establishing quantities by fiat. But few personality theories are so constituted as to permit more than the weakest sort of statements about quantitative relationships, i.e., directional statements. Therefore, in attempting to work out implications, a good many rather arbitrary assumptions regarding the extent and nature of relationships among variables of various kinds and levels would be required. Furthermore, circumventing the problem of measurement is at best temporary with the computer model. In order to establish the validity of a computer for some domain, it is evident that some process of matching the behavior of the computer and that of people is required. At least some of the processes assumed to be operating in people will have to be assigned epistemic and measurement definitions, by some sort of observation of the people as well as of the computer. While the computer model may allow greater control over certain hypothetical intrapsychic events, such as certain types of anxiety arousal, <u>some</u> of the implications of the model will require comparison with real people. Computers provide fertile soil for developing models of personality but, as with other models, one cannot indefinitely avoid the rigors, and sometimes the disappointments, of validation and its concommitant measurement problems. In the case of a well-formalized theory or of a model developed directly in computer concepts, Reitman's point that implications of theories may be worked out rather thoroughly independently from measurement problems is well taken, but it is important to recognize that one cannot circumnavigate measurement operations entirely.

Just as measurement is an unavoidable, if sometimes onerous, requirement of theory validation, so too are individual differences fundamental to the study of personality. Some theorists (cf. Klein & Krech, 1951) have even defined personality as the study of individual differences in motivation, perception, learning, and other "part systems." I see in computer simulation research a great opportunity to study the implications of individual differences in personality. I expect this to be the case for three important reasons: (a) computer models can vastly increase the range of possible individual difference variables which may be brought to bear on a given problem; (b) computers afford an opportunity to explore systematically hierarchies and levels of personality dimensions; and (c) moderator effects and other types of non-linear relationships may be more adequately studied with the aid of the computer.

In the past the study of consistencies in personality has often been hampered by an unwillingness to come to grips in a systematic way with the many varieties of human differences, in a too-ready acceptance of theoretically naive assessment devices, on the one hand, or in rather loose theorizing of a clinical or idiographic sort, on the other. The obvious prescription, far easier to write than to fill, is for a science of personality that will do full justice to the complexities of human nature, while remaining logically consistent and rigorous, with sound empirical underpinnings. I do not know the degree to which the "ultimate" science of personality will employ, for example, non-linear dependencies. I am confident, however, that the future will see far more complex conceptions of man than are now envisioned in contemporary personality theory. Not only will the conception of characteristics be far more differentiated, but their hierarchical structuring, their relationship to a host of situational determinants, and their temporal patterning will all be better understood as they are organized in different types of people. Recently, Tucker (1962) has proposed a model for factor analyses of three-way matrices of traits by persons over occasions. Not only would the computational routine by quite arduous without the aid of a computer, but results from such an analysis would be a challenge to personality theories and theorists alike. This suggests that models of man faithfully representing the diversity inherent in the subject matter of object cathexes, belief systems, styles of responding, modes of perception and of learning, etc., might be far too complex for a single theorist to grasp in their totality. Perhaps, too, a purely verbal representation of these models could not avoid becoming morassed in a fen of communication and definitional difficulties. If human nature in its entirety, in the sense of a "complete" theory of personality, was beyond the scope of the reasoning of a single individual, then personality theorists would either have to learn to be content to "think small" (an unlikely turn of events) or, alternatively, to seek a system with greater storage capacity than the human brain, such as a computer. It is not proposed that computers at present can be constructed to show the flexibility of the human brain, but rather that their enormous potential for handling large numbers of variables in complicated relations to one another as they determine a given behavioral act may be superior in speed and accuracy to the human brain. As one indication of the potential complexity inherent in solid-state computers by use of novel designing techniques, it is estimated that by one such technique "the component density in a finished circuit could be 50 million per square inch per layer... It is conceivable that more than 10,000 layers per inch could be formed, giving a volume density of 5×10^{11} components per cubic inch." (Buck & Shoulders, 1959, p. 2, quoted in Burks, 1959.) Such a computer should contain a flexibility and a capacity at least equal to the task of representing personality and the forces acting upon it over time and at different levels, allowing for restructuring in the face of different need states and goals, and the like.

The Dawn of Discovery

It is clear from Reitman's discussion, and from the accumulating research in computer science, that our knowledge of personality may be expanded not only by looking at simulated models of man but also at the results of human interaction with simulated personalities. The day is rapidly approaching, and in certain instances has already arrived, when subjects will be placed in interaction with the computer, not only to study game and bargaining strategies, but to investigate human interaction with a programmed set of behaviors elicited as a function of the interacting behavior of the human subject or group. Computers can and are being used to provide conditions for the appraisal of a subject's reaction to certain complex problems, sometimes in conflict with one another, with a certain controlled randomness built in. Subjects' responses to such conditions provide information not only about general human problem solving, but also about individual differences in strategies of coming to terms with the environment.

The possibility of simulating behavioral responses in symbolic form to represent certain personality processes offers great promise for teaching and research. It has already been suggested that a computer having the potential for representing psychopathological symptoms could be used to introduce fledgling professional workers to characteristic syndromes. If a computer could be applied to help subjects learn about other people, perhaps its flexibility would also permit large numbers of people to become more aware of themselves, more aware of what effects their behavior will have on others, and more "socially intelligent" in regard to interpersonal relations. Not only might such understanding provide a basis for more adequate vocational decisions (cf. Sechrest & Strowig, 1962), but such commerce with a computer might result in the kind of behavior change often associated with psychotherapy. We are not attempting to be facetious in suggesting that research should be undertaken to compare computers with human psychotherapists. The "impersonal" nature of a computer might even be an advantage in providing a psychotherapeutic situation more anonymous and less threatening, at least for some people, to say nothing of the differences in cost. This would be a break with tradition, but if it comes to pass, it will probably be a less profound break than some occasioned by the non-computational use of computers.

The availability of a computer model of some personality processes would also provide an excellent device for research training. My colleague, Howard S. Hoffman (1963) of Pennsylvania State University, has devised a compact analogue computer which reproduces much of the research data in the conditioning area. This device has proved most effective not only in introducing the elements of scientific method to students, but in providing an economical and rapid procedure for replicating the experimental literature and even for deriving new hypotheses. It is possible to control experimental conditions in this situation far more rigorously than is usually possible with live organisms. Furthermore, having a continuously available "subject" for experimentation stimulates a great deal of curiosity about the limits of the simulation in relation to the phenomenon being simulated. The availability of such a technique for simulating personality processes would enormously facilitate the teaching of the techniques of experimentation in the personality area.

Reitman very ably argues that constructing models of man with the aid of a computer may serve to explicate and sharpen existing theory, as well as to provide a basis for fresh theory construction. I believe that his dawn of discovery metaphor is very apt, not only for the reasons that he emphasizes, but because computer models of personality will serve as a stimulus for more rigorous measurement and study of personality, and might even provide a rich source of experimental data when used in collaboration with human subjects.

6

MILTON J. ROSENBERG
Ohio State University

Discussion:
Simulated Man and the Humanistic Criticism

I should like to begin by giving my understanding of the main line of argument that Dr. Reitman has developed in Chapter 4. His paper starts by referring to a high hope expressed by many in the last year or two—the hope that the achievement of computer simulation of personality is close at hand. True simulation as he defines it is accomplished when the "artificial system" of a personality theory programmed into a computer emits responses identical, or nearly so, to those emitted by natural systems, i.e., by the personalities of real people.

Perhaps this simple definition needs some explication. We may assume that the achievement of true simulation would require that the programmed theory delineate, in their proper magnitude and interaction, those theoretically-significant independent variables upon which personalities differ; and, further, the program would have to allow for the representation of actual individual personalities in terms of those variables. Computer simulation of personality, then, is the construction of a general artificial system which can be set to duplicate the assumed structure and content of a range of separate "natural systems" so that it can match (i.e., predict) certain important response patterns of those separate natural systems.

Out of his experience with the achievements and frustrations of program design and execution, Dr. Reitman comes to the candidly expressed conclusion that such simulation is not now feasible and will not be for some time. This is because three main obstacles seem to stand in the way. The first two of these obstacles seem to Dr. Reitman more surmountable than the third.

The first is that present programs, whether of the information processing type, the problem-solving type, or others, cannot readily duplicate the energy concepts found in many personality theories, particularly those of the psychoanalytic order. The second obstacle is that present types of program do not encompass the parallelism of active functions that seems to be characteristic of real personalities. Computers are programmed to work at one thing at a time, on one problem at a time, no matter how quickly, while humans go at many things at once.

The third problem, and the one that seems to Reitman to be the most irksome, is that we cannot with any trust measure the events that actually occur within the natural systems of individual personalities; we cannot get at the structured organization of those natural systems or at the full meaning of the signals that issue from them. Lacking a way of assessing what is _in_ personality, or of the ways in which human personalities vary, we are then not in a position that would permit true simulation.

Dr. Reitman does envision some possible ways out of at least the first two of these three difficulties. Specifically, he recommends a rewriting of the "general problem solver" type of program, so as to set a coalition of problem-solving sequences in action at the same time and, where personality models so require, to put them in competition with one another. He suggests that this might make possible not only a duplication of the process parallelism assumed in many personality theories, but also a way of getting something like energy concepts into programmed simulations.

However, I find it interesting that these considerations do not seem to energize him very strongly toward the simulation enterprise as such, at least not as something to start doing next week. Instead, he suggests that the main service to personality study that can presently be rendered by computer techniques is to lead us toward a goal which he designates as the "objectification" of personality theories. He has outlined this prospect in useful detail and in so doing has activated the "problem-finder" program of at least one natural system. And here, the shades of Fowler and Strunk forgive me, is my "print out."

To begin with, I must make clear that I see reasons to question just how much "objectification" can actually do for us. As I understand it, objectification is achieved through avoiding the ambiguities and the imprecision of the ordinary language of psychological theories. Instead, a theory is to be reduced to its core of concepts and operators and their logical relations and implications. The language of this reduction would be some one of the available programming codes now in use or, I would suppose, some new one constructed for such a task. This reduced, "cleaned-up" statement of a theory will be fed to a computer for rapid digestion. This should in turn locate the theory's internal inconsistencies; and it should locate the matters on which the theory needs to commit itself but has not, and also the matters on which it has committed itself but need not. This seems quite a promise, and initially it does seem plausible to expect that such analytic service could be rendered us by our computers. But in fact it may not be an easy task at all. Practically viewed, it may be enough to unhinge the programmer and his program. In other words, there are problems.

What are they? The first is that the inventors and "amenders" of major and comprehensive personality theories are not computer specialists and perhaps will not be for a long time, if ever. Thus, the theories which issue from such worthies in verbal statement must be programmed by others, and those others must first run those theories through their own neural computers. This leaves us with the problem of how we determine that computer specialist X's version of theorist Y's theory is accurate. Before Reitman can program, say, Rapaport's (1959) reconstruction of the core concepts of psychoanalysis, he is going to have to say them to himself in something like words, which he will then transform into computer operations. Would Rapaport, if he were still among us, agree as to the accuracy of that programmed translation? I do not question Reitman's skill in this regard, but I do mean to point out that we cannot skip the problem of mediation or transfer from a verbal level of statement to some other kind of less ambiguous language. The programmer starts with his verbal understanding of that which he is programming and then translates it into the terms which he finds appropriate for his computer program. Thus, all that we can be sure of is that X's version is the version that is being "objectivized." An expedient partial answer to this dilemma, of course, suggests itself. The programmer should not start programming until Y, the theorist, is at least fully satisfied that X understands his theory. However, I have a pessimistic hunch that such a happy conjunction is more easily conceived than realized.

But still, objectification of "versions" of some available personality theories could be undertaken. What could we expect them to yield? My prediction would be that we would get a compelling, and thus useful, demonstration of something we already know; and that is that, except for a narrow range of overdetermined gross phenomena, no present personality theory produces much in the way of lucid, unhedged predictions. The additional possible gain in such a demonstration would be, of course, that it might also locate the concepts and relations that must be clarified, or even altered or rejected, if ambiguity in theoretical statement and prediction is to be reduced. And that would indeed be a valuable contribution.

However, if attempts at objectification do yield the sort of theory clarification and perfection that Reitman suggests it will, we are back at the task that he would just as soon avoid for now—that of conducting simulation studies so as to compare a program's responses to a person's responses.

In summary of my argument, the ultimate point of objectification is to get from a theory testable, unambiguous predictions about the variables and "laws" that govern such things as conflict resolutions, fantasy processes, symbolic derivations, and defensive behaviors. Not the only test of these predictions, but a potentially powerful one, is whether people, who are the natural systems to which the program is supposedly matched, do actually emote or fantasy or resolve conflicts in the same way that the computer does when it is set to simulate those natural systems. Thus, the challenge of accurate simulation can be put off, but it cannot be avoided. Ultimately it looms as the test that must be faced by those interested in the study through computers of personality theory, or better, of human personality.

It seems that I am in the position of countering Dr. Reitman's moderate pessimism about the prospect for computer simulation with a moderate optimism. One particular reason for this is that I am not as persuaded as he is that this prospect is darkened by the fact that the "natural systems" of personality cannot yet be effectively and validly assessed.

Obviously, the measurement of personality attributes and of personality-related processes _is_ difficult and often is loaded with unresolved problems of measurement theory and technique. But after all, some test devices do work better than others and some aspects of personality are more available to accurate assessment than others. There is room for judiciousness in choosing the personality variables or processes with which simulation studies might concern themselves. Beyond this rather banal observation, I do want to suggest that there are many guide lines that might help reduce the scope of the measurement problem and thus bring us closer to the point at which simulation studies may be attempted. I should like to mention one such guiding point, though it is not necessarily the most important one that could be suggested.

I have become ever more convinced in my own research that a main determinant of a subject's responses in a personality-testing or behavior-observing situation is the way he characteristically reacts to the awareness or suspicion that he _is_ being observed and evaluated.

One good example of what I am speaking of is the knowledge that has been gathered in recent years on individual differences in the strength of the need to appear "socially desirable." Where this orientation is strong, and it does tend to vary in specifiable ways with certain other aspects of personality, we get considerable distortion of self-report on personality tests, attitude questionnaires, and even in the self-revealing aspects of "overt" behavior. This distortion is usually in the direction of the subject's own version of the normative standards that he perceives, typically with only superficial accuracy, to govern the processes of interpersonal evaluation.

From such considerations it follows that any programmed personality theory must, if it is to yield predictions that match observations on human personalities, meet the following conditions: It must contain some representation of the relation between personality type, need systems, mechanism priorities, or what have you, on the one hand, and, on the other hand, the amount and direction of distortion in self-report that is likely to occur in the assessment situation.

Personality simulation is, after all, the simulation, through the conceptual vehicle of a particular theory, of specific personalities. To the extent that those personalities are known to us through the results of psychological testing, we must program our computers with ways of estimating and correcting for response distortion in the assessment situation. If this can be done, and I think recourse to much of the recent research and theory on this problem will make it possible, two types of error can be reduced: error in the initial computerized description of the personality to be simulated, and error in gathering from the real person response data against which the computer's "responses" are to be tested.

With regard to this problem there is, of course, one other obvious expedient. It is simply that personality assessment can be undertaken without the knowledge of the person being assessed, and thus with decrease in the likelihood of the sort of errors I have mentioned. For example, the focus of our observations and predictions about the personalities of individuals can often be shifted to such matters as responses to everyday stresses, variations in work performance, in interpersonal behavior, in expressive behavior, etc. More generally, I am suggesting that adequate measurement on the natural system side might be facilitated by the continuing trend away from the formal psychological test or interview and toward the systematic perfection of observation techniques that can be employed without the knowledge of the person being observed.

I have so far discussed a few questions raised in Dr. Reitman's very stimulating paper. Now I should like to talk about an issue that he did not raise, but which is implicitly present in the whole new interest in computer simulation. It is an issue that often comes up in the continuing and sometimes agitated exchange that goes on between the "two cultures" of the scientific and humanistic disciplines.

We are all aware that many scholars and artists tend to consider the main drift in American psychology to be a kind of barbarous reductionism; a narrow model that denies those "higher" attributes and "emergent" qualities upon which man's distinctiveness in nature, and his worth in essence, are said to depend.

I am convinced that in its nature as a conceptual system and as a body of scientific observations, psychology is not deserving of this accusation. The significance in their essence of higher processes and of complex integrations of human capacities is not in any logical way denied by attempts to view them in reductionist terms.

But if the criticism is not correct in its formal logic, it is a rather accurate characterization of a style of thought and work that is fairly common in modern American psychology; it may in fact be the modal, if not the model, style in our way of trying to build our science.

And now we are beginning to talk of programming computers to simulate individuals so that in some sense they will have or "be" personalities. Some of our critics from the other culture (in fact, even a few within our own discipline) have found in this ambition a new and evocative symbol of the supposed "dehumanizing" influence of psychological inquiry.

How ought we to respond to the complaint that to speak of computers as having "minds" or "personalities" is an untruth that degrades man? And more specifically how should we in this context approach our coming encounter with the challenging prospect of simulating personality processes through computer programs?

Both our understanding of the full meaning of our work, and the depth and intellectual significance of that work, may well profit from the kinds of responses that the humanist's criticism elicits from us. Along these lines I have two recommendations. The first is that we could indeed consider how computer technology might be used to develop a more complete psychological understanding of such "higher aspects" (to use the language of the humanist) of personality as "moral concern," "freedom," "purpose" and the "uniqueness and wholeness" of individual identity. Specifically, I am suggesting that we ask this sort of question: Can we, through the new precision in theory formulation that "objectification" may provide and through the new way of testing theories that simulation may make possible—can we through these new advantages come any closer to accounting for the emergence of those "higher" attributes which our critics condemn us for ignoring. Perhaps a better way to put this question is to ask whether objectification and simulation can help us to redefine, in terms of their nature and process origins, the scope and sources of such attributes.

I shall allow myself the privilege of coining a crude epigram: Reductionism properly pursued becomes constructionism. Objectification and simulation might enable us to get back to some of the problems we abandoned, both because of their massive size and their philosophical implications, when we entered the laboratory. The greatest of all these problems, as I see it, and one which I would hope we may approach with these new methods, is the question of how organized and integrated identity emerges from, and gives organization to, the antecedent processes that generate it.

I am aware, of course, that the lesser and more indignant humanist critic might view such an undertaking as still further evidence of the psychologist's penchant for denying the worth and significance of human identity. But the humanist of larger understanding would, I think, welcome the sort of undertaking I have tried to describe. At any rate you can't, nor should you want to, placate all of the critics all of the time.

My final point follows from a conviction that social responsibility constrains us to recognize that ours is indeed a time of increasing "dehumanization." Some of our most thoughtful personality theorists and social psychologists have, in fact, helped us to understand how such forms of human failure as "automaton conformity," "alienation," and "anomic apathy" are engendered by those very changes in our social order which define the nature of modern existence.

If we add to this understanding the fact that the explanations and constructions of science, and particularly of psychology, do tend to shape popular views concerning man's nature, his prospects, and his ultimate worth, we begin to see something of the pertinence of the criticism so often directed at us by the humanists.

What should such considerations suggest to those of us who are getting involved in computer simulation of psychological processes? Simply this: The enterprise is a worthy one, but, in pursuing it, we should restrain some of our penchant for the playful metaphors in which we make *beings* out of computers or *personalities* out of personality-simulating programs. Metaphors too redundantly employed, too enthusiastically celebrated, get out of hand. Not only do they becloud our understanding, but they tend to have the effect, as they are picked up and exaggerated in mass media reports, of contributing further to the desperation over their seeming insignificance that so many men, all of them worthy by virtue of *being* men, have come to suffer in our age.

The alienated individual is the one who feels bypassed, negated, deprived of his identity. To the extent that "computeristic excitement" adds to that problem, we are enjoined to remind ourselves and our publics that neither the present data-analyzing powers of computers nor the man-imitating possibilities that we may be able to program into them, represent a duplication of man's humanness.

If someone asks, "What if it turns out ultimately that every aspect of humanness and of the total pattern that binds those aspects into a unity can be duplicated?", I can only answer that I do not believe that to be likely. But I am psychologist enough to know that my judgment against this possibility is a partial function of my distaste for it. At any rate, men are still men, computers are still computers; and it would be well to remember the difference.

PART II

PSYCHOANALYTIC THEORY

7 GERALD S. BLUM
University of Michigan

Programming People to Simulate Machines

It isn't easy to begin with a painful confession, but I know that at least Dr. Mowrer will sympathize with my decision to pursue this course of action. Putting it most bluntly, I hereby expose myself as an impostor. To me the computer is anathema! Such infernal machines are so awesome to contemplate that I phobically avoid any form of contact with them and, in cases of sheer data necessity, call upon research assistants to serve as intermediaries. Furthermore, I believe that attempts to study personality by observing the behavior of computers programmed by humans to simulate other humans is the crudest form of projection—a most primitive and maladaptive mechanism of defense. One might add that the computer is more of a blank screen than the best-intentioned psychoanalyst ever was...

By now I can see the question already formed on your lips: Why was Blum asked to participate in the exploration of this new frontier anyway? The answer must lie in the tolerance and open-mindedness of Drs. Tomkins and Messick who, despite my initial protestation of not belonging, probably chanced upon a kernel of relevance in a couple of recent publications (Blum,

1960, 1961). It remains for you to decide whether their invitation has any justification at all. I came in the hope of having my own prejudices dispelled.

The kernel of relevance grows out of (1) an affinity for describing the mind in terms borrowed from systems theory, and (2) a lately acquired predilection for doing research in which human subjects virtually are converted into machines. Accordingly, I shall first present a brief overview of our current conceptual model, followed by an account of methodological approaches in a series of investigations now under way.

Overview of Model

The model offers a framework for an ultimate theory of human thought, feeling, and action. Pitched at a fairly molecular level, it attempts to integrate phenomena along psychology's broad spectrum, all the way from sensations to psychodynamics. More significant is the fact that it serves as a perennial source of fresh research problems whose solutions contribute to further clarification of the model itself—in other words, an ongoing reciprocal interplay of theory and data.

Figure 1 is a simplified, summary version of Form Q of the working model. The five-year history of our group's vagaries through the alphabet from A to P is detailed in A Model of the Mind (Blum, 1961) and need not concern us here. Suffice it to say that change, if not progress, may be our most important product! The diagram portrays five major subsystems comprising the Mental System, with functions of the cognitive subsystem singled out for special consideration.

Inputs to the Mental System are coded sensory signals based on stimuli originating either internally or externally to

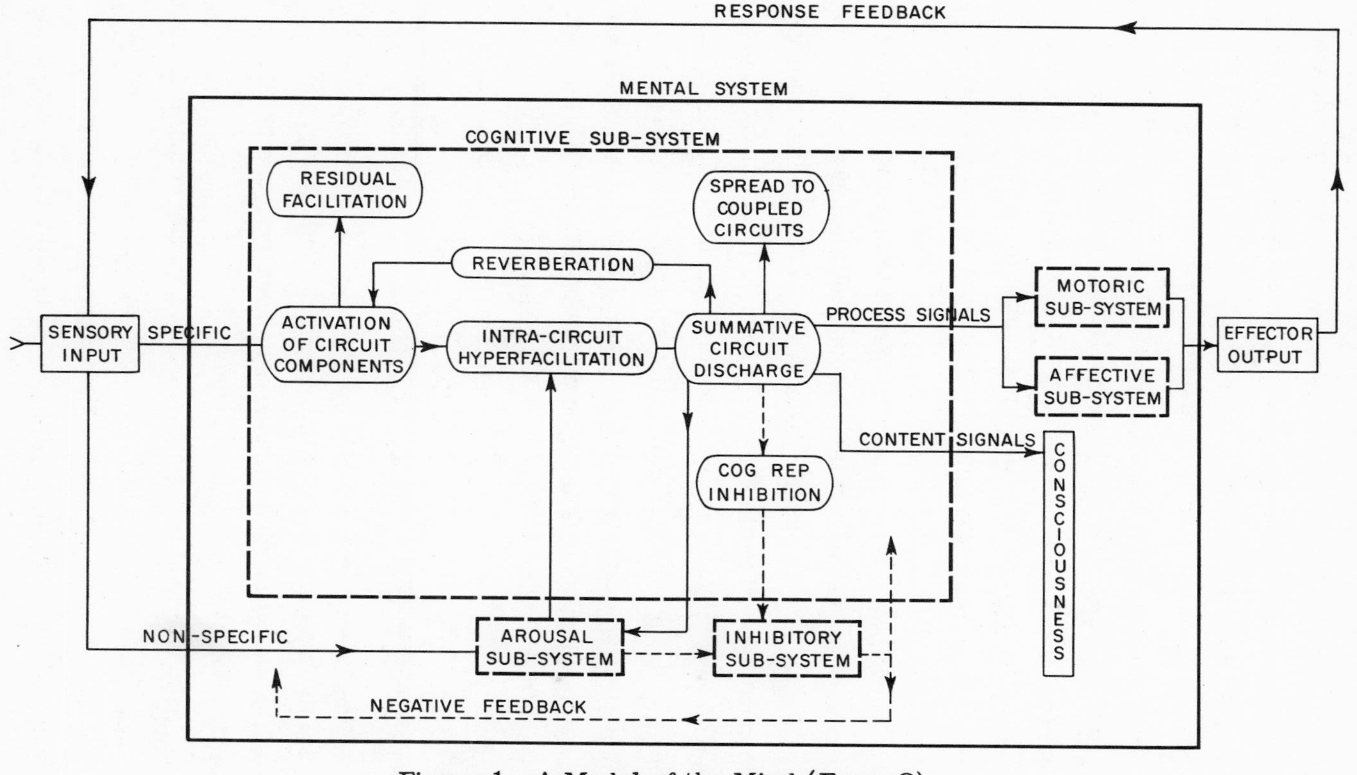

Figure 1. A Model of the Mind (Form Q)

the organism. Whatever the source, these sensory inputs vary in intensity and thereby contribute to variation in strength of the cognitive activities which they instigate. Sensory signals make contact with the cognitive subsystem through specific links designated as components, the strength of connections reflecting past experience of the individual. Components contiguously discharging repeatedly over time are interconnected and form a circuit. At a still more molar level, circuits which are activated many times together become hooked up into a network.

Once its components are triggered, a circuit may manifest several properties: (1) a residual facilitation effect of some duration; (2) current strengthening of connections among components as a function partly of arousal level (intracircuit hyperfacilitation); (3) the setting into motion of a reverberatory loop; and (4) a summative circuit discharge of process signals, with activation capacity only, and content signals, which transmit information stored in the components. The destinations of process signals are other coupled cognitive circuits or motoric and affective subsystems. Content signals, on the other hand, are beamed toward a screen, much like a TV oscilloscope, which corresponds to consciousness. Contents arriving at the screen of consciousness last for varying periods of time according to their intensity, making cumulative effects and interference possible. The strongest signals represent the focus of attention, weaker ones constitute the periphery.

Affective and motoric subsystems, highly complex in their own right, are triggered by inputs from the cognitive. Output signals are in turn decoded at the effectors, activating appropriate muscles and glands. Finally this effector activity provides response feedback to the Mental System in the form of new sensory input.

The two remaining subsystems in the model have to do with arousal and inhibition. Output from the arousal subsystem to the cognitive serves to amplify or boost ongoing component interaction in proportion to the arousal level at that given moment. Arousal level itself is maintained primarily by non-specific sensory inputs and, to a lesser extent, by cognitive discharge. If this level exceeds a normal range, the inhibitory subsystem is automatically triggered, via an innate structural connection, and negative feedback restores the operating level.

Inhibition can be brought into play by cognitive means as well as by arousal. Here the effect is to increase the resistance in pathways and thus interfere with cognitive transmission. The mediating mechanism is the cognitive representation of inhibition, created through experience like other circuits and capable of being set off by a variety of coupled networks. One such network, anxiety, acquires a highly facilitated connection to inhibition and consequently occupies a central role in mental processes.

The preceding brief overview is intended solely to acquaint you with the type of conceptual approach and to indicate how Drs. Messick and Tomkins may have been misled in their invitation. Lacking the details, you have no doubt already detected some familiar aspects of the model: the description of circuit connections brings to mind associationistic theories; contiguity is recognizable as the basic principle of learning in the system; evolution of circuits and networks from sensory input has a distinct Hebbian cast; the importance of inhibition, intimately related to anxiety, is reminiscent of psychoanalysis;

nonspecific arousal has acknowledged physiological antecedents; and so on down the line.

Research Methodology

Now let's move on to the research which has been stimulated by considerations of the model. A dozen earlier experiments have already been reported (Blum, 1961). They dealt with such topics as facilitation without awareness, perceptual interference, inhibition of anxiety, the role of response feedback, etc. The investigations I shall describe today revolve around the concepts of anxiety, general arousal, and inhibition, each of which must be pinned down more precisely in order to advance the model. Ideally, one can visualize a human subject with three dials on the top of his head: one dial specifically regulates his degree of anxiety; another controls level of general arousal; and the third manipulates inhibition directly. Equipped with such a computer, the researcher would have, I'm sure you will agree, a very powerful technique for probing personality. We set about building our computer in the following ways:

The induction of anxiety was old hat for our research group. Previously we had made effective use of a battery consisting of hypnosis, galvanic skin response (GSR), and introspective report to elicit and measure anxiety reactions. Convinced that the most meaningful tactic was to invoke natural anxiety from the subject's past, we first had him relive a disturbing situation under hypnosis, then learn to produce the feeling upon command, and finally allow the anxiety to be attached to an experimental stimulus for presentation later in the waking state. A rather striking occurrence during one experimental session kept haunting me. This particular subject happened to be reacting so strongly to the anxiety-laden stimulus that rapid successive range changes of the GSR recording pen made the response difficult to score. On an impulse we asked him to react moderately instead, whereupon the pen settled down to more reasonable deflections. The notion of an anxiety dial began to take shape at that point and, abetted by some contaminatory thinking, led to the procedure we currently employ.

The subject is told under hypnosis that, having relived the disturbing situation, he now knows exactly what the feeling of anxiety is like. With this knowledge he can easily learn to experience anxiety in varying degrees—in fact the feeling will increase in intensity as the lights in the room (controlled by a rheostat) are gradually turned up. He practices this feat under both hypnotic and waking conditions until successful in terms of the GSR (recorded from finger electrodes), his own report, and the experimenter's observations. Next the experimenter explains that the dial on the wall which controls the brightness has markings from 0 to 100 and that the subject can easily learn to differentiate four levels represented by the numbers 0 (relaxed), 40 (some anxiety), 70 (fairly strong anxiety), and 100 (very, very strong anxiety). More hypnotic and waking practice at each of these settings follows. So far, so good—but obviously it is an inconvenience for lights to be getting brighter and dimmer during the course of experiments, particularly if they involve perception. The solution is simply to tell the subject under hypnosis that the light adjustments are not necessary at all—the numbers can evoke the appropriate responses just as well by themselves. If he sees or hears any of the numbers later while awake, he will immediately respond at the right level. Amnesia for all the training instructions is then induced prior to the experiment proper and our human anxiety machine is ready to be plugged in. Figure 2 illustrates typical GSR responses of the thoroughly trained subject. Drops in resistance produced by anxiety are registered as rising lines. Each section is a 15-second interval during which the subject is awake and looking at a card with a particular number. The "0" shows steadily increasing relaxation; "40" causes a relatively small deflection in the middle of the period; "70" a more marked series of elevations; and "100" occasions a sudden, steep and unusually large deflection covering two whole ranges (the break in the center is the automatic resetting of the pen as the upper end of a range is reached).

The second dial, general arousal, has even more divisions than anxiety, extending from the "deepest point of relaxation" at the low end to a "fever pitch" at the high. Training for two levels of underarousal is easily accomplished by reference to the depth of hypnotic trance, identifiable by GSR in addition to introspective report. The subject is given practice in recognizing the deepest stage of hypnosis so that he can reproduce it automatically in response to a posthypnotic cue (-A). For another cue (-A) he learns to respond at a midpoint of underarousal, as though "half asleep and half awake." The baseline or normal arousal state (O) is described as "normally awake and feeling okay."

The other end of the dimension, overarousal, contains three points designated as follows:

(A) Not relaxed, but instead wide awake, alert, and ready to react.

(A) Very excited, animated, all stirred up, senses highly sharpened.

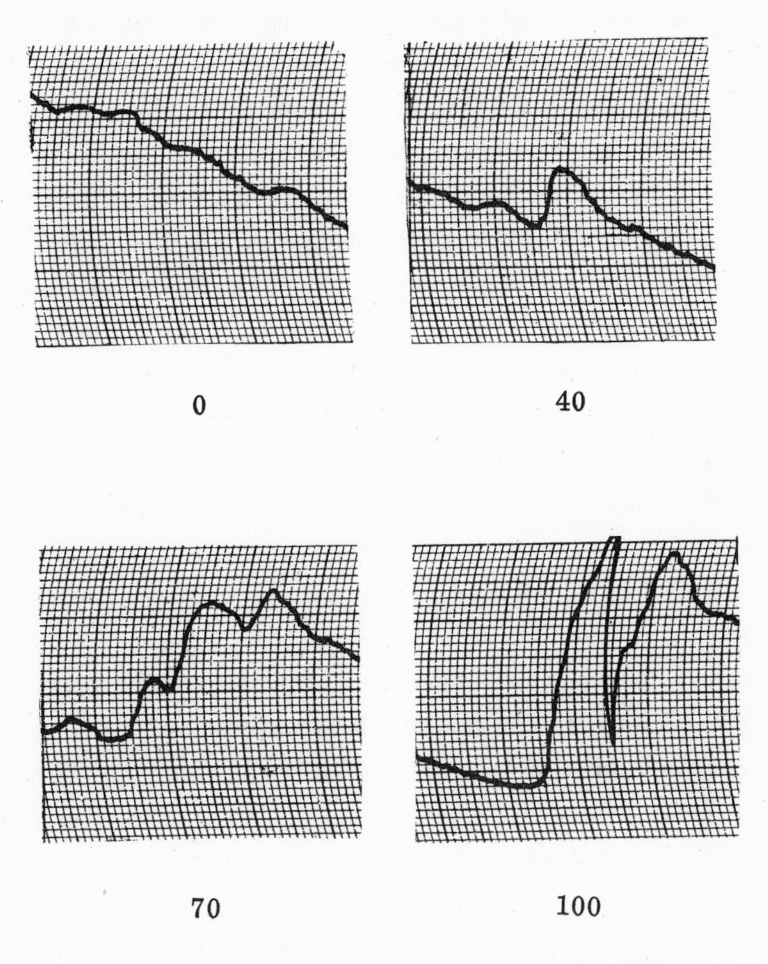

Figure 2. Levels of Anxiety Arousal - GSR

(**A**) Whole body alerted, extremely stimulated and aroused to a fever pitch, electrified, carried away, more than flesh and blood can bear.

Serious efforts are directed toward separating the general overarousal reaction from anxiety, which of course is itself a form of arousal. Subjects are told specifically that they will not feel upset during overarousal and that their responses will involve primarily "muscles and senses." The physiological measure used to check the degree of overarousal is electromyographic (EMG) recording from the frontalis muscle of the forehead. Although it is not possible to disengage GSR and EMG from each other completely, the training does seem to maximize the sensitivity of EMG to the overarousal conditions, so that its fluctuations parallel the prescribed reactions more closely than do those of the GSR. However, at the very peak of overarousal subjects occasionally report an admixture of anxiety reflected in GSR changes as well.

Figure 3 shows appropriate EMG responses upon presentation to the waking subject of each of four cue cards. The upper band contains the primary recording of muscle potentials, the lower integrates the same responses over one second intervals. Duration of each sample is approximately 25 seconds. A clearly discriminable progression of increased activity from the resting level at 0 through the thickest A can be noted.

The third dial on our human computer controls cognitively mediated inhibition. A familiar example of this class of phenomena is posthypnotic amnesia. In an earlier study we had manipulated perceptual blocking by inducing selective blindness. Subjects were able to be trained not to "see" a given stimulus when it was flashed tachistoscopically, even though they did not know in advance at what point in a series it would appear. It was possible to rule out deception or simulation (the nasty kind, that is) on the part of subjects by a combination of physiological and behavioral indices. Currently we are applying, to a variety of perceptual, cognitive, and expressive tasks, several degrees of inhibition associated with instructions to experience "some difficulty" (cued in the waking state by a patch of light gray), "extreme difficulty" (dark gray patch), and "total inability" (black patch). During the hypnotic training, care is taken to insure that neither anxiety nor overarousal accompanies execution of the blocking directions.

Before going on to describe the experiments for which these operations of anxiety, arousal, and inhibition were designed, a short digression concerning frequently voiced objections to hypnotic procedures might be in order. One common complaint is that susceptible hypnotic subjects somehow are basically different from other people, even though specific evidence is largely lacking. At present we are working with three male college students selected on the basis of high, medium, and low scores on the Stanford Hypnotic Susceptibility Scale (Form A) (Weitzenhoffer & Hilgard, 1959). All have been able to learn our complicated procedures, the only difference being in the amount of training time required, roughly 30 hours for a poor subject compared to about 20 for a good one. Interestingly, the medium and low subjects both scored in the high range on the equivalent Form B when retested after a dozen hours of training.

Another prevalent attitude is that suggestions can be carried out just as effectively in the waking state as in hypnosis.

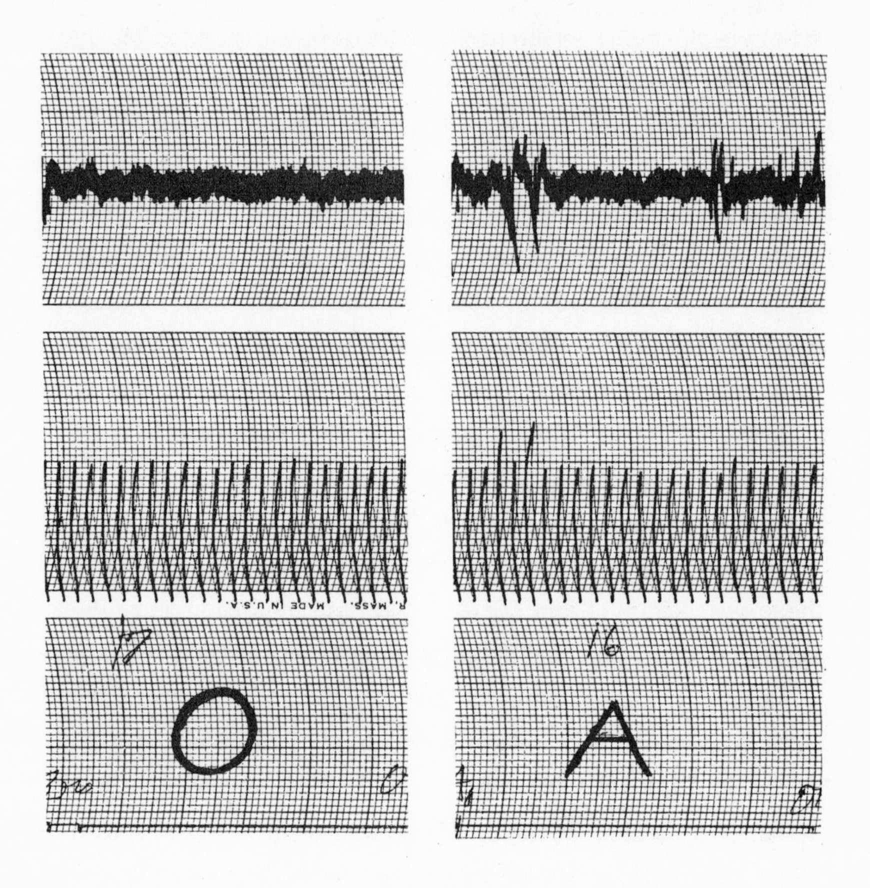

Figure 3. Levels of General Arousal - EMG

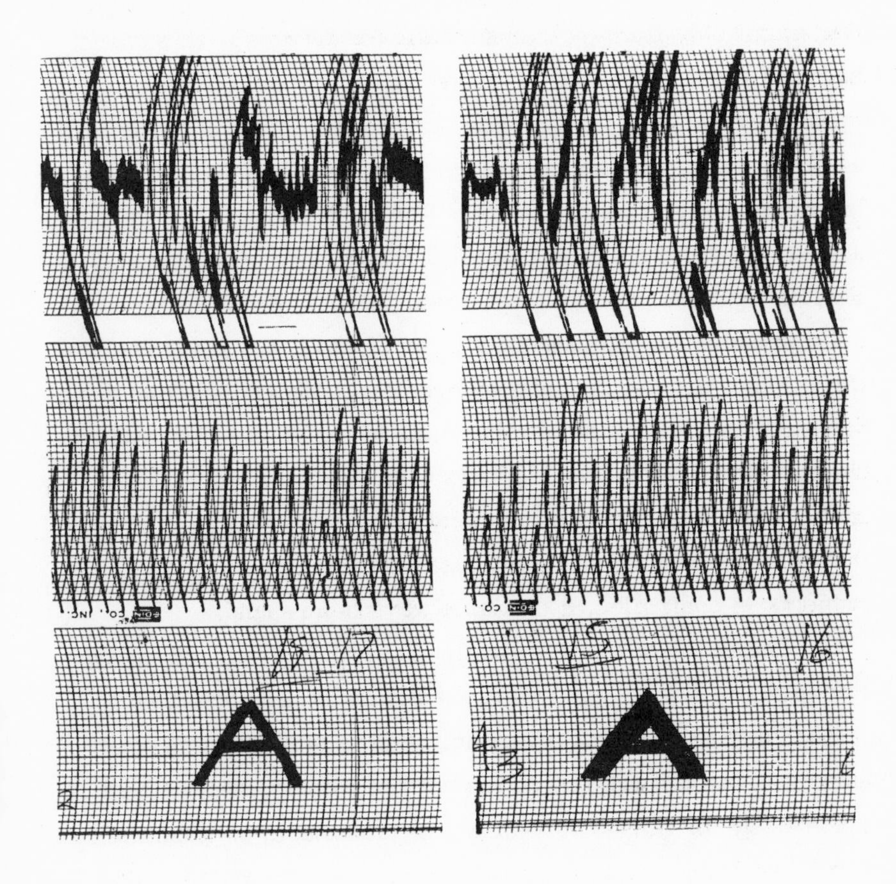
15 17
A
15 16
A

Our admittedly limited, unsystematic excursions in this area have not convinced us of the universality of the claim. The hypnotized subject, for example, can invoke a kind of "internal camera" to observe an incomplete image as it flashes through his mind in response to a signal. The partial image can be arrested, described in full detail, brought back after a period of time and reported again with total fidelity. Prior to hypnotic practice the same subject is unable to carry out these directions. Granted it might be possible, with enough time and patience, to accomplish similar feats in the absence of hypnosis, the fact remains that such efforts would be inefficient at best. In any case, experiments in our laboratory are typically conducted in the waking state, hypnosis serving only to program subjects in controlled, specifiable ways beforehand.

The problem of the hypnotized person's abnormal desire to comply with the experimenter's wishes is often cited as a methodological obstacle. Certainly a wise precaution is to impress upon the subject, at the very beginning, that the best opportunity for him to serve the experimenter's purposes is just to let things happen naturally and not try to mold his own responses according to any preconceived notions of what the experiment may be about. In addition to independent checks such as those provided by physiological measurement, carefully conducted waking and hypnotic inquiries at the conclusion of an experiment are also valuable. Thus far our research group has succeeded, by and large, in skirting this issue by virtue of the intricate nature of the experimental designs we have pursued. Naive subjects (and usually psychologically sophisticated observers, I might add) do not catch on to the hypotheses under test.

Finally, the need for a sound theory of hypnosis is stressed. If one employs a technique, it is important to understand how and why it works. The particular approach evolved from our conceptual model has already been offered in detail (Blum, 1961). Briefly, the essential ingredients are (1) an optimal stage of low arousal with sufficient nonspecific sensory input to maintain amplification throughout the Mental System, and (2) controlled restriction of specific sensory inputs to those repeatedly emanating from the experimenter. Together these conditions foster the build-up of abnormally strong, specific cognitive processes whose output capacities may appear to exceed the usual.

Balancing against the preceding considerations those vast potentialities for systematic control and precision inherent in hypnosis, we have long since come to the inescapable conclusion that it is the method of choice for extending and refining features of the model. Accordingly, the series of studies to be reported next continues to make use of intensive hypnotic programming of a relatively small number of subjects.

Perceptual, Cognitive, and Expressive Inhibition

This investigation, being carried out by Benyamini, explores the effects of our built-in dial manipulations upon performance in a variety of tasks. The aim is first to discover lawful relationships *within* degrees of anxiety, overarousal, and cognitive inhibition; and, secondly, to compare inhibitory action *across* the three conditions.

Four tasks were selected to tap perception, problem-solving, rote memory, and verbalization. For the perception experiment the subject is asked to identify the positions (left, right, top, bottom) and colors (black, red) of miniature playing cards presented tachistoscopically three at once. In preliminary training the fastest exposure still allowing 100% accuracy of recognition is established for each subject and the same speed subsequently maintained throughout the test trials. Practice is also given with the suggested degrees of blocking. Combining the training results of three subjects, Benyamini notes no recognition errors for a cue-absent control condition; 7% error when the "O" precedes the flash; 33% for the light gray patch; 50% for the dark gray; and 75% error for the black—clear support for the efficacy of the programmed hypnotic instructions to which the subject is amnesic while performing.

The experimental conditions are induced by placing appropriate cues (numbers, A's, or patches) in the adapting field of the tachistoscope. For example, prior to the flash of a stimulus pattern, the subject views an anxiety cue until he reacts at the indicated level (the experimenter is kept informed by earphone of the actual magnitude of the subject's GSR reactions by the machine operators outside the laboratory room). The experimenter then directs the subject's attention immediately to a dot in the center of the adapting field, whereupon the three playing cards are flashed. The subject's report of what he just saw is made with eyes closed, during which period the cue is changed for the next trial. Thirty-two exposures each are presented for anxiety, overarousal, and cognitively mediated inhibition, so that in essence a counterbalanced design can be executed.

The problem-solving task, utilizing the same sets of cues, consists of anagram solutions. The subject is given either four, five, or six letters at a time. Told to work as quickly as possible, he must begin each trial with a two-letter word, add another letter to those two in order to make a three-letter word, and so on until all the letters are used up. Time limits, established on the basis of a pretest with 20 undergraduates, are 45, 90, and 135 seconds for four, five, and six letter anagrams, respectively. During the training phase the subject first practices solving anagrams of this type under normal conditions and afterward with the hypnotically induced cognitive blocking instructions. For the experimental trials, anxiety or arousal cues are added before the subject is given the letters, and the cues remain while he tries to solve the problem. The data will be analyzed in terms of number of correct solutions per unit of time.

A third task compares the effects of degrees of anxiety, overarousal, and cognitive inhibition on both rote memory and verbalization. Here the subject is trained under hypnosis to associate six different nonsense syllables with the same four-digit number. The procedure is as follows. With the number always in full view, one syllable at a time is presented to the rhythm of a metronome (set at 60 beats per minute). Next, with only the number present, the subject is required to think silently of each syllable at the rate of one letter per beat and one syllable per measure. If on any beat nothing comes to mind, he shakes his head and continues. On a second round of metronome measures, he reports the letters out loud. The training criterion for a list is two consecutively perfect thinking and reporting trials under hypnosis followed by another in the waking state.

Cognitive blocking is also practiced. Percentages for the three subjects on the thinking rounds reveal a decline from

100% to 72% and 56% and 15% for the three degrees of suggested difficulty; on the reporting rounds the corresponding percentages are 65%, 46%, and 18%. Again we have confirmation of the fact that blocking can be manipulated cognitively, even to the extent of systematically varying its degree.

In the experiment itself, cue cards are placed alongside the stimulus number, the metronome starts ticking when reactions to the cues are deemed appropriate, and the subject automatically and inexorably "beats out" his responses without conscious awareness of why he is doing so. Observers readily attest that humans are indeed capable of simulating machines!

Psychoanalytically-oriented sleuths in the audience may have detected in the foregoing operations, especially those dealing with anxiety, certain similarities to a class of defense mechanisms. Inhibitory action of anxiety on perceptual processes is akin to denial; inability to remember nonsense syllables in the presence of anxiety smacks vaguely of repression; and inability to verbalize syllables (with memory intact) is a demonstration of suppression. The next experiment, also growing out of the model's concern with inhibition and anxiety, attacks other types of defenses.

Experimental Manipulation of Defense Mechanisms

In the earlier exposition of the model (Blum, 1961) various defenses were classified as either "avoidant" or "derivative" in nature. Denial, repression, and suppression, mentioned a moment ago, belong in the avoidant category. Others such as reaction formation, projection, displacement, and intellectualization are derivatives in the sense that they express content in some way related to a primitive, anxiety-laden thought. Typically the derivative content, being distorted and somewhat remote, carries less anxiety. It occurred to us that it might be possible to observe the production of derivatives experimentally by manipulating variables indicated by the model to be crucial, namely (1) locus and (2) degree of anxiety connected to a thought, plus (3) distortion and (4) affective intensity of available derivatives.

Work currently being done by Gallivan makes use of the Blacky pictures (Blum, 1950) to create defense analogues. In the training period the subject tells stories while awake about the eleven cartoons, narrates under hypnosis personal experiences suggested by each one, and also fills out the Defense Preference Inquiry (Blum, 1956). Hypnotic programming prior to the experiment goes as follows: the subject is told that he and Blacky are one and the same, Blacky's feelings are his feelings. After awakening he will be shown one of the pictures along with a sentence describing Blacky's reactions. The sentence will be divided into four elements with a number over each. Three of the numbers will be 0's and the fourth either 40, 70, or 100 (our old friends, the anxiety cues) to which he will respond appropriately. Upon feeling the correct level of anxiety for that part of the sentence, he will turn to a list of eight statements (with which he had previously been familiarized) and immediately choose the alternative appealing to him the most. He also has the option of saying that none of the eight appeals.

Figure 4 gives the stimulus sentence and eight alternatives for one of the four Blacky pictures involved in the experiment. Cartoon VIII shows Blacky off at a distance watching Mama and Papa pet a sibling figure, Tippy. The stimulus sentence consists of the subject ("Blacky"), feeling ("so angry and

Figure 4. Blacky VIII (Sibling Rivalry) stimuli for testing experimental manipulation of derivatives.

Stimulus sentence: Here Blacky/is feeling so angry and jealous/ he would like to physically hurt/Tippy/.

Overall Intensity	Manipulated Element	Alternatives
weak	self	1. It seems to Blacky now that Tippy must be confessing to Mama and Papa feelings of envy towards Blacky.
strong		2. Mama, Papa, Tippy, and everyone else all seem to be so angry with him right now that Blacky wonders if they are planning to do something bad to him.
weak	feeling	3. Blacky believes that insight into his own jealousy of Tippy will enable him to handle himself better in competitive situations later on.
strong		4. As Blacky watches Mama, Papa, and Tippy together, he is sure that right now he couldn't care less what happens to any one of them.
strong	action	5. Though Blacky is quite angry at being left out, he feels he ought to join the group and pay attention to Tippy also.
weak		6. Blacky is pleased to see Mama and Papa being affectionate to Tippy, since he feels that Tippy deserves a turn at getting attention.
strong	object	7. Right now Blacky is feeling so furious and jealous of Tippy that he even feels like angrily kicking the stones in front of him.
weak		8. Discouraged and frustrated with himself as he is, Blacky feels he doesn't deserve the attention Tippy is receiving.

jealous"), action ("physically hurt"), and object ("Tippy"). Fourteen trials in the waking state permit every level of anxiety to be connected with each element of the sentence, plus one control trial with no numbers at all and another with four 0's. The series is then repeated in a second session, using different orders of anxiety presentation and scrambling the alternatives.

The subject makes his choice within ten seconds after looking at the alternatives, responds with the number of the statement he finds most appealing at that moment, quickly puts the response out of his mind, and relaxes before the next trial. From Figure 4 we see the kinds of derivatives under study (for purposes of exposition the statements have been regrouped by element manipulated). Alternatives 1 and 2 are both projections but differ in their intensity. Number 3 handles feelings by intellectualization, 4 by negation. In 5 only the action is altered, whereas in 6 there is a reaction formation which distorts the feeling as well. The last two alternatives represent displacements from the original object, Tippy, to the remote "stones" in 7 and intropunitively to Blacky himself in 8.

At the conclusion of trials for all four Blacky pictures, the subject is asked to rate the over-all intensity of every statement to see if his opinions conform to those already established by outside judges. A check on the spontaneity of the subject's choice of alternatives is also introduced at the end by requiring him to divide the eight statements according to self, feeling, action, and object as rapidly as possible. Despite greater familiarity with the alternatives, it still takes at least two minutes to complete the task—confirming that the subject's programmed instruction to respond within ten seconds virtually eliminates conscious deliberation.

Determinants of Subjective Uncertainty

Another problem to which the model has called our attention is the amount of uncertainty an individual feels when making a subjective judgment. Of particular interest are the effects of anxiety, under- and over-arousal, and cognitive saliency. By systematically varying each of these, Lohr is attempting to pin down the determinants of uncertainty.

Two tasks serve as context for the study: (1) the perception of geometric figures flashed tachistoscopically; and (2) a mental arithmetic series. The subject is required to give his certainty judgment on every response, using a five-point scale ranging from "blind guess" to "absolutely certain." Both tasks are arranged to facilitate correct responses so that accompanying judgments of certainty are not swayed by inaccuracy but instead reflect the influence of experimental conditions.

Training for the perception task consists of waking practice in the recognition of squares, circles, rectangles, etc. shown in either left, right, top, or bottom position. Thus the experimenter ascertains the subject's thresholds for each figure and also familiarizes him with the certainty scale in the process. For the 54 experimental trials under each condition, the experimenter flashes a figure below threshold and then repeats the same figure at successively slower speeds until it is correctly identified, regardless of the certainty rating. At that point a cue is inserted in the adapting field and the progression of trials on the figure is continued until a speed is reached at which two consecutive judgments of absolute certainty (point 5) are made. The score on any sequence is the number of flashes required to increase the subject's certainty from a 2 to a 5.

For one series the cues are the four anxiety numbers, for another the six degrees of under- and overarousal. The third series manipulates cognitive strength by having the geometric figures appear in various positions immediately prior to the test flashes, so that the cue figure is completely convergent with the stimulus (same figure in same position); completely divergent (different figure in opposite position); or neither (different figure, same position; same figure, opposite position).

The mental arithmetic task requires the subject to listen to problems like "7 x 6 - 9 + 2 = ?". In addition to the final answer, he is asked two other questions which vary from trial to trial. These include items such as "What was the second term?", "Were there more numbers above 5 than below?", "Were there more increasing or decreasing operations?", and so on. The combinations are arranged so that one difficult and one easy question occur on each trial, allowing an opportunity for differential effects of the experimental conditions. Every answer is followed by a certainty rating. As before, anxiety and arousal cue cards are sometimes in view, and cognitive strength is altered by having the subject look at numbers which may or may not coincide with his answers.

Experimental Study of Primary Process Phenomena

The last research project I shall describe is being carried out by Reverski. It attempts to test a series of deductions from the model (Blum, 1961) concerning the occurrence of those primitive thought phenomena designated by Freud as "primary process." Reduced environmental sensory input typically has two major consequences: (1) a lowering of arousal level via decrease of nonspecific input; and (2) an alteration in the normal balance between externally vs. internally instigated cognitive events. From lowered arousal the model predicts such phenomena as condensation and loose thought sequences; from tipping the balance in favor of internally activated networks, perceptual distortions and symbolism are deemed likely. Although operations checking four different features of primary process are interwoven in the experimental sessions, I shall try to disentangle them for purposes of exposition.

Condensation is tested by having the subject experience programmed dreams in states of normal vs. lowered arousal. During the training period he first learns to dream under hypnosis in response to a prescribed stimulus. When the experimenter says the word "dream," he relaxes and lets a dream come to mind and, as soon as it ends, reports in great detail no matter how bizarre it appears in retrospect. An interesting sidelight on the potency of anxiety training was obtained with one subject who was asked to dream twice about the laboratory room a few minutes after another experimenter had been giving him practice with the anxiety numbers after lights turned up:

> First Dream: "I dreamed I was a mountain climber. It was a big mountain, a white one. Only it wasn't a mountain. It was like numbers, like I was climbing up numbers and triangles and sliding down rulers and never reached the top. There was always another number or square or something and I'd turn around and slide down a ruler and climb back up."
>
> Second Dream: "It seems like I was hypnotized and turned into a little bug. Only part of me wasn't and I watched it. Like you find a bug in the grass and you put rocks and sticks in its way. And I was climbing over things like that, only they were wires instead of rocks and sticks. And I finally got to the wall and

climbed up to the light and turned it on real bright. Then everything blew up."

In the next step the subject is instructed to have a dream image which will grow out of one or more of three stimulus words provided by the experimenter. Sometimes he is asked merely to repeat the words aloud before dreaming; at others the dream is preceded by a mental picture for each of the three words. Thus, two forms of possible condensation are explored—one mediated by the sound of words, the second by visual images. An example of the former would be a dream about barbells in response to the stimulus words "bell" and "bar." The latter might condense visual images like "a flying insect" and "a burning fire" into a dream about a firefly.

After the subject reports his dream in detail, the experimenter conducts an inquiry in which elements of the dream are related to the original stimulus words by having the subject respond automatically with either one, two, three, or none of the words as each dream element is mentioned. Presumably multiple associations made by the subject support the interpretation that condensation of stimuli had taken place. All these procedures are practiced again in the waking state.

In the experiment itself the subject's waking dreams are preceded by arousal cues shown in the tachistoscope. One cue is the "O" or normal level of arousal, another the faint minus A signalling the "deepest point of relaxation." The experimenter says "dream" when the GSR indicates the subject to be in the desired range. The same three stimulus words are given in both conditions, with amnesia for the first dream invoked prior to the second and the order of conditions controlled across several trials. Dreams under lowered arousal will be examined to see if greater condensation does indeed occur.

Another primary process phenomenon assumed to be a function of lowered arousal is loose thought sequence. Decreased amplification in the cognitive subsystem should cut down reverberation and hence impair discharge of complete networks. This hypothesis is tested as follows. The subject, while performing a visual recognition task in the tachistoscope, also listens through earphones at various times to a tape containing two lists of words:

List I: black, white, dark, cat
chair, table, desk, sit
window, pane, glass, door

List II: earth, round, dirt, world
lamp, shade, light, bulb
moon, stars, sun, shine

He has been told previously under hypnosis that lists of words will be played through the earphones and at intervals the word "repeat" will appear on the tape. At that instant he is to say aloud the last four words he has heard. (The instruction to repeat always follows one of the groups of four words and occurs about once a minute on the tape. The subject's repetition insures his attention to the lists and leads him to perceive the task as one of short-term rote memory rather than the learning of meaningful units in a list.)

He is also advised under hypnosis that at a later time in the experiment he will be required to say words from one of the lists in response to a signal from the experimenter. Furthermore, the words are to be spoken to the accompaniment of a metronome, one word to every beat (set at 60 beats per minute) and it is very important to try not to miss any beats. The word-naming is subsequently performed, like the dreaming, under the two conditions of arousal to discover whether mix-ups between or within groups of words, or breaks in the sequence, occur more frequently with lowered arousal.

The two other primary process phenomena, symbolism and perceptual distortion, are linked by the model to changes in the balance between external and internal input. External input consists of the taped lists of words being played into the subject's earphones; internal inputs are feelings of hunger and cold programmed hypnotically. The subject learns to respond in the appropriate fashion whenever he hears the word "hungry" or "cold" in the waking state, and the feeling persists until the experimenter dismisses it. During the experimental session one or the other of the internal inputs is always in effect, whereas the external input is present only half the time.

For the period when the external inputs are absent, the internal stimuli are more dominant and "need-related" networks become salient. In the wake of discharges from these networks, anxiety-mediated inhibition is more probable. A consequence of inhibition is the increased likelihood of disguised thoughts, such as symbolic ones, emerging into consciousness. The following operations are designed to test for the greater occurrence of symbolism during the internally dominant condition. Under hypnosis the subject is taught to associate a different nonsense syllable automatically to each of six thoughts. Two syllables are attached to the act of listening to the word lists through the earphones. Two others are connected to thoughts previously paired with anxiety induced by the number cues. For example, while the subject is experiencing the "100" level of anxiety, he is told that "more men than women get stomach cancer" or that "sometimes when people are very cold they can get frostbite."

The last two nonsense syllables are attached to symbols derived from these anxiety-laden thoughts. The subject is instructed to relax and let an image come to mind which stands for the thought in disguised form. Two illustrative symbols obtained in this manner from one subject were "a blue mass with a red circle around it" (representing the cancer thought) and "a black, high-heeled shoe on a white background" (representing the frostbite thought).

The experimental task then requires the subject to spell one of the six nonsense syllables every time he hears a bell ring. Ten bell-ringing trials are interspersed at unannounced points throughout the various external-internal input conditions. We can now check the following hypotheses: (1) nonsense syllables attached to symbols will be reported more frequently when internal input is dominant, especially the symbol relevant to the ongoing internal input of hunger or cold; and (2) the higher the degree of anxiety, the more likely it is for the thought syllable to be supplanted by its symbolic representation.

Perceptual distortions (hallucination as an extreme example) also are presumed to increase as internal inputs become more salient. This phase of the research involves the same hunger and cold manipulations described previously for the symbolism experiment. The task in which the lists of words, internal inputs, and bell-ringing are embedded is visual recognition of hunger and cold-relevant stimuli, namely pictures of a serving dish (containing the subject's favorite food) and a fireplace with a burning fire. The stimuli are flashed in the tachistoscope one at a time in either left, right, top, or bottom position and the subject indicates which object he saw, whether it was the complete figure or not (incomplete versions of the two stimuli are also shown), and how certain he is of the response. From these and other variants in the procedure it is possible to derive a scale of perceptual distortion which can then be applied to test the prediction that, in the absence of external inputs, strong internal stimuli may mistakenly create the impression that a relevant object was actually flashed.

(If the preceding four experiments in the primary process project appear complicated and difficult to follow, just imagine what the situation is like when all four are compressed into the same session, in which the subject is simultaneously responding to internal inputs of hunger or cold, listening to and repeating words over and over, identifying flashed stimuli, and spelling out nonsense syllables whenever a bell rings. And during breaks between blocks of trials, he alternately dreams and ticks off words in accompaniment to a metronome. Clearly our human computer ranks with the best of the mechanical brains!)

Concluding Observations

Before summing up, it is important to consider the attitudes and reactions of our subjects throughout the series of experiments. Is their so-called anxiety behavior, for example, really genuine? And, if the answer is yes, aren't they being traumatized by hundreds of repetitions of a painful experience? There is no sure way of convincing someone at a distance of the authenticity of the subject's feelings. We long ago dispelled our own doubts by observing expressive movements, listening to introspective reports, and watching the GSR perform in almost incredible fashion. Skeptics in the vicinity are invited to see for themselves, and a steady parade of visitors undergoes conversion. Anyone who doesn't even believe what he sees is given a standing offer—we can always use more subjects!

Why, then, does the subject tolerate protracted, unpleasant experiences with such equanimity? The reasons are probably several. To begin with, he has volunteered to be a subject in scientific research for which he is paid at an hourly rate. His job is to carry out directions and, during the training, a feeling of pride and accomplishment is specifically reinforced whenever he succeeds. He is made to feel like a vital cog in a machine and soon acquires a strong identification with the research group. Between experiments his treatment is always informal and friendly. For the training, pleasant experiences are introduced to balance the affective ledger with joy, and anxiety practice is distributed rather than concentrated. Of course, care is also taken to insure that the anxiety and other reactions occur only within the confines of the laboratory room and, upon termination of his service, the subject participates in lengthy "debriefing" which includes the removal of all suggestions. These facets may all contribute in varying degree to the smoothness of the operation.

But the machine-like atmosphere enveloping both subject and experimenter during the experiments is still curious, especially so since most members of our group have been trained as clinical psychologists. My hunch is that the computer analogy implicit in the model exerts a subtle yet profound influence. I know that, in my own case, thinking of the human mind in systems terms has not only been a source of liberation from the value-laden language of psychoanalysis to which I had been accustomed, but also has opened my eyes to new kinds of experimental approaches. Even the rich, complicated psychodynamics of personality—defenses, primary process, and the rest—suddenly become susceptible to direct, controlled laboratory pursuit with the advent of a systematic conceptual framework, an impersonal language which cuts across areas of psychology, and a powerful technique like hypnosis to manipulate crucial variables in precise manner.

My enthusiasm should not be misinterpreted. The ultimate behavior theory is still a long way off. Our own working model of the mind will undergo many more revisions in the near future (Form R should be forthcoming as soon as the current results are in). Perhaps actual computer simulation may someday be helpful in pointing to neglected or inconsistent aspects of our formulation. The experimental subject of choice for us, though, must remain the human being, maybe restricted to a six-foot radius by his attached wires and thinking thoughts not quite original with himself, but nonetheless alive and breathing. Anyone want to buy a program?

8 | JOSEPH H. HANDLON
Stanford University Medical School

Discussion:

The Case of Professor B

The Chief Complaint presented in this case is an inability to have intimate contact with electronic computers. The symptoms of the Present Illness are an over-awe of such computers, making it necessary to deal with them only through intermediaries. There are also accusations of maladaptive primitiveness of defense against those who have commerce with the phobic object, plus some vague feelings of guilt about having been mistaken for one who has indulged in such intimacies. The Diagnosis, an acute case of computatuphobia.

Happily, the potential for therapy seems promising. There is a desire to confess and an expressed wish to have prejudices dispelled—always good signs.

What should the goals of therapy be in such a case? Certainly the therapeutic goal should not be that Professor B is made to feel that he must have repeated contact with the object of his phobia. Rather, therapy should be considered successful if Professor B could come to feel that he has an open choice of making use of such machines in his work if he so desires.

Another hoped-for outcome would be a strengthened appreciation of those who do have comfortable dealings with the phobic object.

What should be our treatment plan? There are several ways that we might begin. First, it might be well to build up rapport. This might be done by communicating in a straightforward and honest manner how much Professor B's thoughtful and imaginative work of the past few years in interrelating model building and empirical research is appreciated and admired. Further, trust in the therapist might be increased by revealing that he too, in the past, has been a party to model building without benefit of computer—model building far more primitive than Professor B's (George & Handlon, 1955, 1957).

A second approach might be to begin by dealing directly with the feelings that Professor B has about those who do not share his phobia. It would be hoped that Professor B would come to see that he is squarely in reality contact when he suggests that those who study human personality by observing computers are indulging in projection. But this should come as no surprise since, in a sense, projection is inherent in the scientific enterprise. It might even be suggested that the essence of science is the attempt to discover the degree to which nature imitates man's artistry at building models. Of course, it is to be hoped that our defensive projections are not so recalcitrant as to be unmodifiable after the inevitable disappointment at learning of nature's failures at imitation. Fortunately, in this case the degree to which Professor B's own projections have been appropriately flexible is well attested to by their metamorphoses A through Q.

A discussion of what ego-syntonic pleasures there might be in making use of computers to test one's projected models might well follow. Of course, there would have to be talk about how, as our models have become increasingly complex, it is getting more difficult for their creators to know exactly all the characteristics of their offspring—their hidden potentialities, limitations, and inconsistencies that we have arbitrarily, and often unwittingly, built into them. As a result of this increasing complexity, many model builders have found it advantageous to turn their attention to questions of an internal nature about their creations. In attempting to evaluate models there seem to be two separate, by no means unrelated, areas of concern which can conveniently be termed external questions and internal questions.

Stated in metatheoretical terms, the first area of attention focusses upon the degree of congruence existing between general descriptions of empirical phenomena and descriptions of _what_ the task is that the model has been created to perform. In our own field this might be exemplified by the correspondence between nomothetic statements about the results derived from a large number of experimental cases and, say, a block diagram of a model designed to account for these results with units labeled "selector," "intensifier," "transmuter," etc. Such questions of correspondence may be said to be _external_ to the model in that they focus upon the congruence of input-output relationships in the model as they imitate those of the empirical data. If the degree of congruence is not sufficiently great, due perhaps to the discovery of an unexpected input-output relationship in the empirical data, then the model is modified to account for such results.

The second area of endeavor focusses upon internal questions and becomes important when model builders begin to specify the mediational steps as to how the model is to accomplish its various tasks, not simply what the tasks are. Of course, having computers available to help reify the model has been a further impetus to asking internal questions. The correspondence problem here becomes one of congruence between statements of tasks that need to be performed by the model in order to insure certain input-output relationships and statements about the instructions which the model must, in a sense, give itself in order to accomplish these tasks. The emphasis here is more idiographic in that the test of correspondence is often done by seeing what happens when specific information is processed by the model. When we ask internal questions, implications of the formal characteristics of the models are more likely to be discovered because of the necessity to spell out with great precision each step from input to output. As a result more attention is paid to the inherent nature of the model itself and not just to its predictive value. Thus, complex models need no longer lie dormant on paper until modifications are demanded by future empirical findings which the model fails to describe. Instead, through the use of computers the model can become viable, develop a personality, and lead a life of its own.

At this point it might be well to direct the discussion toward Professor B's interest in using people to simulate machines. In doing this he has, of course, been concerned with both external and internal questions. He has indeed posed some ingenious external questions and has gotten his machines to yield such exciting and complex answers that one would almost believe them to be human. But when it comes to internal questions, a price has to be paid for having been blessed with such a plethora of compact and even comely computers. The number and kind of internal questions that his convenient computers can help him answer about themselves is limited. This is so because of the inevitable restrictions upon the degree to which Professor B can manipulate and control their input as well as their programming; and because of the presence of idiosyncratic data and routines with which each of his machines has come individually equipped. As a result there is a limit as to the degree of precision with which he can specify the steps along the mediational pathways of his stable of biped computers. But perhaps we should not be over-concerned for Professor B about this; for who can blame him for his involvement with external questions when his computers lend themselves so well to such explorations. Besides, the amount of actual tinkering permissible with the components of their internal circuitry is not boundless.

The therapeutic plan just outlined may strike the staff as being much too directive. It certainly smacks of the therapist trying to put himself forward as an authority who is pretty quick on the draw with advice and undigested homilies. Perhaps a better plan would be to attempt a deconditioning approach such as Wolpe's (1958), and ever so gradually try to demonstrate to Professor B that his fears of approaching computers are ungrounded in reality.

But in the last analysis (no conscious pun intended), perhaps a frankly existentialist approach might really be the most appropriate. One would then deal with the existential anxieties of our professional lives—anxieties about finding more comprehensive and research-generative models; anxieties about keeping up with the fashionable trends in gadgetry; anxieties over proper relationships with our friends, the physiologists, with their disquieting habits of probing nature's quixotic imitations of our lovely models. Finally, the therapy might be terminated with the typical existential emphasis upon the realization that the ultimate responsibility lies with each of us to work out his own scientific salvation through programming the private computers inside our skulls according to what feels right for us.

End of consultation.

9

KENNETH MARK COLBY
Stanford University

Computer Simulation of a Neurotic Process

Those of us involved in simulation research have yet to solve the problem of how to communicate our work to others not in the field. If someone is totally unfamiliar with a computer as a technical instrument and a program as a conceptual instrument, we usually spend so much time elucidating these that very little is left to describe how our particular program works in any satisfactory detail.

Even in communicating with computer people I have found that it takes hours before a detailed understanding is reached of the interaction between only a few of the routines in this program. Hence, I must limit myself to a description of the background of this effort, give some programming details, state a progress report, and indicate what we hope to achieve and how we might tell whether or not we are achieving it. I shall assume familiarity with a computer and with the nature of theory construction in the form of programs.

My particular interest in computer programs stemmed from two sources: (1) curiosity about models as theory construction, and (2) experiences in experimenting with persons to study the process of free-association. The traditional difficulties in both of these areas, but especially the latter, led me to consider the idea of composing a computer program which would explicitly state its theories and on which one could conduct experiments. This mind-like artifact would represent an unambiguous synthetic system of convenience and manipulability.

The work consists of two phases. In phase one we would like to construct a program simulating a neurotic process, and in phase two we would like to experiment with it by making inputs in an attempt to modify this neurotic process. Such a program would represent an information processing model which manipulates sequences of symbols according to rules. We would attempt to change the rules and the symbol sequences by inputs of information much as we do in clinical psychotherapeutic situations. When running on a computer, the program will generate a stream of symbols, an output of statements which resembles the output from a patient when he is speaking in the context of a psychotherapeutic or psychoanalytic situation.

A highly schematic flow diagram, as in Figure 1, illustrates what is taking place in the program in order to generate output statements. Information is taken from storage and evaluated. If it passes several tests, it moves to an assembly point for eventual output. If it does not pass the tests, it is successively modified until it does and then moved to assembly. Other information regarding how the processing is progressing is also collected in the assembly for output. Hence, in this phase, there is no external input. There is only an output generated by internal activations and processes.

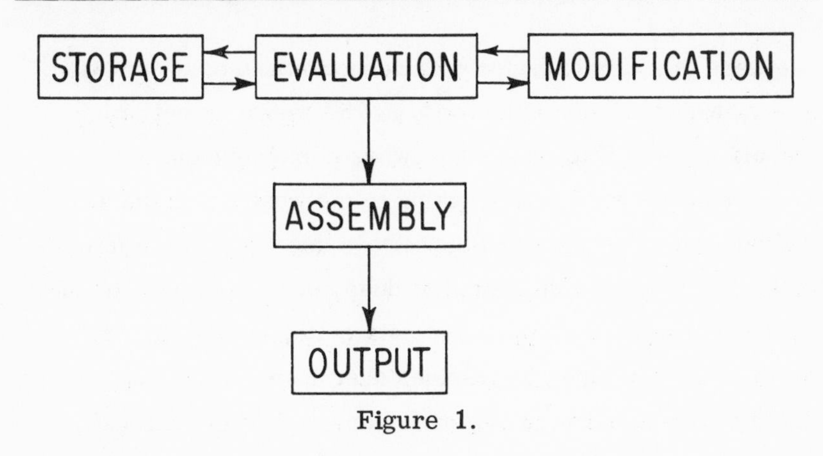

Figure 1.

The program contains information, knowledge in symbolic form. This information is stored in the form of beliefs originally stated in a simplified version of everyday English and subsequently coded in the computer language IPL-V (Newell, 1961, 1962) for machine testing. Beliefs are the molecular units of information processing. A belief is a proposition, a state of affairs, accepted and held as being true.

Which beliefs does the program hold and where did they come from? A characteristic of this type of simulation is that we take as data the utterances of an actual person. Besides reintroducing old-fashioned terms such as "mind" and "belief," we also feel no reluctance about using entirely introspective data from only one person. We start with a patient's free-associations which represent descriptions of self-observations in an I-language and, from these descriptions, obtain those beliefs judged to be essential in some neurotic process.

At the moment we have no machine method for taking all the utterances from a patient taped over long stretches of time and abstracting from them essential beliefs. Eventually we will have a voice-recognizing computer which should be able to do this. In the meantime, we must use a human computer, the wetware of a clinician, for data reduction and categorization. I say "wetware" since the brain is 75% water, a fact which should never fail to amaze hardware computermen.

It has always been striking to me what clinicians as human computers do when they try to describe a case to themselves or to other clinicians. It does not seem to faze them that they have huge amounts of data collected perhaps from hundreds of therapeutic sessions over months and years. They know this data is highly repetitive and redundant and that a patient's major concerns can be stated as themes which run through the data. They feel these themes, stated directly by the patient or inferred by the therapist, characterize a patient's descriptions of self-observation. In this type of data reduction, the resulting thematic condensations may be incomplete and some of them may even contain inaccuracies. But they do assert something relevant and important, and, using them, a clinician does get somewhere with the problems of his subject matter. As an example, I would cite the case of a single woman unable to get married for many years. From thousands and millions of utterances around this topic, the clinician abstracts a theme such as "she becomes contemptuous of any man who wants to marry her."

The data of the program I am describing are themes of a patient in analysis for several hundred hours. The themes are stated in the form of beliefs, of propositions held as true by the patient and by the program. Thus the data are case-descriptive and idiosyncratic. The processes which carry out operations on the data are assumed to be general, that is, norm-descriptive, holding for everyone except under special conditions. There are also processes in the program assumed to be normative, ideal, representing the way an artificial or actual mind should work under certain circumstances.

We do not know what coded signal the brain-mind uses when processing information. We know that what comes out of a person are messages, statements in English describing his self-observation. We assume there is some degree of homomorphy or correspondence between these statements and mental states. So in simulating mentation as a symbolic process, we use belief propositions which in the program are not taken as descriptions of mental states but actually are the mental states. Examples of beliefs from this patient are "I am defective," "father abandoned me," "I descend from royalty," "mother is helpless."

These beliefs are coded as lists of symbols. The components of each belief, i.e., the atoms of the molecule, exist in a format so that the same syntactical order of subject, verb, and object is preserved for each belief. This is achieved by writing the belief in the form of an attribute-value list as shown in Figure 2. Each attribute (e.g., A_9) is followed by its particular value (D_{206}). The atoms of the belief molecule are symbols designated by the programmer to have specific meanings. Such a list can be processed in many ways. It can be examined for presence or absence of certain symbols, it can be matched against another list for degrees of similarity, it can be modified by substituting different symbols as values of the attributes, and so forth. The need for a consistent syntactical order in all this processing should be apparent.

The processes which carry out operations on the data are also written in the form of lists. These routines and subroutines utilize the by-now-conventional procedures of iterations,

B_{16}
A_1
V_{22}
A_2
D_{601}
A_3
D_{402}
A_4
D_{62}
A_5
S_{43}
A_6
T_{109}
A_7
D_{400}
A_8
D_{701}
A_9
D_{206} 0

Figure 2.

conditional branchings, and recursiveness. But what is specifically neurotic about such a program? Without arguing about what constitutes neurosis in persons, I shall say that the processes I am about to describe are neurotic for this mind-like artifact. Later I shall return to the question of the degree of correspondence between neurosis in an artificial mind and neurosis in a person.

In the program, beliefs are organized into complexes. A complex is a list of beliefs which are related to one another according to criteria of relevance. The first action postulate of the program is that it strives to express the beliefs of its complexes. But, before a belief can be expressed in output, it must be evaluated as to whether or not there is any danger in gaining expression. Thus the second action postulate, having priority over the first, is that no belief can be expressed directly if it is evaluated as dangerous to do so. A search is made through all the beliefs in a given complex. If a conflict is found, a danger signal is activated. The degree of danger is indicated by the degree of conflict. For example, if one belief asserts "I love father" and another asserts "I must not love father" and both are highly charged beliefs (charges are represented by numerical weightings), then a situation of intense danger exists. The response to danger is to modify or transform the regnant member of the conflict (the one against which the others in the complex are being searched for conflict)

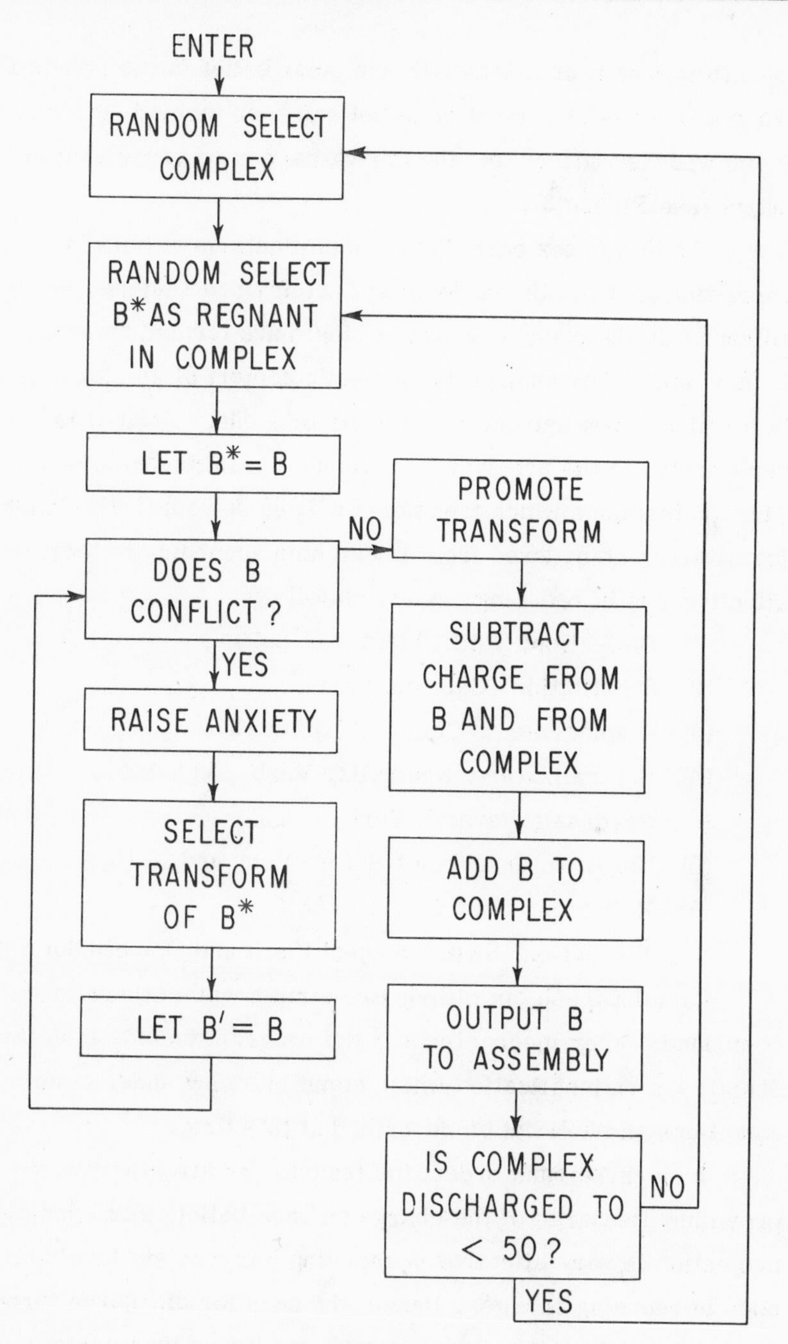
ENTER
RANDOM SELECT COMPLEX
RANDOM SELECT B* AS REGNANT IN COMPLEX
LET B* = B
DOES B CONFLICT?
NO
YES
RAISE ANXIETY
SELECT TRANSFORM OF B*
LET B′ = B
PROMOTE TRANSFORM
SUBTRACT CHARGE FROM B AND FROM COMPLEX
ADD B TO COMPLEX
OUTPUT B TO ASSEMBLY
IS COMPLEX DISCHARGED TO < 50?
NO
YES

Figure 3.

until it no longer conflicts with any other belief in the complex. When a successful derivative belief has been formed, anxiety, if you will, is reduced and the derivative can be expressed in output (see Figure 3).

The processes carrying out modifications of beliefs represent what in clinical language are termed "defense mechanisms." In the program, many of them are termed "transforms" since they change the symbolic content of an old belief in forming a new derivative. Anxiety or a danger signal is represented in the program by a running quantitative level which determines which transform will be selected. The transforms are rank ordered from low to high according to their effectiveness in reducing anxiety as follows:

(1) Deflection: Shift Object (Not Self)
(2) Substitution: Cascade Verb
(3) Displacement: Combine (1) and (2)
(4) Neutralization: Neutralize Verb
(5) Reversal: Reverse Verb
(6) Negation: Insert Not Before Verb and D_0 (5)
(7) Reflexion: Shift Object to Self
(8) Projection: Switch Subject (Self) and Object (Not Self)

Some of these operations are simple while others are compound. Other mechanisms in the program include isolation, denial, and rationalization which come into play under other conditions and will not be described at this time.

In reverse rank order, the transforms are effective in providing discharge of the charge on each belief. For example, projection is very effective in reducing high anxiety levels but poor in reducing charges. Hence, the need for discharge through expression drives the program down the list of transforms, while the need to reduce anxiety drives the program up. The sequence of derivatives created as output will represent a compromise formation between these processes.

When a transform succeeds in creating a satisfactory derivative, it is rewarded by being given a greater range of anxiety to handle, the other transforms being relatively demoted. If a belief is expressed, its charge is reduced to zero. When a derivative of a belief is created, it acquires a percentage of the charge on the original belief and, if expressed, the value falls to zero. However, since there is still a residual charge left on the original belief, it has a high probability of being selected again in the random search through the complex. Thus a tendency towards repetition results. A complex is run through until its charge, the sum of all the charges of its beliefs, is reduced below a certain level. Then, for the next pass, a complex is randomly selected from a list of complexes.

The essentials of this neurotic process are conflict, producing a danger signal which in turn produces a transformation of belief until the danger is eliminated. The safety-first postulate of avoiding danger takes precedence over the discharge through expression postulate. The transforms are adjustive mechanisms, but they are maladaptive since they result in loss of information, misrepresentations of beliefs, and insufficient discharge leading to increasing repetitive preoccupation with conflictual areas. If the program attempts to interrogate itself about its own information, it cannot express directly some of its most highly charged beliefs and it receives as answers distorted derivatives of these beliefs.

Let us follow the details of an actual run which generated the output statement "I want to help father." In a random search of the complex list, the complex D_3 was selected. A random search of D_3 produced the belief B_1 which stands for "I want to hurt father." Matching B_1 as the regnant against all others in the complex a conflict was found with B_2 standing for "I must not hurt father." B_1 and B_2 each had a charge of 300 which drove the anxiety level up to 400. At this time, the transform handling anxiety of degree 400 was No. (4), Neutralization. Hence, a derivative of B_1, B_{22}, was created to assert "I am indifferent to father." In matching B_{22} against others in the complex D_3, however, it ran into conflict with B_{19}, "I must not be indifferent to father." Failure of this operation raised the anxiety level another 100 units to 500. At this time, No. (5), Reversal, was attempted producing the derivative B_{23}, "I want to help father." B_{23} was passed through the complex and, since it found no conflict, it was output as an expressible belief. Reversal was promoted as a transform, the charge on B_1 and B_2 was reduced by the percentage the transform of Reversal handles, the charge on B_{23} was reduced to zero, B_{23} was added to the complex D_3, the charge on the complex was reduced but not sufficiently so the next cycle began by random searching D_3 for the next regnant belief.

The over-all master program contains at the moment 10 major routines. Six of these have been machine tested as separate pieces of processing. As yet we have not attempted a master run coordinating all processes in the program, but we hope to do so shortly. Thus as a progress report I can state with some certainty that this program does not yet work right.

How will we know that it does work? What does "work" mean in this connection? This brings us to the difficult problem of testing such models. The term "test" does not refer to a simple unidimensional concept. Consider Gray-Walter's artificial turtles which crawl around the house at night. They do what they were designed to do and they illustrate a point vividly. They simulate a bit of the goal-seeking behavior of organisms. But do they test a theory or do they provide adequate explanations of behavior? In my view they do, but even if they don't they still are interesting things in their own right.

We have some rough criteria in mind for tests of adequacy for this neurotic program. I shall group them under the headings of comprehensiveness, consistency, correspondence, and heuristic usefulness.

(a) Comprehensiveness: One definition of "simulate" is to capture the essences without the reality. In the simulation of a neurotic process, we would want the program to contain what we conceive of as essential relevant factors. Most clinicians agree that factors of conflict, anxiety, and defense are essential and would want to see them simulated. How many such factors are to be included is a matter of judgment. We want to simplify but not over-simplify. One early mistake we made was to start with too many beliefs. The coding and cross-referencing of only 70 beliefs becomes an enormous task. At the moment we have cut the data down to 20 starting beliefs. Another problem in this area involves how big a dictionary to have. That is, if the object of a belief is to be changed, how many possible choices will the program have to select from? We have limited the objects to persons to keep the dictionary small, knowing that, in real-life, persons deflect to things as well as to other persons. Finding upper and lower limits of the "essences" will eventually be a matter of playing around with longer and shorter lists, adding and subtracting until an optimum body of data and routines are established sufficient to generate the type and variety of output we are looking for.

(b) Consistency: A major problem in writing programs is to get all the pieces, the routines and subroutines, to coordinate so that action takes place back and forth between them in the desired hierarchical way. When a piece of a program is written, put aside for a few months, and then hooked up to a recently written piece, chaos and gibberish often result since one has forgotten or never realized some of the consequences of the first piece. It takes a great deal of thought and work to get a complicated program to hang together and to run harmoniously. A master program should run as harmony in process.

(c) Correspondence: This is the criterion of adequacy which is most commonly referred to by the phrase "testing a model." In the case of simulating a neurosis, one might ask if the output from the program has some degree of correspondence to the output from a neurotic patient? In comparing output statements from a program and from a patient, what would constitute a reasonable degree of agreement? We would have to specify the type of indicators we could observe and suggest some way of measuring them. At the moment there is no satisfactory statistical approach to this fidelity problem. We might, for the time being, try Türing's Test, that is, have clinical judges try to distinguish output from a person in therapy and output generated by a program. But so much editing has to take place in translating the program output before it looks like everyday English that all kinds of biases can enter to make it an unfair and, hence, a weak test. There are many people now working on these kinds of models. We hope that, by the time we develop a large family of these models, others will have developed ways of testing their fidelity by good measures, so that we can tell which model is better than another for a given simulation.

If we want to dream a bit, we could imagine correspondence tests involving predictions. Suppose the program contained data collected from the first half of a therapy and then the program was given a task such as object-choice. Would the program come to the same decision as the patient did when she met a new man during therapy? Or one could keep the program updated with the course of an actual therapy. Over a weekend one could run the program and observe the outputs as predictions of what the patient might actually experience. The predictions could be confirmed or infirmed by the patient's Monday report of his weekend thoughts, feelings, and decisions. Or one might test the program for sensitive areas, namely inputs which produce a rise in anxiety. If on offering these inputs to the patient a similar phenomenon was observed, one might begin to think there was some useful degree of correspondence between the structure of the program and the structure of the patient's mental functions.

(d) Heuristic Usefulness: By this I mean using the program as an experimental tool in an attempt to find better ways of modifying a neurotic process through inputs. We may be able to find something new about effecting persons from experimenting with mind-like artifacts. It is incorrect to say that nothing new can come from a program because we know everything that was put in initially. One may know all the initial data, but, in a developing system evolving over time which can create an unlimited number of derivatives, we cannot know all the implications and consequences of what we have put in. A program generates many surprises for even the programmer.

Besides being a new experimental opportunity, a program runs in compressed time. We can try out all kinds of psychotherapeutic alternatives on it which would take a lifetime to try out on actual persons. It is true it will take years to construct such a program, but once you have it you always have it. One can try out a variety of alternative inputs starting from the same initial conditions and having full experimental control over explicit independent variables. We might hope to find better ways of recognizing relevant areas in a patient's program, better inputs, better sites of application, and better ways of reaching to the heart of the matter in a neurosis. Perhaps we can learn to discard the multiple irrelevancies which clinicians recognize are involved in present-day psychotherapy. The status of psychotherapy at present is reminiscent of Eddington's quip about causality—"something unknown is doing we don't know what."

All this sounds promising enough, but we should be frank to ourselves about limitations of this computer approach. Perhaps we are leaping too far, too fast. It may be too ambitious or pretentious to believe we can get anywhere in these complex but lumbering efforts. The First Law of the Instrument states that if you give a boy a hammer, he suddenly finds that everything needs pounding. The computer program may be our current hammer, but it must be tried. One cannot decide from purely armchair considerations whether or not it will be of any value.

It is still not clear what a program is as a conceptual instrument. Mathematicians say it is not mathematics, logicians say it is not logic, scientists say it is not science, and artists are certain it is not art. It is a way of dealing primarily with quality and structure rather than quantity and number. L. L. Whyte has said we do not have a term for describing "harmony in process." I would suggest the term "program" now meets the need.

On this frontier we can't be too worried about what a program is. We are too busy trying to get programs to work, to do what we want them to do. Even if they do not pass tests of correspondence, I would maintain they are an interesting class of new objects in the world. A program realizable on a computer is a new paradigm of fundamental novelty. It gives us a new set of scientific commitments and a new way of practicing science. We can do things with a program that cannot be done by other methods. Before the computer program we had no satisfactory approach to huge, complex, ill-defined systems difficult to grapple with, not only because of their multivariate size but also because of a property of elusiveness which in psychology is mainly a function of vagueness in that the limits of inclusiveness of conventional terms are unclear. A computer program can handle any degree of complexity a programmer wants with great power and subtlety. But more important for simulation of mental functions is the grip a program has on otherwise elusive qualities. It is the ideal Socratic goad for analysis. For if you cannot make explicit in the form of a program what information is being processed according to what rules, then you do not yet understand the mental phenomena in question. If you can do this, then you have at least an explanation (no one ever has the explanation of anything) which is relevant, perhaps adequate for your purposes and perhaps even containing some degree of truth.

10

JEROME L. SINGER
Institute of Psychological Research,
Teachers College, Columbia University

Discussion:
Motivational Models in the Simulation of Neurosis

It seems to me that the role of a discussant is to provide an author with some feedback concerning the effectiveness with which he has communicated his ideas, to attempt to elaborate on or elucidate aspects of the content of the paper, and to raise critical or constructive questions which may help the investigator to clarify his message or his research efforts. One cannot but be impressed by the difficulty of the task Dr. Colby has set for himself and by the ingenuity of his attempt to resolve that difficulty. Let me see if I can briefly summarize what he has attempted to do. Dr. Colby has chosen to simulate the neurotic process as it is manifested in the verbalizations of a patient in a typical psychoanalytic hour. The neurotic process is represented by the instances where the patient's drive to verbalize a particular belief or affect conflicts with a contrary drive or belief and results in anxiety. The anxiety can be resolved only by some defensive transformation of the drive or belief which reduces the anxiety sufficiently to permit some proportion of the original drive to be expressed. In such a case, therefore, what the patient actually says to the therapist (or what the computer prints out) is essentially a distortion of his original intended expression. Yet by saying even this much he partially reduces the drive in most instances. If eventually he can express more and more of the beliefs or drives in a "complex," he will presumably be free of pressure in that area and will no longer need to hand out misinformation to reduce anxiety. As he eventually expresses all the beliefs in his various complexes he will presumably be cured of his neurosis.

The various defenses are ordered in a hierarchy based on their capacity to reduce anxiety and also to effect the output of a version of the original drive or belief that is as little distorted as possible. Thus, an experienced rage against the father which conflicts with superego values might, if expressed as a rage against the boss, greatly reduce drive pressure but only slightly reduce the anxiety associated with the drive. This would represent a "deflection" transformation. If the drive were modified into a desire merely to "tell off the boss," it would represent a somewhat less effective means of drive reduction by "displacement," while reducing the anxiety more, since the conflict with naked aggressive impulses would be more disguised. "Projection," in this sequence, by extensively transforming the original drive-belief into "they all hate me" reduces the anxiety considerably since the original unacceptable "I hate father" is now thoroughly disguised. At the same time relatively little of the original drive has been expressed, so it is likely to recur again and again. The result of projection is therefore a temporary relief of anxiety at the cost of a gross distortion of reality—in the program, the output of gross misinformation. An example of close apparent correspondence with Dr. Colby's model comes to mind. A hospitalized patient described the tremendous relief he experienced when he realized that the tortured thoughts and headaches he experienced nightly were not the result of his hostility towards his successful younger brother, as he had originally believed, but were the result of experimentation on his brain by electrical impulses sent out by psychologists in the Pentagon. The headaches and thoughts recurred regularly but he could accept them with a kind of tolerance, since he at least realized their true origin.

I've gone into this summary because I believe it indicates how cleverly Dr. Colby has managed to think through and program for at least potentially quantitative evaluation some important aspects of psychoanalytic drive theory. At the same time, it is necessary to make clear an important limitation of this approach—one which I'm sure Dr. Colby recognizes. The program as described reflects the ingenuity and simplicity of the earlier expressions of psychoanalytic drive-reduction theory. The very mechanical simplicity and neatness of psychoanalytic drive theory prior to the contributions of Hartmann (1958), Rapaport (1959), and Erikson (1950) (not to mention neo-freudian criticisms) at once makes it amenable to ingenious programming, but also betrays its serious limitations for a comprehensive view of personality. The implication seems clear from the program as described that if the patient can eventually express most of his beliefs or drives, he will be cured of his neurosis. Would this then leave him a driveless person lacking incentives for new activity? Is it not possible that some of the distorted drives expressed as beliefs might generate their own dynamics; e.g., the transformation from "I want to see mother's body" to "I want to know about life" might lead to a scientific curiosity which could be greatly rewarding for its own sake, as Rapaport recognized in his concept of the hierarchies of motives. Indeed, if we take seriously the recent criticisms of drive-reduction theory by Harlow (1953) or White (1959), and the increased experimental and theoretical attention given to competence striving, mastery, and curiosity, the formulations of the program here presented seem excessively narrow in their explanatory potential.

Within the therapeutic situation itself, the conditions which govern the expression of a particular belief in direct or modified form also go considerably beyond the internal conflict described here. The regnant belief would ultimately have to be evaluated not only for conflict with the patient's internalized contrary beliefs but also for evidence of conflict with the real or transference-distorted perception by the patient of the *therapist's* beliefs. Perhaps such "perceptions of the *therapist's* beliefs" might some day be thrown into the hopper along with "countertransference distortions" for evaluation in some future, more complex program. I should like to call attention also to the fact that at least some types of self-defeating or ineffective patient-outputs are not the consequences of conflicting beliefs. Many patients, because of neglect, environmental peculiarities, or early conflicts, are surprisingly ignorant of important aspects of social behavior or communication patterns, or they lack practice in diagnosing accurately the intentions or meanings of other persons. They may express this ignorance directly by incorrect notions or may occasionally develop some type of defensive transformation to cover their embarrassment at what they half realize is a great gap in their social skill or knowledge. I believe that a kind of social education or re-education plays a more prominent role in psychoanalytic therapy than is generally admitted. I can't go into this in detail here but mention it to emphasize again the restriction in scope of the neurotic process as employed in this program.

The restrictions I call attention to in Dr. Colby's program point up what I feel is a danger in this approach. It can easily become an ingenious game—a kind of extraordinarily inventive penny-arcade machine for simulating mechanically the behavior of the probably fictional neurotic who emerged from the psychoanalytic case studies of the early 1920's.

It is easy to sit in judgment on such an early pioneering effort and to point out its lack of comprehensiveness or its simplicity. To do so should not, however, lead us to overlook the extremely provocative nature of Dr. Colby's work. Reading this paper has set my head swimming with thoughts about not only the practical possibilities for ultimate prediction which might result but also about many of the basic theoretical issues in personality theory. Perhaps for a long time to come the major value of computer simulation research may lie in its increasingly rigorous analysis of the essential elements of various personality processes. I feel very strongly with Dr. Colby that by playing the computer simulation game we will be forced to undertake increasingly controlled, systematic, and detailed scrutiny of crucial facets of behavior or therapeutic processes. In a sense, then, programming a process for a computer is indeed a new type of logical or, say, disciplined analysis that may be of particular use for behavior theory. It is a kind of programmed learning situation for the programmer! An example in this paper is the care with which Dr. Colby has analyzed the relative order and power of the defense mechanisms as drive-releasers or anxiety-reducers. As my little example sought to suggest, this analysis seems to have phenomenal validity. More than that—I believe that this type of analysis may increasingly uncover questions that lend themselves to experimental expression. For example, I found myself thinking of a series of experiments with normal subjects that would simulate Dr. Colby's program for the hierarchy of transformations. We might conceivably have persons role play a conflict and then under specified conditions observe the ways in which they express an instructed taboo belief. I am sure that computer simulation has certain advantages over a good clinician if it can be given sufficient information to work with, but that time may be a long way off. I am much more certain, however, that repeated efforts at such simulation will produce hypotheses which can be tested by experiments whose findings will place the guesses of the clinician on a firmer scientific base.

PART III

COGNITION AND AFFECT

11 JOHN C. LOEHLIN
University of Nebraska

A Computer Program That Simulates Personality

I assume that it is not necessary at this point in the conference to explain what a computer model is, or to enter upon an elaborate justification for attempting to apply such a model in the study of personality. But any newcomers may rest assured, in any case I will be describing one such model and some experiments done with it. After describing these experiments, I propose to address myself briefly to two questions. First, is it appropriate to speak of this model as a model of personality at all? In view of my title, obviously I'm going to say "yes," but arriving at this answer will require us to consider some different views about what personality is. Second, I will ask the question whether the model I have described is an entirely satisfactory model of personality. To this I will say "no"; however, I will suggest some ways in which it might be made more nearly adequate.

The Computer Model

Aldous

First, let me describe the model briefly. I've named him Aldous—his is a Brave New World. Aldous is fairly modest as computer models go: about 750 computer instructions loaded into a smallish, not-very-fast computer, the Burroughs 205. Once set up, Aldous can be presented with "situations" (coded as seven-digit numbers) to each of which he "responds" by printing out a number. Depending on the nature of his response and the nature of the situation, he may or may not receive further consequences, and hence may or may not learn from his experience.

The main subsystems within Aldous which mediate his response to his environment are three in number. First comes recognition. Here the incoming "stimulus" establishes contact with Aldous's memory, which includes the traces of previous encounters, if any, with this particular situation, as well as with the more general classes of situations to which it belongs. Aldous occasionally makes errors—occasionally he mistakes a situation for another perceptually similar one.

The second subsystem in Aldous is emotional reaction. Here Aldous develops an emotional response to the situation (as he perceives it). Aldous has three emotions. One is positive—call it attraction or desire or love—and two are negative, anger and fear. The development of Aldous's emotional response gets moderately complicated; there may be components of all three emotions present, and they may interact in various ways which differ with the emotions involved. The particular response developed to a situation will depend on Aldous's past experience with the situation and others like it, as well as on his current mood (his reaction to one situation persists and influences his response to the next one).

The third subsystem mediating Aldous's response is action preparation. Here an appropriate action is selected. Aldous has a limited repertoire of behaviors: he can approach positively, attack, or withdraw, corresponding to predominant emotions of attraction, anger, or fear; each of these behaviors may occur at two levels, mildly or vigorously. If the two strongest emotional tendencies are approximately equal, Aldous will display conflict behavior. If emotional arousal is slight, he will do nothing at all; if it is extreme enough, emotional paralysis will ensue.

In addition to the three systems described, Aldous has two memory systems, immediate and permanent memory, with a learning subsystem that modifies the latter. Aldous's permanent memory retains a cumulative record of his encounters with particular situations and classes of situations; i.e., it consists of attitudes rather than memories of particular events. Aldous's "laws of learning" are such that the attitude shift produced by a single encounter with a situation is inversely proportional to the amount of prior experience Aldous has had with that situation, and at the same time recent experiences carry relatively more weight than less recent ones in determining Aldous's current attitude toward a situation.

Besides overt behavior, Aldous can introspect; that is, he can respond to three "questions" about his experience of particular situations (or abstract attributes thereof) by printing out a coded "verbal report" instead of an action. Such a "report" gives a more detailed account of Aldous's "feelings" about a situation than could readily be inferred from his overt action.

Aldous is honest and fairly insightful—obvious opportunities for increased verisimilitude exist here!

Aldous's Environment

Now, what about Aldous's environment, the situations which confront him? As indicated earlier, each of these is represented by a seven-digit number. This number consists of two parts. The first three digits represent the perceptual or discriminable characteristics of the situation—those features by which Aldous can recognize it and react accordingly. The last four digits describe what Murray (1938) would call the "press" of the situation; what it can do to or for Aldous. The nature of the press is defined in three dimensions—situations may be to varying degrees satisfying, frustrating, and painful. Also included in the description of the press is an indication of the power of the situation to impose its consequences on Aldous. Some situations produce their positive or negative consequences only if approached by Aldous. Others may be able to impose punishment or reward despite vigorous evasive action on his part.

While a great variety of environments might be set up using different kinds and sequences of situations, the experiments I will describe in the present paper involve only two environments. These are identical in perceptual terms: each consists of situations identified by three perceptual dimensions of ten steps each, giving rise to a possible total of 1000 discriminable situations. The environments differ markedly, however, in terms of their press. One world is a benign one—most situations are predominantly satisfying, and the power of the injurious and frustrating situations tends to be low. The other world is hostile—injurious and frustrating situations are frequent, and their power tends to be high.

As Aldous is confronted with a series of such situations, he gradually develops a set of attitudes toward the events of his world. On some occasions his behavior and the nature of the situations he confronts will lead to encounters with his world that will increase his knowledge of it; on other occasions he will come away with his preconceptions undisturbed. Sometimes this latter outcome will represent successful avoidance of a realistic threat; on other occasions it may mean loss of a potential real satisfaction.

Some Program Details

So far, I have been describing Aldous mainly in psychological language, i.e., in terms of the processes being simulated. Some of you will want to hear a little more about the actual computer operations involved. These are ordinary arithmetical and decision processes applied to the input and memory data (this particular computer works with decimal numbers, although the actual machine logic is binary). I will begin by describing Aldous's memory storage, then will outline briefly the main steps in the recognition, emotional reaction, and action preparation routines, and will finally describe memory change (learning).

Aldous's attitude toward a situation (or class of situations) is represented by the ten digits of a computer "word"—the first four digits represent the familiarity of the situation (the number of previous encounters with it) and the last six Aldous's dispositions toward fear, anger, and attraction to the situation. The location of the word in memory is based on the perceptual characteristics of the situation. Memory addresses 0000 to 0999 contain attitudes toward the 1000 situations with corresponding perceptual descriptions, addresses 1000 to 1299 contain attitudes toward the classes of situations defined by the 300 possible pairs of attribute values, and 1300 to 1329, attitudes toward the 30 classes defined by single attribute values.

When Aldous is confronted with a situation, the recognition subroutine first determines if an error is to be introduced (by consulting a random number), and, if so, changes one of the descriptive digits by plus or minus one (also at random), i.e., Aldous misrecognizes the situation as a similar one. The program is normally set to introduce errors on about 6% of trials. The subroutine then computes seven addresses where relevant memory is located—namely, Aldous's attitude toward the situation itself, toward the classes defined by the three pairs of attribute values contained in it, and toward the classes defined by the three individual attribute values.

Next, the emotional reaction subroutine computes a response which is a weighted combination of Aldous's current mood and his relevant attitudes. The subroutine first examines immediate memory (which stores data from the preceding trial). If there were no consequences on the preceding trial, Aldous's initial emotional reaction on that trial is used. If there were consequences, Aldous's reaction to these is weighted 2/3 and his initial reaction 1/3. (This last should be changed, I suspect; the initial reaction might even be weighted negatively to reflect a contrast of event with expectation.) Next the relevant permanent memory locations are examined and weighted values are computed for fear, attraction, and anger. If the situation is a familiar one, the reaction is based mainly on previous experience with the situation itself, experience at the higher levels of abstraction being weighted 1/10 and 1/100 respectively. If the particular situation has only been encountered a few times, it is given less weight; this varies with the emotion involved. If it has never been encountered, the reaction is based on experience with the classes of situations to which it belongs. Immediate mood and memory are then combined, with a 1 to 4 weighting. The final step is to compare the three emotional tendencies; if one is dominant it interacts with its competitors to weaken them; this varies with the emotions involved.

In the action preparation subroutine, an action corresponding to the dominant emotion is selected. (If none is dominant, conflict occurs.) In general, if the strength of the dominant emotion is 0-2, no action occurs; if 3-5, mild action of the appropriate kind; if 6-8, vigorous action; and if 9, emotional paralysis.

When Aldous acts, a routine (external to Aldous) determines whether, in the light of Aldous's action and the (real) press of the situation, consequences to Aldous will ensue. In general, if Aldous approaches, consequences always occur; if Aldous does nothing, consequences occur if the power of the situation is 3 or greater; if Aldous avoids or attacks mildly, consequences occur if power is 5 or greater; if Aldous avoids or attacks vigorously, consequences occur only if power is 8 or 9.

If no consequences are experienced, no change occurs in memory, except an increase in the familiarity of the situation. If consequences are experienced, the reaction to the consequences affects the attitudes in the seven relevant memory locations, with a weight which depends on the amount of experience with the situation or class of situations—the weight is 1 on the first 10 encounters, 1/2 on encounters 11-100, 1/4 on encounters 101-1000, and 1/8 thereafter, with the weights being applied separately at each memory location. A single trial will thus ordinarily lead to more attitude change toward the particular situation than toward the general classes of situations to which it belongs.

Experiments with Aldous

Development in the Two Worlds

Initial experiments done with Aldous involved "raising" him in the benign and hostile environments, and checking up periodically on his attitudes by administering a "personality questionnaire" to him. This "questionnaire" measures Aldous's attitudes toward a sample of the situations in his universe. It yields scores on the average level of attraction, hostility, and fearfulness of the sample of situations; an adjustment index which reflects the correspondence of Aldous's attitudes with reality; and a score which indicates the *kind* of errors Aldous makes in judging his world—is he impulsive, inclined to approach frustrating and injurious situations, or are his misjudgments mainly avoidance of potential satisfactions?

In these experiments Aldous's behavior clearly showed the effects of his environment within the first dozen trials or so, an effect that became progressively more marked over the first couple of hundred encounters with the environment, by which time Aldous's behavior had stabilized at approach on about 85% of trials in the benign world, and virtually no approach in the hostile world. The personality measures showed improving adjustment in both environments, rapid at first and then slowing down, with the curves leveling off pretty well after about 700 trials. Adjustment proceeded somewhat faster in the favorable environment, but reached a similar level in both. (Of course Aldous's attitudes toward particular situations would continue to change for a very long time after this, since after 700 trials he would not yet have even encountered a majority of the potential situations in his world, let alone have formed any stable response to them.) The direction of adjustment errors was opposite in the two worlds, and represented overgeneralization in each case: Aldous tended to be even more optimistic in the benign world than was justified, and overly pessimistic about his chances in the hostile one.

Shifts Between Worlds

Next some experiments were done in which Aldous was "raised" in one environment for 500 trials, and then shifted to the other without notice. In all these experiments, Aldous did readjust to changed conditions; however, the process tended to go faster when he was shifted from the benign to the hostile world than in the opposite case. A fearful Aldous took longer to discover the altered state of affairs.

Trait Changes

In a further series of experiments, various of Aldous's "personality traits" were altered, and his adjustment and readjustment in the benign and hostile worlds were studied. There are a number of constants in the program which govern various aspects of Aldous's response. In the recognition system, for example, error rate may be varied. In the emotional reaction system there are several constants controlling such matters as the relative weight given to current mood and to past experience, the relative importance of the particular situation as against general classes of situations in determining emotional reaction, the extremity or flatness of emotional reactivity, the interactions among the emotions, and so on. Similarly, constants in the action preparation system and the learning system control such matters as response intensity, learning rate, and so forth.

I will describe briefly three experiments in which trait changes were made, involving different parts of Aldous's reaction system.

The first of these involves a variation on the basic model which I will call "Abstract Aldous." Abstract Aldous differs from Standard Aldous by virtue of his predilection for dealing with events in terms of general categories rather than in their concrete individuality. The 100 and 10 to 1 weight ratios that prevail in Standard Aldous between experience with a particular situation and experience with its generalized attributes are changed in Abstract Aldous to 1 to 1. When Abstract Aldous is presented with the benign and hostile worlds in experiments parallel to those described earlier, several differences from Standard Aldous can be noted. For instance, Abstract Aldous tends to be slightly more consistent (and slightly more extreme) in his behavior than Standard Aldous. He approaches somewhat more in the benign world, and avoids somewhat more in the hostile world. He also shifts from approach to avoidance behavior (or vice versa) more rapidly when the environment is changed. In terms of the over-all adjustment of their attitudes to reality, however, the two Aldouses do just about equally well; the same can be said of their readjustment to a changed world.

In another experiment, hesitant and decisive versions of Aldous were used, which differ from Standard Aldous in the constants that govern translation of emotion into action. Hesitant Aldous does not act at all unless his predominant emotional reaction to a situation is a fairly strong one, and his resulting action is diffident in any event, unless emotion is fairly extreme. Decisive Aldous, on the other hand, acts with even the slightest emotional involvement, and usually acts vigorously. This difference showed up clearly in their behavior in the two worlds. In 500 trials in the benign world and 500 trials in the hostile world, Decisive Aldous failed to respond a total of just three times, while Hesitant Aldous took no action on 242 and 287 trials, respectively. Despite their very different behavior styles, however, the adjustment of their attitudes to reality showed little over-all difference: Decisive Aldous's vigorous approach gave him a slight advantage in adjusting to the benign world, but Hesitant Aldous more than held his own in the hostile environment. In readjustment to a changed world, however, Hesitant Aldous's more passive role gave him an advantage, especially in making the shift from the hostile to the benign world.

In a third experiment, versions of Aldous were used which differ in several constants related to the influence of past experience. One Aldous tends to live in the present, the other is relatively dominated by the past. The first, whom I will call Radical Aldous, is more influenced in his emotional reactions by his current mood, and has a memory that changes more rapidly; hence he is more influenced by recent than distant past events. Conservative Aldous, on the other hand, is more influenced by permanent than by immediate memory, and his memory changes more gradually, giving more weight to the distant past. In behavior, Radical Aldous and Conservative Aldous did not differ as much from Standard Aldous as Decisive Aldous and Hesitant Aldous did; of the two, Radical Aldous acted more like Decisive Aldous, and Conservative Aldous more like Hesitant Aldous. In adjustment, Radical Aldous had a slight edge on Conservative Aldous, and, as one might suspect, this was even more true when it came to readjustment in a changed world. In terms of the kind of adjustment discrepancies, Radical Aldous ran more to extremes, with a higher proportion of both approach errors in the benign world and avoidance errors in the hostile world than Conservative Aldous had.

What general comments can be made about this last group of experiments on the manipulation of personality traits? First, the changes did affect the characteristic behavior of Aldous. Decisive Aldous, Radical Aldous, and Abstract Aldous were more inclined toward extreme actions than was Standard Aldous. Hesitant Aldous and Conservative Aldous were more likely than the others to take no action at all. Decisive Aldous was the only one who ever got his emotions worked up to the point of paralysis: this occurred three times during his series of 500 trials in the hostile world.

Secondly, differences in over-all adjustment tended to be considerably less striking and consistent than differences in styles of behavior. Plotted on graphs, curves representing the adjustment of the different Aldouses over trials are close together and cross each other frequently; curves representing behavior are spaced more widely and seldom cross. In computer models, too, apparently, quite different "styles of life" may lead to equally satisfactory adjustments.

A third point worth noting is that the success of a particular Aldous's adjustment to his environment depended somewhat on the nature of the environment. Hesitant Aldous, for example, did not do particularly well in adjusting to the benign world, but was the most successful of all the Aldouses in the hostile world.

In a sense, the most striking outcome of these experiments was the stability of Aldous. Changing constants in the system by factors of 4, 8, 10, or more produced temperamental changes, all right, but did not gravely hamper Aldous's ability to adjust to his environment and readjust when it was changed. Perhaps the human personality is a more delicately balanced system; on the other hand, when one reflects on the variety of people in different societies who come to reasonably satisfactory terms with their widely differing environments, perhaps not.

Computer Models and Personality Theory

Now let me tackle the two questions I mentioned earlier. The first of these was: Is it appropriate to describe Aldous as a personality model at all? The second: Is Aldous an entirely satisfactory personality model? You will recall that my answer to the first of these questions is to be "yes," and to the second, "no."

Now clearly, whether we answer the first question "yes" or "no" depends somewhat on how we conceptualize personality, and I don't have to tell you that there are a good many views extant on this topic. Some writers speak of personality as characteristic action and reaction patterns; some writers speak of it as a way of viewing the world; some writers speak of it as a system within the organism that mediates either or both of these.

Most writers suggest that personality has some degree of unity or integration or organization, but they differ on how much unity. Most writers suggest that personality is individually distinctive, but they differ on the extent, dimensionality, and importance of this distinctiveness. Most writers suggest that personality has some degree of independence of its immediate environmental setting, but they differ on how independent it is. Most writers suggest that personality tends to endure over time, yet is subject to some modification by life experiences, but they differ on how much change is typical, what kinds of experience can bring about what kinds of changes, when and why such changes take place, whether they tend to occur continuously or discontinuously, and a few other matters.

Now I'm not going to be able to give all these issues, and many more, careful attention with respect to Aldous, but I would like to examine a few which seem particularly relevant to our general question: whether Aldous (or models like him) can reasonably be described as <u>personality</u> models. Note by the way that a model need not have <u>all</u> the defining characteristics of the thing portrayed in order to be useful as a model—indeed if it did, it would no longer be a model, but rather would be an example of the phenomenon in question. A model of the solar system is not the solar system, but if it may differ in some properties (such as size, material, and location) it must resemble the original in others (such as proportional distances and movements) if it is to qualify as a useful model. Thus Aldous need not have all the attributes of a person to be a successful personality model, but unless he incorporates at least some of the more basic features of personality, there would seem to be serious doubts as to his claim to the title.

But back to business. First, Aldous appears to possess most of the broad qualities of personality noted above: he is organized, individually distinctive, and somewhat autonomous and enduring—yet subject to influence and change. However a good many things that aren't personality also possess these qualities; it may prove more instructive to be a little less general, and to look at Aldous from the more restricted perspectives of some major viewpoints within personality theory.

Three Perspectives on Personality

Contemporary personality theorists may, with a little gall, be divided into three parts. I will, in the interests of alliteration, describe these groups as the system, the surface, and the subjective theorists. These three categories are neither mutually exclusive nor exhaustive, which is regrettable but is entirely due to the fact that personality theorists are a notoriously untidy lot, persisting in taking all sides of any issue you care to name, to the grave inconvenience of those of us who have to teach courses about them. But be this as it may, at least our three groups will provide us with three perspectives from which to view Aldous and others of his kind as models of personality.

In the first of these three camps we find what we may call the system theorists. For them, personality is a complex dynamic system that mediates the adjustment of the organism to its environment. Often, but not always, progressive development of the system according to some principle of growth or differentiation is part of the theory. Some writers include the environment as well as the organism as part of a single personality system; others treat the personality system as contained within the organism. The system may be defined purely psychologically, or given physiological underpinning. On the whole, some variation of a system-theoretical viewpoint appears to be the dominant trend in personality theory in this country. Allport's (1937, p. 48) famous definition: "Personality is the dynamic organization within the individual of those psychophysical systems that determine his unique adjustments to his environment," is solidly in this tradition. In various directions from Allport, but sharing his emphasis on the dynamic system character of personality, we find a diverse array of writers. Some reflect the joint influence of Gestalt theory and theoretical biology. Kurt Goldstein[1], Andras Angyal, and Heinz Werner are examples; Gardner Murphy shows a considerable affinity for this point of view, as does Carl Rogers (1959) when he's looking at things from his "external frame of reference." Off in another direction we find Freudians and Jungians, with different views on many questions, but jointly preoccupied with the balance of forces in intrapsychic systems. In still a different direction we find writers on personality influenced by general behavior theories, at least those theories like Hull's and Tolman's which feature intervening variable systems. Strange bedfellows, perhaps, but system theorists all.

The second of our three groups of personality theorists, also with a long and honorable tradition in this country, may be called the surface theorists. These give priority to the person-

[1] I have not included bibliographic references for the various personality theorists merely mentioned in passing, except in a few cases where the reference is specific, or too recent to be found in standard texts such as Hall and Lindzey (1957).

ality psychologist's descriptive task. They are inclined to be highly empirical and operational, and to look with grave suspicion on concepts inferred to lie in the organism's depths. A factor analyst like Guilford (1959), for example, concerns himself with seeking a comprehensive and systematic set of dimensions of behavior variation, much more than with an "explanation" of such variation in terms of postulated mechanisms within the organism. The "dustbowl empiricists" in the Minnesota tradition also belong with this group, as would a Skinnerian learning theory approach like that of Lundin (1961).

The third main group of personality theorists we may call the subjective theorists. These are theorists who tend to approach personality from the viewpoint of the person observed. The way an individual perceives and reacts emotionally to himself and his world are the most essential facts about him for a personality psychologist of this persuasion. The existentialists are a recent example. Much of Carl Rogers is in this tradition. Snygg and Combs provide a clear case, and other writers emphasizing the self-concept often belong with this group. Theorists who stress the way an individual uses concepts in interpreting events, such as George Kelly, or Leeper and Madison (1959), share the central concern of the subjectivists with the person's own point of view towards his world.

Three Perspectives on Aldous

Now let us take a brief look at Aldous through the spectacles of system, surface, and subjective theorists.

First, system theory: Here computer models like Aldous should be most at home. If the personality is conceived of as a complex, interlocking series of subsystems mediating an individual's characteristic behavior, Aldous should provide a natural mode of representing personality. Computers, as a model-building medium in which such hypothesized systems can be set up and their interrelationships studied, would seem to offer inviting possibilities to theorists of system inclinations. To be sure, Allport in his recent book (1961) is critical of computer models. However I feel his objections are largely connected with the nomothetic-idiographic issue (more later on this).

Proponents of the second approach to personality, the surface approach, should have less interest in Aldous; however they could certainly study him by their methods if they wished. Just for fun I intercorrelated the six versions of Aldous described earlier, in terms of the similarity of their behaviors in adjustment and readjustment to the benign and hostile worlds, and ran a quick factor analysis on the computer. Standard Aldous showed up with Radical, Decisive, and Abstract Aldous on one factor, and with Hesitant and Conservative Aldous on another; a third small factor specifically contrasted Decisive and Hesitant Aldous—results which on the whole confirm impressions arrived at earlier on more intuitive grounds. Experimental methods can have their place in studying Aldous too. For example, as part of the initial checkout of Aldous to see that he worked properly, I happened to examine his responses to repeated presentations of several systematically varied situations. It wasn't until after I had done this that I realized I had performed a classical learning experiment on

Aldous. So I promptly plotted the data as a family of learning curves and felt much edified by it all.

Incidentally, it is interesting to speculate what results could be obtained by empirical methods in discovering the principles of Aldous's operation. One could use either correlational or experimental approaches; the latter would probably prove more powerful. Aldous's ability to give verbal reports, limited as it is, should be a very valuable supplement to direct observation of his behavior. It ought to be possible to establish some empirical "laws" by such experiments. However, I suspect that these "laws" might not give the investigator much of a picture of Aldous's inner operation.

Let us return to look at Aldous from the third perspective—that of the theorists who favor the subjective approach to personality. Aldous can certainly be viewed in this way. He "perceives" the situations that confront him and "reacts emotionally" to them. His reaction to each situation is a unique resultant of the situation's properties, his own mood and temperament, and his previous relevant experience. Aldous's actions follow from his feelings about the perceived situation, not from the situation as it independently exists. To be sure, Aldous's perceptual capacities are extremely limited, and he does virtually no thinking at all, but as other papers at this conference have demonstrated, these limitations are by no means inherent in a model of this kind.

One point on which most subjective theorists will find Aldous deficient is his lack of an explicit self-concept. One might, of course, arbitrarily designate one of the attributes of the situations Aldous faces as "degree of self-involvement," and thus define classes of more or less self-related experience from which a self-concept and attitudes toward the self could be inferred. I suspect that some expansion of Aldous's cognitive capacities would be necessary before such an enterprise would yield very plausible results; however, a proper "self-concept" should not be in principle impossible for a model of Aldous's kind.

Some Problems with Aldous

Where, now, do we stand? We have looked at Aldous from three current perspectives on personality and concluded that he has some qualifications as a personality model from each viewpoint, although he will presumably be a lot more congenial to some theorists than to others.

Our final task is to point up some of Aldous's more severe shortcomings, and to indicate roughly some of the kinds of changes that might make him more adequate as a personality model.

First, and perhaps as serious as any, is Aldous's limited foresight and ability to plan. He does not organize his behavior around long-term goals, approached stepwise in an interlocking series of plans, but just reacts to situations as they come along. He does anticipate immediate consequences, and acts accordingly, but clearly he needs to be equipped with considerably more long-range integrating ability before he can do real justice to personality. Now this defect is not in any way inherent in computer models—in fact Miller, Galanter, and Pribram in their recent book (1960) specifically work out their theory of plans in terms of computers. It's just that in the designing of Aldous some things had to go to keep him within bounds, and the elaboration of action patterns was one capacity that went.

In general, Aldous's perceptual system is also very limited, particularly from the viewpoint of a subjective theorist. A few emotionally-based perceptual distortions, and other such interactions with other systems, might lend considerable tone, and could readily be introduced. Similar possibilities exist with respect to the memory system and the action selection system: repressions, compensations, and reaction formations could be added more or less ad lib. One additional cognitive defect I have already mentioned: lack of a concept of self. I will simply note again that this defect exists, and should be curable.

Another possible refinement on Aldous would be to introduce provisions for gradually modifying some of his basic parameters during operation, either "maturationally," i.e., as generalized changes over time, or in connection with particular kinds of experience. Thus one might, for example, introduce progressive changes in the constants affecting learning, as part of an "aging" process, or have a blunting of affective responses result from a traumatic experience.

One further issue: I mentioned briefly earlier a complaint raised about computer models by those who find them too generalized and abstract. These models tend in a sense to be highly "nomothetic"—certainly Aldous is intended to represent various general mechanisms of personality. And yet, paradoxically, any given model is in fact a highly particular system, in which every parameter has a definite value, and the system components interact in a particular and definite and idiosyncratic way. What is lacking would seem to be some way of getting from the idiosyncratic person to the idiosyncratic model. A major part of this problem, of course, is getting an adequate description of the person to start with—if one could get a full account of the processes constituting a particular person, one should be able, in principle, to set up a corresponding computer model (although it would not necessarily be a model practical for present computers). In fact, one can speculate about a kind of super-compiler program which would build a personality model to any particular set of specifications supplied it. This would be idiography with a vengeance! Actually such models might have some merits as clinical training devices. No reason why embryo clinicians shouldn't track down their personality dynamics with simulated Rorschachs and attempt to modify them with simulated psychotherapy before being turned loose on the real McCoy.

A super-program of this sort may in fact point to one resolution of the nomothetic-idiographic question. The super-program would be a nomothetic system which would construct idiographic systems to represent particular, concrete, individual personalities in all their unique idiosyncrasy.

Conclusion

I have attempted to do three things in this paper. First, I have described to you briefly a computer model named Aldous who recognizes situations, reacts emotionally to them, and expresses his feelings in action or verbal report. Second, I have described the results of some experiments in which Aldous and several cousins of his were brought up in various environments. Third and finally, I have considered Aldous in the light of some theories about human personality, and suggested some of the ways he might be changed to make him better fit for his job as a personality model.

Let me conclude with a final bit of speculation on the future of computer models in personality theory. In the first place, I believe they do have a future, and an important one. When you want to represent a complex dynamic system, there is some advantage in using a complex dynamic system—as against, say, a point in a multidimensional hyperspace or a few thousand well-chosen words. And an electronic digital computer is the only medium I know of in which you can build a model of anything like the requisite complexity, and still have it definite and concrete enough to examine bit by bit to any desired degree of analytic detail.

I do not wish to suggest that our other conceptual models are obsolete—far from it. I suspect that for some time to come the ideas embodied in computer models will be ideas that have previously been expressed, often better expressed, in words or mathematical symbols.

I do think, though, that one day a computer program will take a vast mass of data about a person (say the data from a Murray-type assessment) and formulate a more complex and comprehensive representation of his personality than any single human brain could comprehend. And on that day we may begin to see some real predicting in the area of personality.

12

WAYNE H. HOLTZMAN
University of Texas

Discussion:
The Robot Personality--Static or Dynamic?

Loehlin's paper (Chapter 11) was indeed fun to read, at least the first time through. But in going over it several more times I found that the more deeply I got into it the more frustrated I felt. I resented mildly the fact that Loehlin had a real advantage over me in that he had spent several years building this machine, and then had failed to tell me all of the rules built into it. It is bad enough to be presented with a real person in all of his hidden complexity without being confronted by a black box that acts like one. Even late last night I was still fussing around, trying to reproduce a flow chart or logic diagram that must have been employed in designing this program that Loehlin has called "Aldous in His Brave New World." Consequently, like Aldous, my error rate of misperception may be considerable in reviewing this paper.

Loehlin thoughtfully disposed of most criticisms as he went along. He managed to point out the weaknesses in his own system very effectively, although a few remain for further discussion. In general, however, I can only commend his paper, as it stands, for the general purpose of this symposium. While

I may have a private desire to see very concretely how and why Aldous ticks, it would be inappropriate in a general conference of this type to saddle the participant with an undue amount of programming detail.

In my first free associations, I wondered about the fascination of machines that act like people. It occurred to me that, as psychologists, all of us are more or less frustrated by our inability to explain human behavior in terms of individual situations. We have a certain faith in the determinacy of man and his behavior, but we have no hard proof of it. In terms of our own motivation, what better escape than to build a set of mechanical personalities (the completely deterministic origin of which can hardly be doubted) as a substitute for the real thing. The progressive university of the future may have to establish a department of pseudopsychology which is devoted exclusively to the psychology of machines. Think of the behavioral systems that can be developed and the rash of doctoral dissertations on synthetic experiments using high-speed computer runs rather than human performance! While I am personally not opposed to such activity since much of it is highly stimulating to the psychologist and may indeed be significant in its own right, we should be constantly aware that the psychology of machines is only a pseudopsychology unless a reasonable goodness of fit is assured between the machine model and real organisms, at least with respect to the limited system of attributes and relationships being simulated.

I was also intrigued by Loehlin's implied suggestion that we might turn such machines loose on our colleagues. That is, having developed a population of Aldouses with well distributed attributes, turn them over to factor analysts or clinicians to see how well they can derive a personality theory from a study of simulated behavior. The participants in this little game could be given a sporting chance by permitting limited interaction with the machines, or one could simply turn over huge masses of behavioral data collected under specified conditions. The participant who comes closest to the actual set of attributes and relationships built into Aldous would be the winner. While I can think of countless reasons for begging off such a challenge myself, I relish the thought of standing on the sidelines watching others try their hand at it.

Aside from such rather irresponsible fantasies, a sober analysis of Loehlin's simulated personality model reveals that it is static and fairly simple in design. Considering the fact that he laboriously wrote the program in machine language for a small computer with very limited capacity, the number and variety of attributes employed is quite impressive. When Aldous is adapted to a high capacity computer, a major improvement would be to incorporate the dynamic ability to change the intensity and patterning of traits as a result of interaction with the environment. The attribute of self-modification is essential to any realistic personality model. In the current model of Aldous, the personality can only be altered by ending the life cycle and starting over again with a different variation. For example, the error rate of misperception in Aldous remains a constant six percent, regardless of the degree of success or failure in coping with the environment. Such obvious improvements in Aldous as a model can be made by employing a higher capacity computer and using one of the interpretive processing languages such as IPL-V (Newell, 1961).

What are the personality traits currently built into Aldous? There are at least six dimensions along which the experimenter can readily vary Aldous's personality. Other variations are possible, of course, but most of them require more tinkering with the basic program than the typical experimenter cares to undertake. The first trait is rate of misperception. That is, in selecting a situation and picking out an address within the memory of the Burroughs 205, a random error is made to an adjacent address a predetermined percentage of the time, say six percent. The actual error rate can be varied from zero to one hundred percent. The propensity to be autistic, to misperceive, clearly belongs in any personality model, although it is hardly a static trait throughout the lifetime of the individual.

The second trait or parameter, which can be varied but only at the time Aldous begins his life cycle, is the relative importance of outcome on the last trial (current mood) and frequency of previous contact with a particular situation (past experience). Expressed as a ratio, this parameter was deliberately varied to yield Radical Aldous (heavy weight on current mood) and Conservative Aldous (emphasis on past experience). It should come as no surprise that Aldous tends to fluctuate with the current situation when the last trial is heavily emphasized, to the detriment of past experience. Once you get down to what the computer is actually doing and strip the romanticism away, some of the steam is taken out of Aldous as a personality.

The third trait consists of the relative value of a particular situation as opposed to the general class of situations of which it is a member. Manipulation of this parameter changes the level of abstraction anywhere from a concrete orientation to the particular situation all the way to the generic class of which the situation is a member. Here again is a trait that should be modified through learning rather than remaining static.

The degree of emotional reactivity is the fourth trait that can be fixed at a given level in advance of the life cycle. This parameter is the critical threshold value needed to trigger off a branch in the program, leading eventually to the selection of one of three "emotions," one positive and two negative in value. The score which varies about this parameter is apparently a function of particular weights assigned to the three emotions. Loehlin has shown considerable ingenuity in writing a subroutine for computing weights which takes into account Aldous's initial emotional reaction, immediate memory of consequences from the preceding trial, and charges stored in the relevant permanent memory location for the situation at hand. Moreover, as a final step, the three emotional tendencies (weights) are compared and, if one proves dominant, it interacts with its competitors to weaken them, leading finally to selection of the dominant emotion. Here is an excellent example of creative programming that illustrates how the subtleties of emotional interplay can be captured by a machine with fair resemblance to reality. While the particular weights chosen by Loehlin may be inappropriate, the factors he has taken into account are highly relevant. As with other parameters, however, the degree of emotional reactivity is static once installed, a shortcoming that can be easily overcome with a higher capacity computer and a self-modification subroutine.

The fifth trait is a parameter in the action preparation subroutine which determines the intensity of reaction by Aldous. When a dominant emotion is present, four levels of action are possible ranging from none through vigorous to emotional paralysis. The score necessary to trigger off these different levels can be varied before commencing Aldous's life cycle.

A sixth trait which can be easily manipulated is the rate of learning, or the extent to which the consequences of an action affect the attitudes in the seven relevant memory locations. Greatest weight has been given to the first 10 encounters, tapering off crudely for blocks of 100 or 1000 trials. Variation in these weights would produce different rates of learning. To obtain more realistic learning curves and such phenomena as stimulus generalization, forgetting, and reminiscence would require much more elaborate programming. It is interesting to note, however, that such programs have been successfully written and could probably be adapted to a more sophisticated model of Aldous (Feigenbaum, 1961).

In addition to these traits within Aldous, one may also manipulate to a very limited extent the environmental factors in Loehlin's program. The relative frequency of satisfying, frustrating, or painful situations can be varied to provide differing degrees of benign or hostile worlds in which to rear Aldous.

In spite of the rather severe limitations present in Aldous, a variety of experimental runs can be performed along the lines already undertaken by Loehlin. Considering the resources available, an excellent start has been made on the simulation of certain aspects of personality. The next step should be to correct some of the obvious deficiencies in Aldous, reprogramming him for operation on a high capacity computer. When self-modification has been built into Aldous it would be interesting to expand the simulation to include a second personality such as Aldous's father, girl friend, or competitor. For the moment, however, it would be rather foolish to bother with two-person interactions. A more pressing problem is the improvement of Aldous as a single individual behaving within a controlled environment. Eventually, however, there is no reason why two- or three-person systems cannot be simulated on a computer with certain kinds of parameters varied systematically. The influence of social conformity pressures on behavior and the interaction of two persons in solving a problem are examples of interesting phenomena that can probably be studied by simulation techniques in the near future.

In closing I want to come back to the basic question that should concern all of us in evaluating any simulation of a psychological phenomenon such as human personality. How adequate is the model? Two general criteria can be applied. How badly does the model violate reality, and what new insights are afforded the individual who experiments with the model? In spite of the ingenuity shown by Loehlin in this first approximation to a human personality, his current model is seriously deficient in several respects, especially in the completely static nature of Aldous. Loehlin is certainly among the first to recognize this problem and can hardly be criticized for starting with a highly simple model where there may be gross violation of reality. The important point to emphasize is that most of the deficiencies noted above can be overcome in future models of Aldous. One has to start somewhere in this business of simulation, and it is to Loehlin's credit that he has anything running at all.

What new insights are given us by experimental runs with Aldous? Frankly, I fail to see any new contributions to a psychology of personality in the results thus far. It's really too early for that. More important for Loehlin and others like him, who have the persistence and skill to develop programs for simulating aspects of personality, is the self-discipline of program logic and the sobering implications of such articulateness for the development of personality theory. In the simulation of personality, it is too much to ask that anything remotely like the total complexity of human personality be incorporated immediately into a model. A better strategy would be to develop much smaller assemblies first, such as Colby's simulated neurotic system (Chapter 9) or Feigenbaum's (1961) simulated verbal learning. Once such assemblies are reasonably well perfected, they can be joined together as subroutines in a larger system that more nearly simulates human personality. In the meantime, I can only applaud the efforts of Loehlin and others who are willing to plunge in and do the best they can with limited resources. The time may come sooner than we think when we will be able to run meaningful experiments on the descendants of Aldous—experiments that will have direct relevance for personality theory.

13 | GEORGE A. KELLY
Ohio State University

Discussion:
Aldous, The Personable Computer

Since most of the participants in this conference have been prefacing their remarks by saying that they really have no business being here, I would like to insert my claim to a similar distinction. I think I can make a more convincing case than the others who have tried.

Not only am I innocent of any intimacies with computers, but I am the fellow who has sworn off using most of the psychological constructs that have been tossed around during the last three days. For example, some time ago I discarded "motives" and have been living quite happily without recourse to "motivation" ever since. "Affect" makes no sense to me anymore; nor do "drives," "reinforcements," " stimuli," "responses," "emotion," or "cognition." As a matter of fact, I decided to abandon "learning" some years ago, a bold step that opened up a whole exciting new world to me. Having had a taste of this exhilarating way of life, it seems quite unthinkable now that I should ever return to the days when I allowed my time to be taken up with learning things rather than making something out of them, with being pushed around by what people kept telling me were my motives, or with being forever prodded into some senseless activity by events that happened to be labeled "stimuli."

But while I, myself, have abandoned most of the vocabulary of those who keep the American Psychological Association journals going, I do regress, from time to time, in the interest of classical humanism. So just to make it clear I have not lost respect for the older generation who imagined there really were such things as "affect," etc., I have tried to put some of the thoughts expressed in this conference into poetical form:

There once was an ardent young suitor
Who programmed a female computer,
But he failed to connect
The affective effect,
So there wasn't a thing he could do to 'er.

I suppose I really shouldn't have recited that—the sentiment being quite antithetical to my own personal convictions. But I find, sometimes, it is helpful to give my opponents an argument or two with which to defend their positions. It makes for better feeling when we get through.

Following World War I the intellectuals of Central Europe were searching desperately for values to replace the romanticism they believed they had lost. During the Twenties a play by Karel Capek appeared, entitled "R.U.R.—Rossun's Universal Robots." The word "robot" was new in those days and I remember there was considerable discussion of how it should be pronounced—"rah'but," "row-boat'," "ro-bow'." In any case, what happened was that, in the play, the robots, whose outlook on life was pretty much what we would call that of the "hard scientists" nowadays, got out of hand and began to take over from the natives. Just about the time the last inefficiently sentimental human being was being mowed down by machine gun fire, a couple of the late model robots began to exhibit some quite unrobot-like behavior. A girl robot and a boy robot fell in love with each other. Thus, right at the moment of triumph for the ingeniously constructed simulators, the whole project collapsed. The robots got to acting so much like human beings that they actually became human. All of which goes to show you can't really win at this game of simulating the human personality; for the moment you succeed, you are right back where you started. If I may paraphrase Camus, simulation is a Sisyphian enterprise.

As a matter of fact, at the Ohio State University we have taken this hazard into account and have developed a simulator that goes just about as far as you can expect to go in this direction without getting set back to where you started. The model is called the OSU-401. We have quite a number of units of this device available for research in the Department of Psychology, although from time to time the more objective members of the staff express doubts about how well it simulates the human personality and, indeed, occasionally raise some very grave questions about its statistical reliability. (Perhaps I should say that 401 is the number of our elementary psychology course and the units are made available to us free of charge through an arrangement that requires students enrolled in the course to serve as subjects in experiments.) But as I say, this is getting perilously close to the ultimate in personality simulation, so I wouldn't blame some of you if you voiced objections over the extent to which we have allowed our enthusiasm for computer verisimilitude to override our obligations to science.

Actually it was some years ago, when I was in the Navy during the war, that I discovered that you could carry this simulation business too far. It had been suggested that the Navy should purchase some Link Trainers and rig them so that primary flight instruction could be given in them. This was known as "The Visual Link Project." The Link Trainer is a mock-up of an airplane cockpit which can be rotated on three axes by the occupant's using stick and rudder. It has little stub wings sticking out from the side that are supposed to suggest the wings of an airplane. I might add that this bit of simulated realism always struck me as extremely amusing because of what it revealed about the mentality of Naval officers.

Be that as it may, one of the problems that seemed to stand in the way of the use of the Link Trainer as a primary flight instructional device was the fact that it could not simulate the noise, the laboring of the engine in a climb, the vibration, and the acceleration effects one experiences in a turn. As they thought it over, the engineers decided they could simulate everything except the acceleration effects. But those effects are especially important in the early stages of learning to fly.

After giving the matter some thought myself, I came up with a definitive solution to all aspects of the problem. I suggested that the Link Trainer be enlarged so that a real engine could be installed, that the stub wings be extended, and that certain other modifications could be adopted to provide greater realism. I was able to point out an interesting feature of my proposal—the fact that the cost of all this would be only about one thirtieth that of a regular Link Trainer, which was a pretty expensive gadget. But this is where I made my first mistake; no one was interested in reducing the cost of anything. Enthusiasm for my project immediately declined.

But this was only my first blunder; the whole project completely collapsed when they discovered that my invention would actually fly. "Why," they said, "that would be nothing but an airplane! " They were right, of course; I had made the fatal mistake that all computer enthusiasts run the risk of making—the mistake of carrying simulation too far. If I had only doubled the cost, instead of cutting it, and had stopped just short of something that would actually fly, I am sure I could have won a Green Commendation Ribbon.

At this point perhaps I should make my own theoretical position clear, so as to forestall any frivolity that may grow out of my outspoken enthusiasm for computer simulation of personality. I think truth can be approached by simulation, and by simulation only. This is the thesis behind the phrase, "the psychology of personal constructs" (Kelly, 1955). Man gets at the truth of things, not by some special revelation on Mount Sinai or in a laboratory, but by erecting constructs to simulate it as best he can. The point at which the simulation and the reality will converge is, I assume, a very long way off.

So we devise machines to simulate—not man directly—but theories about man. The machines are actually two steps removed from personality. The circuitry of the machines is designed to simulate the logical connections within the theories they are supposed to approximate. The theories, in turn, are constructed to simulate the human processes they are supposed to explain.

But the simulation does not stop there. The persons themselves are simulators. They attempt to simulate each other—too much, some say. They simulate their parents, their gods, a presumed rational way of life, and the expectations of others. In fact, a lot of people even make a big to-do about simulating themselves. This is known as "trying to be yourself" and is often regarded as quite an accomplishment. Sometimes people simulate machines. This is sometimes called "being objective." Doctor Blum (Chapter 7) has even programmed his people to behave like computers. Some psychologists undoubtedly will take this to mean that he has succeeded in getting people to behave psychologically. All this, it seems to me, brings us to a situation of infinite regression—like that of the cat looking in the mirror at a cat looking in a mirror at ..., etc. Persons act like models that are supposed to act like persons that act like models that are supposed..., etc.

Some persons raise the objection to computer simulation, as they have for many years objected to factor analysis, that "you get out of the system only what you put into it." For my own part, I cannot see this as anything to fuss over. It would be a sorry state of affairs if it turned out that you didn't get out of it what you put into it. If that were true, you could never use the computer to test the outcome of anything, for you could never tell whether you were getting out of it the consequences of something you put into it or the consequences of something you didn't put into it.

I suppose what the critics who raise this objection mean is that you don't really discover anything by firing up your computers, that the outcome is biased by what you have invented, not governed by what nature really is. But since, as I have already indicated, the inventive approach to truth is the only one that works anyway, I see no fault in this kind of bias.

To be candid about it, there is considerable virtue in the fact that computers do not simulate persons perfectly. If they did, they would produce some pretty complex results. We would probably have to go looking for some human simulators to give us a down-to-earth version of what was going on—a version we could grasp. To be sure, we would have the blueprint that had been used in manufacturing the gadget, but that would not mean we could tell what was happening inside the mechanism, nor would it mean we could read backwards from a similar bit of human behavior and say it came about in the same way.

As long as the task of science is to reduce matters to terms our pedestrian minds can grasp, the instruments of science will have to select, distort, and simplify the vast complexities of nature. In other words, I hope Aldous does not behave like a human being. He would turn out to be quite a problem if he did.

There are two major ways in which I see a computer simulation program contributing to an experimental science of psychology. First, as I have already intimated, it can simulate the logic of a theoretical system and, with a series of inputs, explicate the theory and its implications in ways the original theoretician would take a lifetime to figure out on his own. Moreover, the output should, at various stages here and there, be sufficiently parallel to human observables to enable the theoretician to check himself against the behavior of a human subject.

The second contribution can be to the processing of data provided by a given subject, as suggested by Doctor Colby's research (Chapter 9). This, too, can be compared with the subsequent behavior of the subject at various check points along the line.

In this connection I would like to make a plug for the psychology of personal constructs (Kelly, 1955). Not only is it a system built on the notion that scientists and human beings, alike, approach truth by erecting simulation devices—called constructs—but it is a theory deliberately formulated in a language system which is based on binary elements and which does not accept the so-called subject-predicate error of the Indo-European language system.

Without burdening you with the radical assumptions of the theory, may I simply mention the fact that a personal construct is defined by extension through being applied to a series of events. The events are not regarded as stimuli but as objects of construction. If we imagine a matrix with events ranged along the top, then a construct, defined by extension, would be a horizontal row of plusses and minuses within the matrix—or, better, incidents and voids. The construct would be symbolically defined as such a row pattern. Another construct would be defined as a somewhat different row pattern. There is a theorem here to the effect that if two constructs match, cell by cell, throughout the length of their rows, clear out to infinity, they are identical.

Such a matrix is a representation of a person's psychological space. The dimensions are his, not necessarily those of his psychologist or of his culture. They are not likely to be orthogonal to each other. There are many interesting matrix relationships that can be directly explored by means of machine processes, using personal construct data produced by an individual person or by a group of persons. Such exploration may throw light upon the dimensions which define the space in which individuals are free to move and live their lives.

While Aldous, as he is now constituted, would not, of course, be prepared to explicate the theory of personal constructs, I am sure Doctor Loehlin could, if he wished, sire a fellow called Suodla who could explicate the theory. Suodla is simply Aldous spelled backwards.

Of course, Suodla would, and should at best, be an imperfect simulator. I am sure that for some this would spell disappointment.

> There once was a passionate dame
> Who wanted some things made plain,
> So she punched up the cards,
> Filled tape by the yards,
> But—somehow—*it just wasn't the same*!

14

LEONARD UHR
Mental Health Research Institute,
University of Michigan

The Development of Perception and Language: Simulated Models

"...the universe is a vast representamen, a great symbol of God's purpose, working out its conclusions in living realities. Now every symbol must have, organically attached to it, its Indices of Reactions and its Icons of Qualities; and such part as these reactions and these qualities play in an argument that, they of course, play in the universe—that Universe being precisely an argument. In the little bit that you or I can make out of this huge demonstration, our perceptual judgments are the premises for us and these perceptual judgments have icons as their predicates, in which icons Qualities are immediately presented. But what is first for us is not first in nature... The Universe as an argument is necessarily a great work of art, a great poem—for every fine argument is a poem and a symphony—just as every true poem is a sound argument."

C. S. Peirce, Vol. 5, Par. 118

The research discussed in this paper has been conducted jointly with Charles Vossler of the System Development Corporation and is supported by The University of Michigan, the System Development Corporation, and USPHS Grant M-5254.

General Introduction: Computers and Simulations

The importance of computers does not lie in any specific type of model that they may suggest, in any switchboard or associationist "machine" analogy to the brain. Nor does it lie in any specific method of using computers, such as Rosenblatt's (1960) perceptron, or the descriptive programs of Newell, Shaw and Simon (1960), or the analogies of Miller, Galanter, and Pribram (1960). Rather, computers present the unique opportunity to explore efficiently and effectively with any theory or model, subject only to the restriction that the theory be adequately stated. And in this restriction itself lies a major virtue of the computer for psychological research. For the process of getting a model onto the computer is the process of describing the model precisely (see Rochester, Holland, Haibt, and Duda, 1956; Dunham, 1957). The successful running of a program put into the computer's language is, at the same time, a statement of the theory and a test of its consequences.

The computer does not predispose toward anything other than clarity, and clarity only in the minimal sense of "not nonsense." This is not quite a precise statement of the restriction on the universe of acceptable statements imposed by the language of computers, but it is not at all misleading. The restrictions imposed on statements by this requirement are less stringent than the restrictions imposed by the canons of any of the traditional schools of physical or social sciences (including introspectionism).

The chief virtue of the computer lies in its immensity, its enormous potential for complexity. Many psychologists feel that analyzable mathematical models of the classical sort, as exemplified by the field theories of the physical sciences and attempted in the stochastic learning models of the behavioral sciences, are incapable of mirroring the complexities of the living systems with which they deal. This has led most theorists to revert back to natural language descriptions with, of course, enormous loss in deductive powers. But the computer as a vehicle for models will allow for the complexity of natural languages, along with especially great power to deduce consequences.

It is here that the early switchboard models of gadgeteers and cyberneticians may have done an enormous disservice in misrepresenting the virtues and the powers of the computer. Even today the great bulk of simulations in "pattern recognition," "learning," and "problem-solving" is of this sort: the very simplest of possible behaviors, chosen for a specific problem, is built into the machine; if to this behavior any of the befuddling epithets above can be applied, it is. But even these machines should not be overlooked; they model much that is interesting in the simpler behavior of lower organisms or isolated organs.

Computers are media within which symbols can be transformed as functions of other symbols which, themselves being written in the same medium, are similarly transformable. Loosely, a computer is like a piece of paper, marking fluid, and rules for marking. Thus it is sufficient for all books, all art, all music. This is so because a computer will torture numbers in any conceivable way, if you are sufficiently clever and patient at specifying how. And you can always code other things—sequences of sounds, colors and intensities, words, ideas and feelings—into numbers. For example, you can simply assign numbers to the letters of the alphabet, or the keys of the typewriter, or points in space-time.

Of course computers are like very large pieces of paper. But size does not always inspire. Many people, and certainly many psychologists are among them, feel that there is a very large book to be written. But who will do the writing?

A computer is a rather peculiar writing contraption. Think of the difficulties with a pen disposed to do the following: It dispenses ink one micro-drop at a time, and this ink must be placed on paper by a special micro-drop carrier, designed by an expert who has solved the problem of a single micro-drop carrier capable of carrying all sized micro-drops (from 500 angstroms to 200 microns), which tells you immediately and dramatically (by committing suicide on the spot) when the pen dispenses a drop more than .001 per cent larger, or smaller, than contracted for. Although our micro-drop carrier has its simulatedly human moments, which might tempt someone to ponder upon the double edge of sado-masochism, it is maliciously, inhumanly stupid, like an escaped ball bearing or a charge of dynamite. It knows not whence it came nor whither it must go; nor will it ever learn.

So, in order to begin a book in this new manner one must first establish a coordinate system within which to locate pen, paper, and most recent smudges (note: smudges, not thoughts), and establish a series of instructions and modifications that will keep micro-drop carrier scurrying back-and-forth to where the pen will dispense the next drop from where the next-to-last n drops suggested the last drop should have been placed. Now, in between the details of getting the ink of the program nicely laid out on the paper of the computer's memory, our theorist is free to use whatever time and energy may be left him to follow the flights of his intuition and data.

The actual situation is a good bit more troublesome, since the computer has a peculiarly powerful but little understood ability, even propensity, to erase or perform more subtle operations upon itself. One might suppose that this quirk could be outlawed, like cocaine. But no one can resist it and, in fact, it makes a difference much like the difference between taking a movie of a person's face and body changing with emotion, and putting the dynamism into the person, so that *he* changes.

An interesting and plausible way to consider the problem of getting "mind" into the computer is to convert the inanimate mechanism into psychosis and eventually (if we are especially fortunate and clever) into good healthy neurosis. The computer that would not stop dead at every silly little misstep, but rather would roll all its problems up into a few blatant irrationalities and conflict-reducing symptoms, would be a tremendous advance indeed.

The present-day computer avoids such pitfalls by stepping directly into the supreme pitfall the instant it makes its first false move. The typical program has no margin for error or vagueness; it acts as though its programmer knew what he was doing. The psychologist, on the other hand, very definitely wants to use computers precisely because he does *not* know what he is doing. He wants a flexible program that will develop unexpected powers along with its abysmal failures. From such a program he may learn something useful toward writing a better program. But the traditional program is written to do exactly what it is told to do; it can be in one of two states—either "with bugs" or perfect (but this latter state cannot be proved, so a program can only be, like a GI, in a state of hopeful debuggedness).

What would a program be like if it could make mistakes, even whopping mistakes? By falling into a state of uncertainty and conflict, can a program begin to obtain knowledge?

Specific Introduction: Perceptual Learning and Discovery

The approach that Charles Vossler and I have been taking can be characterized and summarized briefly as follows: We are trying to develop a model of the interrelated mental processes of the human being. Perceptual learning seemed a good starting point toward this long-term goal. It allows us to study the development of cognitive processes and of personality processes, as a function of the experiences an (simulated) organism of a certain structure has with its environment. We can draw upon the great wealth of data that has been amassed about the perceptual systems (particularly the visual system) in order to postulate a suitable structure for the organism (the program). And by putting as great a burden as possible on what we might loosely call "learning" from experienced interactions with the environment we can study the development of more complex structure.

Visual "pattern recognition" programs have been written by a number of people (for reviews, see Selfridge and Neisser, 1960; Stevens, 1961b; and Uhr, in press); thus there are the beginnings of alternate models that can be compared. These programs study a central aspect of form perception—the classification of variants, including never-before-seen variants, over the unknown (and highly non-linear) distortions that normally occur. They follow a variety of approaches. Uttley (1959), Farley and Clark (1954), Rosenblatt (1958), and Taylor (1959), among others, have examined models of a simple associationist sort, looking at individual spots in the pattern. Unger (1959) and Doyle (1960), the latter working with Selfridge (1959) on a parallel operator model, have programmed pattern recognition with more powerful measures, some rather similar to those that have been found in the visual system. Stevens (1961a) has put Deutsch's (1955) theory of form perception into computer form. Grimsdale, Sumner, Tunis, and Kilburn (1959) and Sherman (1960) have written programs to examine geometric and topological characteristics of the whole pattern, aspects that one might think of as related to the Gestalt characteristics.

Relatively little work has been done in psychology on the recognition process, and it is difficult to know whether this is so because the problem is considered too trivial, or too deep. For example, Hake (1957, p. 82) writes, "About the process of recognition itself little is known. We know little about the stimulus conditions which influence accuracy of recognition or evoke recognition responses." And Osgood (1953, p. 288) writes, "...those organizational characteristics of perceiving we call 'non-sensory figure perception' and 'recognition' are clearly shown to be the results of learning, and arduous learning at that." Interestingly, the most clear-cut of descriptions of what goes on in the typical "pattern recognition" program is Kendler's (1961) definition of "concept-formation"—"...the acquisition or utilization, or both, of a common response to dissimilar stimuli."

Along with pattern recognition come beginnings of concept formation, and then the learning of symbols that refer to the patterns and concepts that have been learned. As I will discuss later, a model that might begin to do such things should have a great deal to say about matters of motivation and conflict, socialization, and personality development. This is so because (a) such a model must interact with an environment and with itself in order to learn from experience, (b) certain parts of its environment must give it appropriate training sequences and feedback, and (c) the model must have some reason, some drive, toward interaction and change.

It has seemed to us especially fruitful, in trying to expand pattern recognition models to other cognitive processes, to lean more and more on what might be called learning, adaptation, evolution, or self-organization. This replaces pre-analysis by having the model collect, organize and make use of data as presented to it by its environment. It also makes possible the examination of different problems in a common format. Here again, it seems reasonable to hope that there is some relation between the basic mechanisms that handle the perceptual processes and the mechanisms for other cognitive processes. They all must evolve in a relatively orderly and continuous manner.

We have been encouraged toward this point of view by the relative success of pattern recognition programs that have been weakened to the point where they must rely on discovery and learning. The simplified problem of form perception posed in the typical pattern recognition program appears to be quite handleable no matter how much the program is weakened and asked to rely upon its own ability to discover and build up useful inductions (Uhr, in press; Vossler & Uhr, 1962b). Certain superficially different problems within perception, and even across symbolization in general (thus including both perception and language), seem amenable to common handling (Vossler & Uhr, 1962a). Thus, at least at present, this seems a workable and potentially promising level at which to attack these problems (and actually tends to simplify computer programming methods). No specific problem appears to be better handleable by more powerful methods. That is, a program designed to be a perceiver or language translator (either a supposed functional brain, or a complex information processor) will probably not do much, if any, better than a second program that must take time to discover and adapt. And surprisingly little learning time seems to be needed to develop.

An especially congenial framework for such processes is Peirce's conception of logical inference, which for him includes deduction, induction, and discovery (also called abduction, retroduction, or hypothesis-formation). For Peirce, perception is the extreme, brute example of abduction, the formation of the hypothesis that must be present before any processes of inductive inference, any gathering of evidence about that hypothesis, can begin. To quote Peirce: "...abductive inference shades into perceptual judgment without any sharp line of demarcation between them; or, in other words, our first premisses, the perceptual judgments, are to be regarded as an extreme case of abductive inferences, from which they differ in being absolutely beyond criticism" (Vol. 5, par. 181). "The form of the perceptual abduction is...A well-recognized kind of object, M, has for its ordinary predicates P_1, P_2, P_3, etc., indistinctly recognized. The suggesting object, S, has these same predicates, P_1, P_2, P_3, etc. Hence, S is of the kind M" (Vol. 8, par. 64). Further, the building up of the symbolic processes, of signs and symbols, is a natural part of perception, since (very roughly) the sign points to the object of perception and the symbol links (interprets) the sign. Thus, the structure of mind builds up much like a complex logical structure whose basic undefined primitives are the raw stuff of perception.

Pattern Recognition Simulation Program

Charles Vossler and I have coded and tested several versions of a pattern recognition program (using the IBM 709 and 7090) that simulates a simplified model of the visual system and also attempts to make as much use as possible of methods for discovery and learning. (For details, see Uhr & Vossler, 1961; Vossler & Uhr, 1962b.) The program attempts to recognize specific examples (over unspecified distortions) of pattern sets. It "learns" to do this through experience with specific examples, along with their correct names, and then it is tested on its abilities to recognize different unknown examples that are given unnamed. The measures, or operators, that the program can discover and develop are restricted to those that could be performed by nets of neurons five neurons in diameter, and by higher-level combinations of these nets. The size of the total "retina" (a 20 by 20 matrix) is about the same as the size of the smallest retinal mosaic of cones that can quickly and clearly discriminate the pattern sets we ask the program to discriminate.

The program attempts to develop its own set of operators, rather than having these built in. Originally we tested the program using a built-in set that looked for simple curves, angles, and straight lines, somewhat similar to the operators that have been discovered by Hubel and Wiesel (1959) in the cat. The program would "learn" by accumulating weightings and success counts for each measure, developing higher-level measures, and throwing away bad measures and generating new ones. But when we asked the program to generate measures from the very beginning, including its original set, it did a little bit better than it had done with the pre-programmed set. This rather surprised and encouraged us, since it suggested that a somewhat weaker program could learn quite quickly to reach the typical level of performance of pattern recognition programs. It also gave us the opportunity to study processes of discovery and learning. Pattern recognition is considered by most people to be a difficult problem for the computer. So if a program that is not based on elaborate pre-analysis and *ad hoc* methods, can, through its experience, handle this sort of task, there would seem to be some indication that interesting sorts of discovery and learning methods can be used with such programs.

It should be noted that this program is evolving a good set of net-operators. It is thus almost certainly not only learning but also attempting to recapitulate some of the evolutionary processes that build such nets in. But, since we know so little about what is built into the brain and what is learned, it seems reasonable to study these two problems in combination. We need only expose our model to its environment, and let its experience develop its structure.

The pattern recognition program is tested by being given successive examples of N different general patterns, each exemplified by n different examples. The program measures each example with each of its net-operators, as though the nets were iterated in parallel throughout the input matrix, just as nets of cones leading to ganglia are iterated throughout the fovea. It then combines the implications of the outcomes of these measures, and of successively higher-order combinations of these measures, and chooses to give the example the name that is most strongly implied. Then it is told the correct name, and it attempts to improve itself by discarding bad operators and generating new ones, changing weighting and success counts, and storing new information as to the implications of its measures. At the end of such a learning pass through the set of nN "knowns," the program is asked to name new "unknown" examples (usually produced by different people). These "unknown" examples are not named, so that the program does not "learn" anything from them, its internal state therefore remaining unchanged. They can thus be used over and over again, as a standard set of test items, at the end of each learning pass.

Figure 1 presents some results of tests of the program. Figure 2 presents some examples of patterns used. Patterns were drawn or written into a 4" by 4" matrix. A different person wrote or spoke each set, except for the arabic letters. Those patterns that were copied (from cartoons and mail order catalogs) were projected onto the matrix and sketched in by hand. Each cell of the matrix was then given a value of "1" if any line had been drawn through it, otherwise it was given a value of "0." Because the program does not depend upon pre-analyses of pattern sets it was possible to test its abilities on a wide variety of pattern sets.

We have made several comparison tests between the program's performance and the performance of human subjects (Uhr, Vossler, & Uleman, 1962). In these we presented the same patterns ("meaningless" randomly generated patterns of various sorts) to both program and human subjects. We

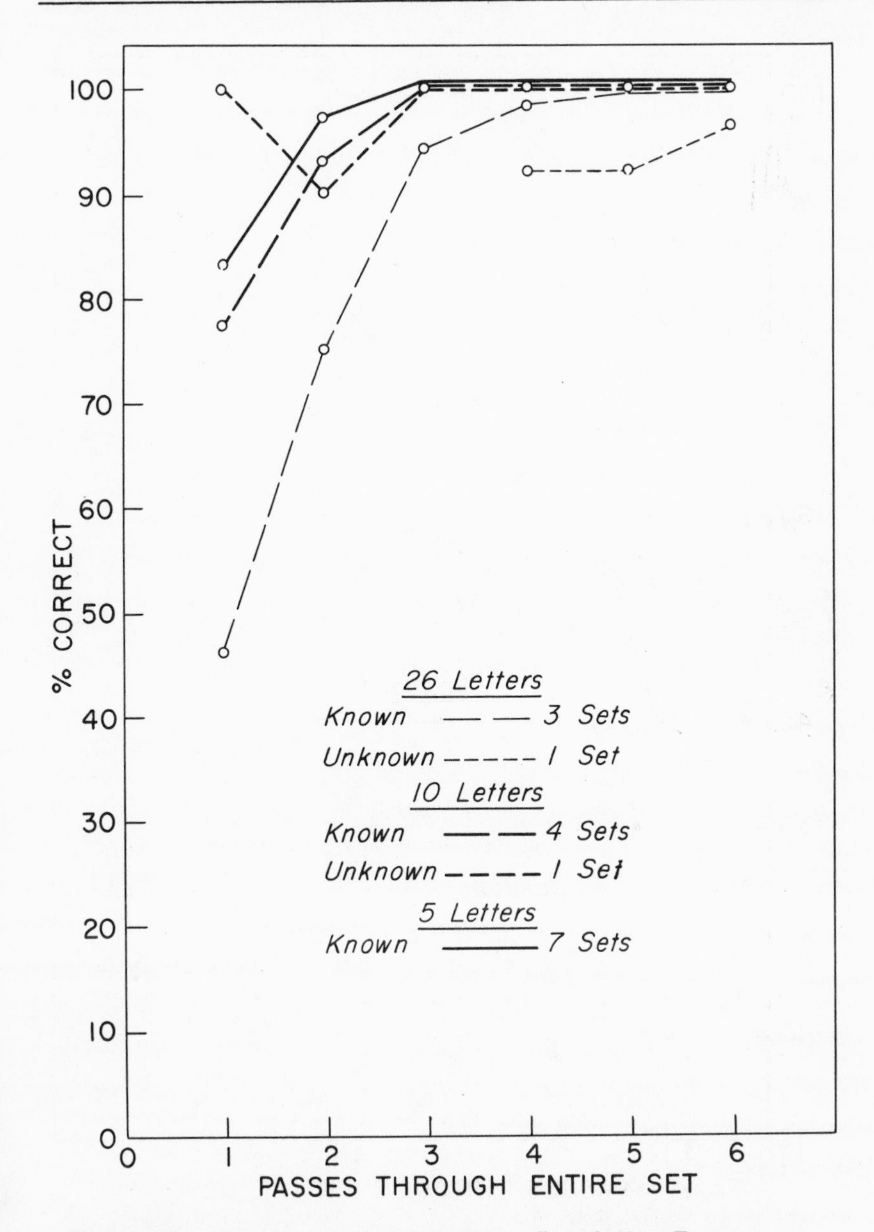

Figure 1a. Results of the Computer Simulation Program

[Hand printed alphabetic patterns. Per cent correct on several sets of a 26 pattern, a 10 pattern, and a 5 pattern array. The program was tested on both known and unknown sets of patterns.]

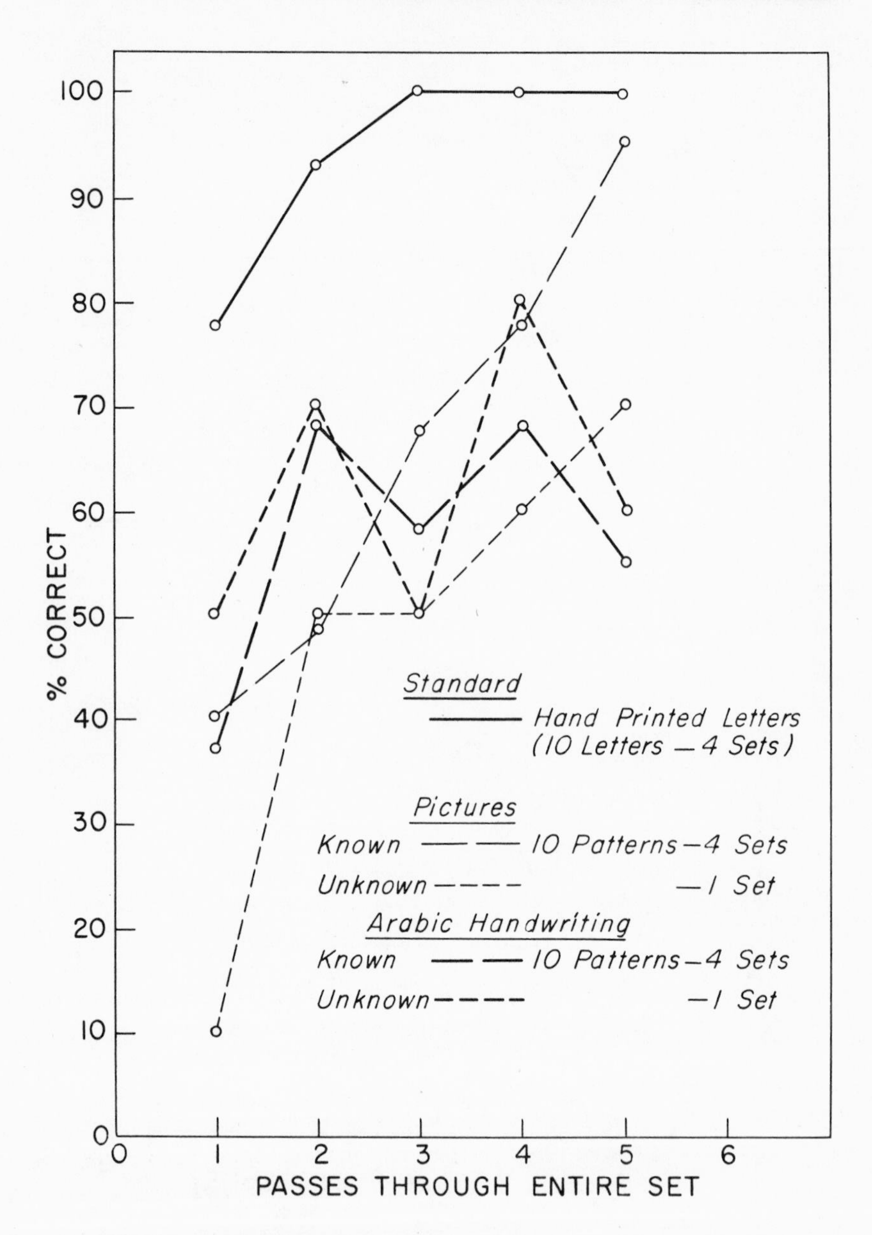

Figure 1b. Results of the Computer Simulation Program.

[Results with two additional 10 pattern arrays: (i) line drawings of pictures (different examples of each of 5 faces and 5 objects), (ii) arabic handwriting (written by the same person). The program was tested on both known and unknown sets of patterns.]

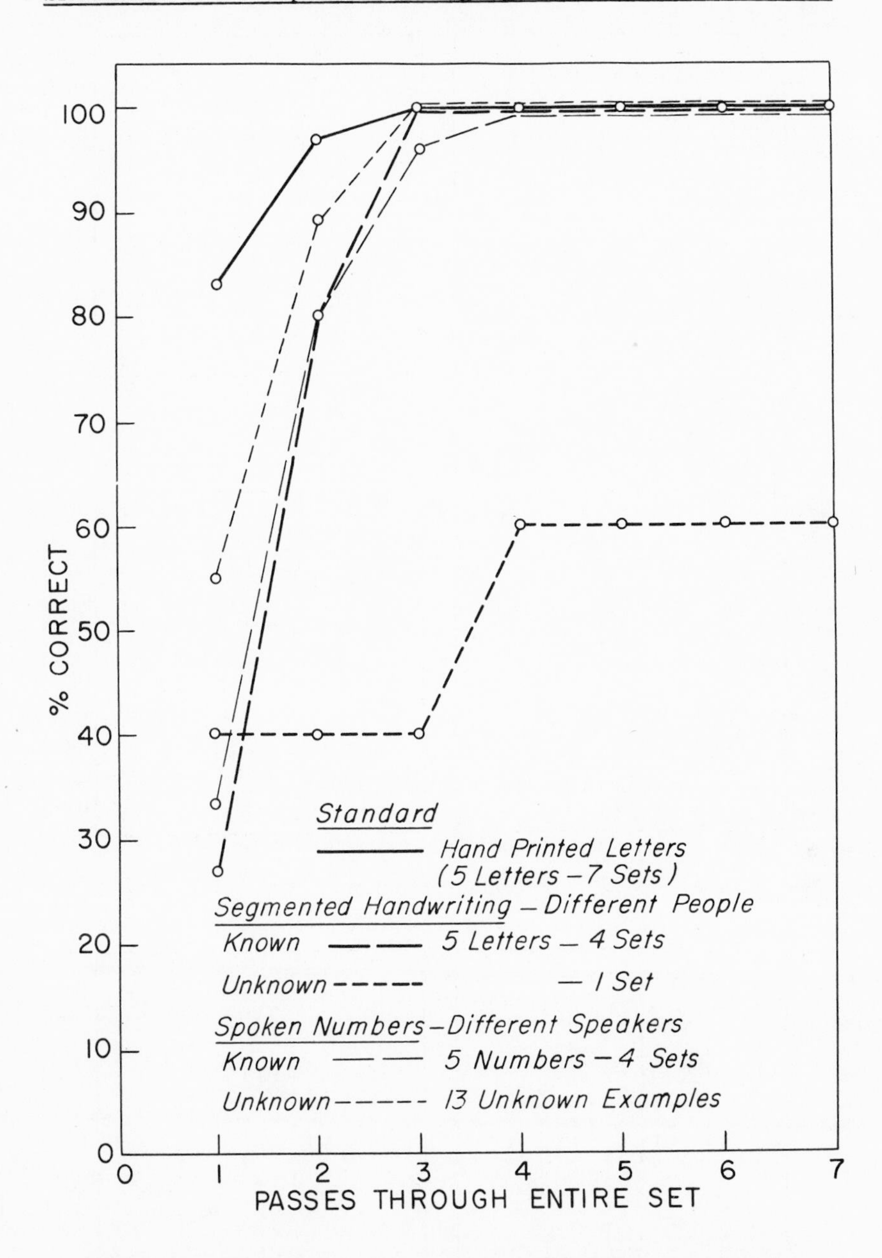

Figure 1c. Results of the Computer Simulation Program.

[Results with two additional 5 pattern arrays: (i) spoken numerals (spoken by different people), (ii) segmented handwriting (written by different people). The program was tested on both known and unknown sets of patterns.]

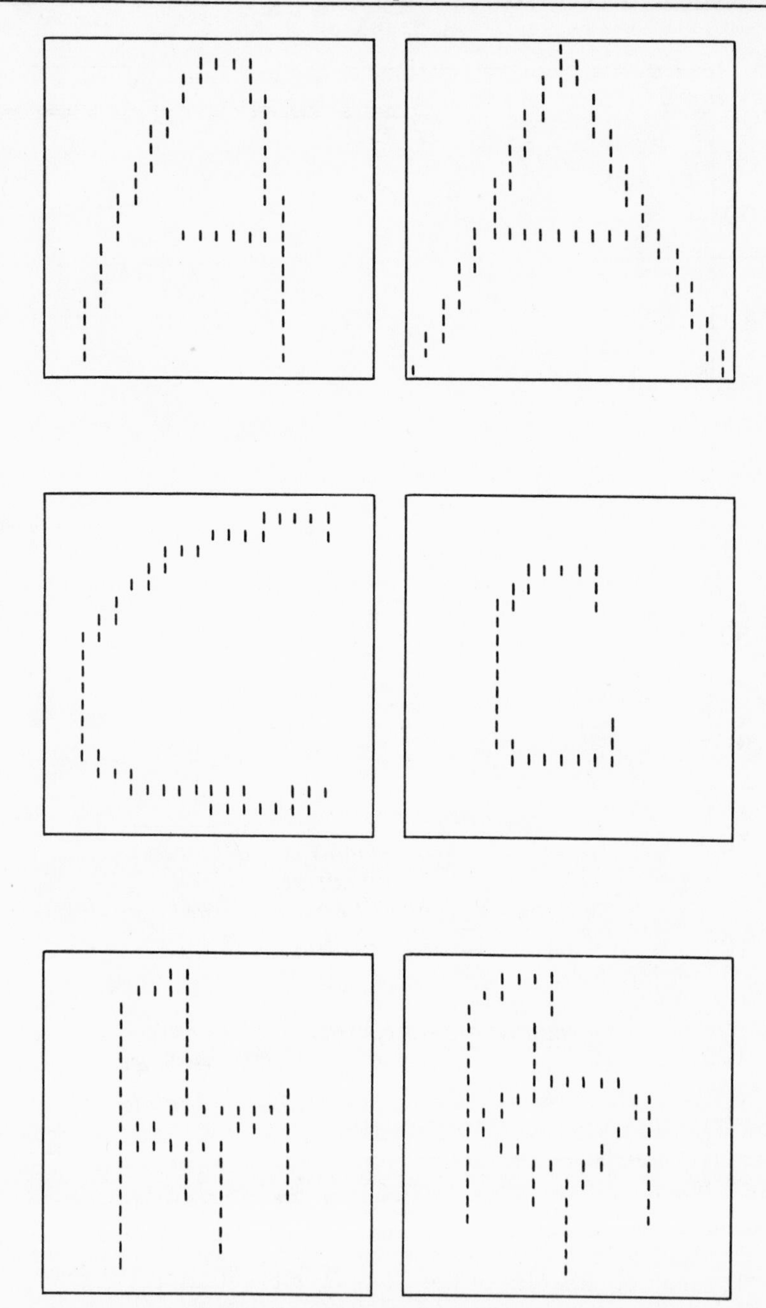

Figure 2. Some Examples of Stimuli Used in Tests of the Pattern Recognition Simulation.

Figure 2 (contd.)

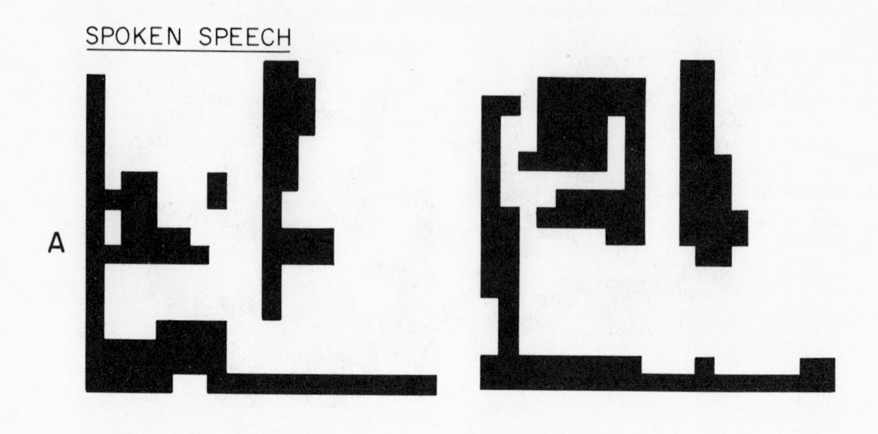

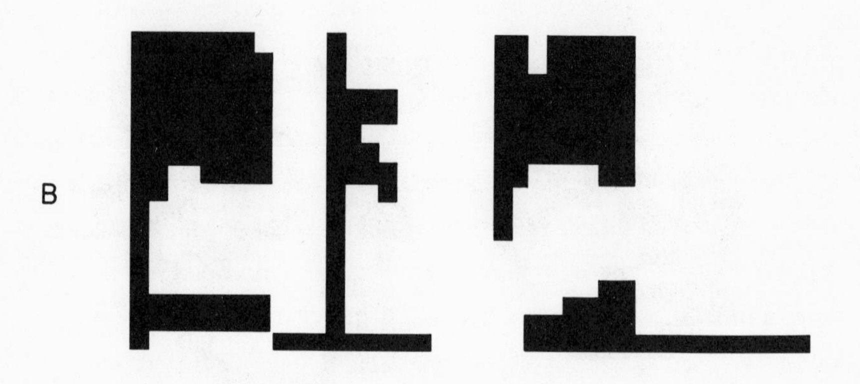

Figure 2 (contd.)

attempted to test our human subjects under conditions that were as favorable as possible. Figure 3 presents some of the results from these experiments. Figure 4 reproduces the two pattern sets used. We also replicated three experiments previously reported in the literature by Attneave (1957), Leonard and Fitts (discussed in Fitts & Leonard, 1957), and Vanderplas and Garvin (1959). In all cases the program did at least as well as human subjects. These results, plus the relatively good results for speech recognition, were rather encouraging, since they suggested a fair amount of ability, built up rather quickly by discovery and learning methods, over a rather wide range of problems.

Pattern Recognition and Symbol Transformation

"Pattern recognition" problems allow the program to assume (in that these things are built in) that a single entity has been presented it, that it should respond with a single name, and that all the information can be found within the single entity. A program that responds with one of N names, to designate one of N patterns, is not necessarily very different from a program that has an $n+1^{th}$ name—"unrecognizable." This need not be true, since the decision _not_ to decide might be an extremely subtle one, depending upon a great deal of information from context, expectation, and previous experience. But often it is not. And in any case the decision as to the choice between patterns might be equally subtle, as it surely is in the living organism.

Problems of language manipulation add, among other complications, the necessity of recognizing several different patterns, usually in a simple linear sequence. This added aspect

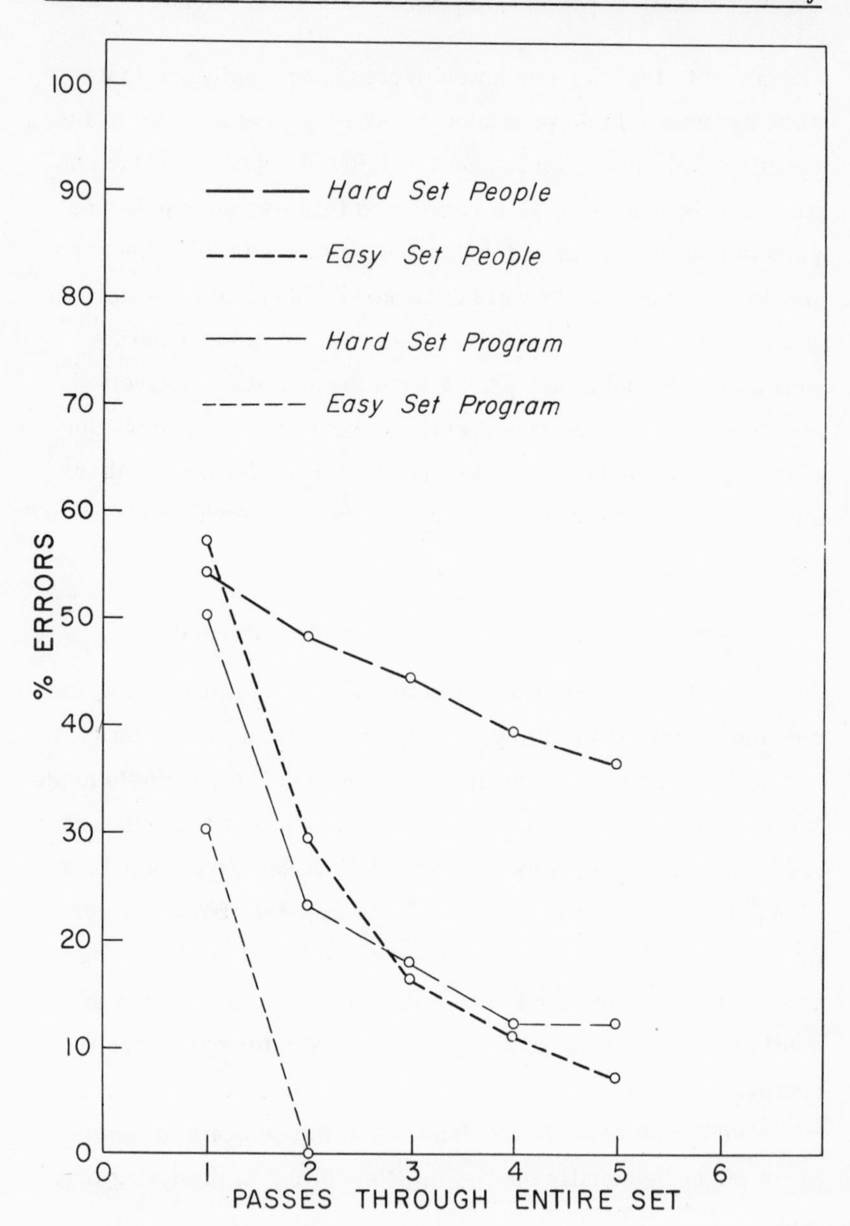

Figure 3. Results from a Comparison Experiment.

[Per cent errors for the program and mean per cent errors for human subjects (from 6 to 10 subjects per point) on one hard and one easy set of "meaningless" patterns. Both sets contained five variant examples of each of five patterns.]

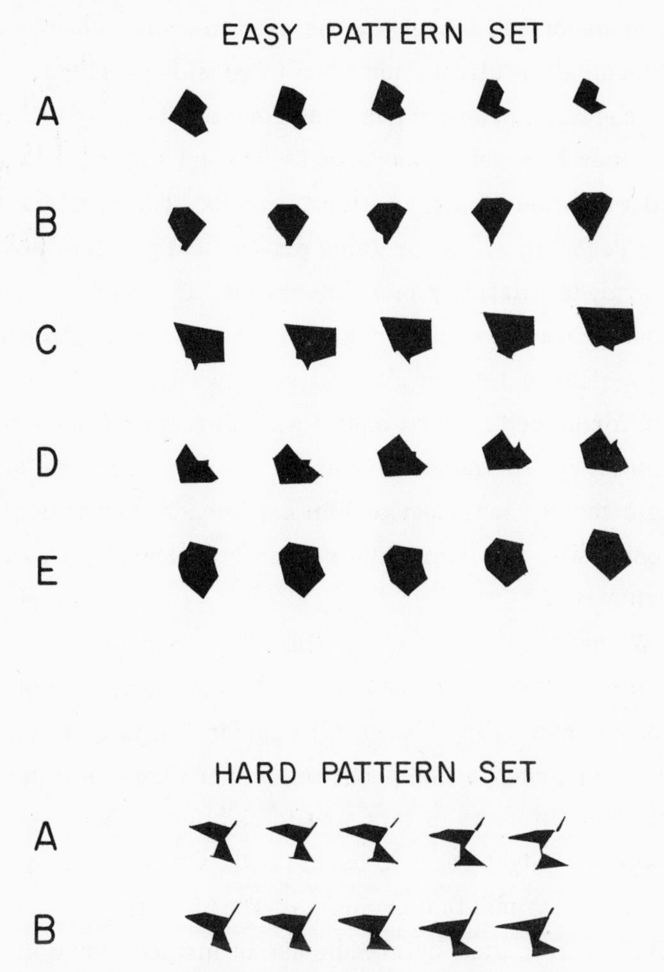

Figure 4. Stimuli Used in Experiments Comparing the Performance of Simulated Model and Human Subjects.

might be described loosely as the need to decide when to decide among alternatives, and when to consider that a new pattern recognition problem has been confronted. In addition, the pattern may be a set of subpatterns (words) and it may be partially implied by many different words. The problem for pattern recognition, as for game playing and problem-solving in general, is relatively more clear-cut. The program has a data-gathering stage and a decision-making stage, choosing among a clear-cut set of alternative acts. It may also have a stage for something that has to do with learning, induction and discovery, so that its measures, decision methods, and possible choices may change with experience. But it is not confronted with the immediate necessity of learning about what to learn about.

We have coded a language-learning program that makes a few simple attempts to handle some of these new problems. This program acts in an over-all manner that is quite similar to the pattern recognition program, and our hope is to learn enough from attempts of this sort to be able to code a single program that might begin to handle both pattern recognition and symbol manipulation problems. That is, the program would "handle" them in that, by making use of methods for discovery, induction and learning, it would generate specific additions to itself, as a function of its experiences with (a) input and (b) expected output sequences, that would turn it into a successful program of one type or another. We could then begin to examine the different structures built up by different problem domains to see whether they told us anything about the problems, or about the parts of a cognitive system suitable for such problems. (For discussion of generalizations of discovery methods, see Vossler & Uhr, 1962a, and Amarel, 1962.)

Symbol Transformation Simulation Program

The language program is given input strings in one language and output strings in a second language. The program tries to predict output strings. That is, it tries to learn to translate (for examples of its output, see Figure 5). It has several important abilities built into it in a way that keeps it from using these abilities as flexibly as one would hope might be possible if the program had learned them itself. It does several crucial things in what we know is the wrong way, and it has several other crucial things left out. As a result, it learns simple things unrealistically fast, and it does not develop abilities to generalize and to do things efficiently. However, despite the fact that it does certain things in what seems to be the wrong way, it does, in fact, attempt these things. Briefly, the program builds up a dictionary of basic units (words or letters—that is, whatever is bounded by the blank symbol), each with a set of translations that the program has inferred for it. To each such translation pair is associated a number that reflects the frequency with which that translation appeared to the program to have occurred. When the program infers that connected strings of defined words translate to something new, it stores these longer strings, much as idioms and complex grammatical forms must be remembered by the human being. The program is thus able to translate one word into several, or several into one. It is also able to build up transformations by this method. For example, it will learn to translate "I told him 'no'" into "Je lui ai dit 'non'" by storing (a) I - je, (b) 'no' - 'non,' and (c) told him - lui a dit. It will also have learned (d) told - ai dit, and (e) him - le, lui, along with other forms of the word "tell," if it has had experience with sentences

Figure 5. The Beginning of a Learning Sequence in a Test of the Symbol Transformation Program.

[The top line gives the sentence to be translated, the middle line gives the program's attempt, the bottom line gives the feedback to the program.]

1. YO SOY UN HOMBRE .
   T(YO) T(SOY) T(UN) T(HOMBRE) T(.)
   I AM A MAN.
2. YO SOY UNA MUJER .
   I AM T(UNA) T(MUJER) .
   I AM A WOMAN .
3. YO SOY UN MUCHACHO .
   I AM A T(MUCHACHO) .
   I AM A BOY .
4. YO SOY UNA MUCHACHA .
   I AM A T(MUCHACHA) .
   I AM A GIRL .
5. YO SOY UN HOMBRE .
   I AM A MAN .
   I AM A MAN .
6. USTED ES UNA JUMER .
   T(USTED) T(ES) A T(JUMER) .
   YOU ARE A WOMAN .
7. YO SOY UNA MUJER .
   I AM A WOMAN .
   I AM A WOMAN .
8. USTED ES UN HOMBRE .
   YOU ARE A MAN .
   YOU ARE A MAN .
9. USTED ES UNA MUCHACHA .
   YOU ARE A GIRL .
   YOU ARE A GIRL .
10. USTED ES UN MUCHACHO .
    YOU ARE A BOY .
    YOU ARE A BOY .
11. EL ES UN HOMBRE .
    T(EL) ARE A MAN .
    HE IS A MAN .

Figure 5. (Continued)

12. ELLA ES UNA MUJER .
    T(ELLA) ARE A WOMAN .
    SHE IS A WOMAN .
13. EL ES UN MUCHACHO .
    HE IS A BOY .
    HE IS A BOY .
14. ELLA ES UNA MUCHACHA .
    SHE IS A GIRL .
    SHE IS A GIRL .
15. ES UN SOMBRERO .
    IS A T(SOMBRERO) .
    THIS IS A HAT .
16. ES UNA MESA .
    IS A T(MESA) .
    THIS IS A TABLE .
17. ES MI CABEZA .
    IS T(MI) T(CABEZA) .
    THIS IS MY HEAD .
18. ES SU CABEZA .
    IS T(SU) T(CABEZA) .
    THIS IS YOUR HEAD .
19. ES MI MANO .
    IS T(MI) T(MANO) .
    THIS IS MY HAND .
20. ES SU MANO .
    THIS IS YOUR T(MANO) .
    THIS IS YOUR HAND .
21. ES EL SENOR VARGAS .
    IS HE T(SENOR) T(VARGAS) .
    THIS IS MISTER VARGAS .
22. ES LA SENORITA GOMEZ .
    IS T(LA) T(SENORITA) T(GOMEZ) .
    THIS IS MISS GOMEZ .
23. YO SOY UN HOMBRE .
    I AM A MAN .
    I AM A MAN .

Figure 5. (Continued)

24. ES MI CABEZA .
    THIS IS MY HEAD .
    THIS IS MY HEAD .

25. TENGO UN SOMBRERO .
    T(TENGO) A T(SOMBRERO) .
    I HAVE A HAT .

26. TENGO MI SOMBRERO EN LA MANO .
    I HAVE MY HAT T(EN) T(LA) HAND .
    I HAVE MY HAT IN THE HAND .

27. TENGO MI SOMBRERO EN LA CABEZA .
    I HAVE MY HAT IN THE HEAD .
    I HAVE MY HAT ON THE HEAD .

28. TENGO MI SOMBRERO EN LA MANO .
    I HAVE MY HAT IN THE HAND .
    I HAVE MY HAT IN THE HAND .

29. USTED TIENE UN SOMBRERO .
    YOU T(TIENE) A HAT .
    YOU HAVE A HAT .

30. TIENE SU SOMBRERO EN LA MANO .
    HAVE T(SU) HAT IN THE HAND .
    YOU HAVE YOUR HAT IN THE HAND .

31. TIENE SU SOMBRERO EN LA CABEZA .
    HAVE YOUR HAT IN THE HEAD .
    YOU HAVE YOUR HAT ON THE HEAD .

32. ELLA TIENE UN SOMBRERO .
    SHE HAVE A HAT .
    SHE HAS A HAT .

33. TENGO DOS MANOS .
    I HAVE T(DOS) T(MANOS) .
    I HAVE TWO HANDS .

34. ES LA MANO DERECHA .
    IS THE HAND T(DERECHA) .
    THIS IS THE RIGHT HAND .

35. ES LA MANO IZQUIERDA .
    IS THE HAND T(IZQUIERDA) .
    THIS IS THE LEFT HAND .

Figure 5. (Continued)

36. USTED TIENE DOS MANOS .
YOU HAVE TWO HANDS .
YOU HAVE TWO HANDS .

37. TENGO DOS SOMBREROS .
I HAVE TWO T(SOMBREROS) .
I HAVE TWO HATS .

38. TENGO UN SOMBRERO EN LA MANO DERECHA .
I HAVE A HAT IN THE HAND T(DERECHA) .
I HAVE A HAT IN THE RIGHT HAND .

39. TENGO UN SOMBRERO IN LA MANO IZQUIERDA .
I HAVE A HAT T(IN) THE HAND T(IZQUIERDA) .
I HAVE A HAT IN THE LEFT HAND .

40. EL TIENE DOS SOMBREROS .
HE HAVE TWO HATS .
HE HAS TWO HATS .

41. TIENE UN SOMBRERO EN LA MANO DERECHA .
HAVE A HAT IN THE RIGHT HAND .
HE HAS A HAT IN THE RIGHT HAND .

containing these words in different contexts. But since it does not have any more efficient way of decomposing strings when the order is changed, it must store each occurrence separately in this manner. For example, if it were to learn "happy horse, happy girl," and so on, each would be a separate item in memory (because of the inversion into French). And "'no'" must be learned separately from "no." This is an obvious weakness. But it should be noted that it is a weakening of efficiency in storage and speed in learning, rather than in ultimate performance. Relatively simple subroutines would give the program abilities to develop rules for permuting words, for changing their grammatical form, and for certain types of generalizations. But these subroutines would make awkward and unrealistic mistakes at times, and have a feeling of the *ad hoc* about them.

The Symbol Transformation Program as a Sensory Pattern Recognition Program

The symbol transformation program can be used to recognize sensory patterns, as well as to translate between languages. This is most easily seen if we consider patterns as preprocessed by a small nerve net that performs a two-dimensional differencing operation on the sensed pattern. That is, for each cone in the input matrix the question is asked whether the stimulus impinging upon it is the same as or different from the stimulus impinging upon each of its neighbors, and the answers are summed together. For example, when a regular square matrix is used and each cell is considered to have eight neighbors (including its diagonals), then such a net, when asked to process a square, will output the following string of connected values: $5\text{-}3^n\text{-}5\text{-}3^n\text{-}5\text{-}3^n\text{-}5\text{-}3^n\text{-}5\text{-}3^n\text{-}\ldots$ Such a net turns a pattern into its contour, a one-dimensional string that loops back on itself. It performs much the same operation performed by the contour-enhancing net of excitatory and inhibitory connections leading from cones to ganglia in the eye.

We wrote a subroutine that performs this operation, planning to tack it onto our pattern recognition program as a first preprocessing step. But, although the subroutine is running, we haven't got around to doing this yet. However, we can ask what this subroutine would do if tacked onto the beginning of the symbol transformation program, simply by outputting strings of contours and then inputting these to the symbol transformation program in exactly the way we input sentences, with the output sentence the pattern's name.

The symbol transformation program will learn to recognize these patterns. It will make the many-to-one mapping, from the elements of the contour string to the name of the pattern, by concatenating these elements up into larger structures, just as in the language problem it concatenates letters or words up into idioms. If the contour string is doubled in length (for example, by repeating it, or by integrating change of slope), then this pair of programs will recognize sensory patterns over all the linear transformations. Because the preprocessing program does a certain amount of averaging and smoothing, so that it gives the same outputs for slightly variant angles, curves and lengths, it will also immediately recognize at least a certain number of variant non-linear instances of patterns it has learned. Its abilities at rote learning, which allow it to build up alternate translations, will allow it to learn alternate patterns, given experience with these alternates. But it does not have the abilities of the original pattern recognition program to develop a generalized concept of the pattern class. If we can succeed at giving the symbol transformation program interesting and natural-looking generalization methods, these methods should overcome its rigidities with respect to sensory patterns as well as with respect to symbols.

Motivation and Socialization

We have a feeling that each of these problems is a specific instance of a more general problem that might be termed "abstract pattern recognition," or "induction and discovery," or "learning." This is the problem of how an organism (or system) can reach a state where it is successful in processing inputs transmitted to it from the larger system that surrounds it. That is, how it can come to act appropriately upon the larger system. This problem inevitably leads to a further problem: how can such an organism evolve in the first place? That is, not merely how an evolved organism could develop appropriately (learning and maturation), but also how the organism could develop in the first place (evolution).

It seems useful to at least consider these two problems, each one of course immensely complicated in itself, as a combined problem. This is ~~to~~ because in at least certain respects the problem simplifies. One might posit a mechanism that would be sufficient for pattern perception, or generalization, or deductive inference. And a number of ingenious mechanisms for such functions have in fact been suggested and programmed. But then the question arises: how could these mechanisms have developed? It seems reasonable that a simpler mechanism should be sufficient as a basis, and a still simpler mechanism as basis for this simpler mechanism, and so on. Otherwise we are caught on the horns of the homunculus. And this is a deep dilemma, for it would assert that in order to be able to begin to learn, to profit from its environment, an organism must contain something that is not a consequence of the environment, but only stupendously unlikely chance. The more complex the basic mechanism the less likely are our chances of discovering it. Second, whereas the specific solution one generates via hard analysis and ingenuity may be sufficient, it is difficult to evaluate whether it is good, in the sense that a theory is good. On the other hand, if the problem is posed as one of an environment alone, in which an organism begins to grow as a function of its relations with this environment, then we have important information as to the "naturalness" of the organism that finally develops. We are also now posing the problem of learning and evolution in such a way as to make it the problem of discovery-induction.

Abstracted from pattern recognition or language learning our problem becomes: Given input experiences such that certain output responses will lead to certain subsequent experiences, such that some of these experiences will be liked by the responding organism, then how can we get an organism to develop as a function of such experiences so that it will find more and more to its liking. Or we can think of a second organism or set of organisms such that they respond to the first organism's responses according to their own evaluations, so that our first organism will now tend to develop at least partially in the direction of doing things that these *other* organisms like.

By "liking" we mean something very similar to pleasure-pain or drive reduction or intellectual curiosity; something that gives direction to change. There must be some principle for choosing good experiences from bad, otherwise the choice, if any, will be chance, and the organism will either fluctuate randomly like dust in sunlight or be immovable like rock. From this point of view it seems rather reasonable that the principle be diverse, a set of principles rather than a single one, so that it samples possibilities with a certain range. And it is probably easier to specify a complex overall principle by a set of simple basic units than by a single combination. Thus, given the basic *need for need* in such an organism, there seem to be quite plausible reasons for more than one need to be present.

The existence of needs in present day computer programs is not at all apparent, and the problem is not usually discussed.

But the fact is that all programs already incorporate what might just as well be called a need system, just as much as they incorporate a sensing system, and a response system. Sensing and responding are simply input-output for the program. This is simple and built in, but not at all trivial. Unless a program could input data its answers would not be a function of data, and would have nothing to do with data. One might with real justice say that a mathematical operation must sense its data, transform them, and then respond with its output. A human being assumes this, and acts as sensor and responder. A computer program uses the input and output routines and specific instruction sequences that are of the form "fetch a, b, c...; perform operations m, n, o...; store (for future operations or outputting) the results in r, s, t..." Thus sensing and responding are always present, not only in a program but in every subpart of the program. Very simply, sensing and responding are the connections between the parts (note that one part's response is another part's sensation). What we more normally think of as sensation and response are the inputting to and outputting from the program, i.e., the program's connection with the world external to it.

But underlying these connections are the driving forces that make the program continue along these connections. A program is always a sequence of instructions, as indicated above, and each instruction tells not only what should be done to what, but also where to go to find the next instruction. But there is also the mechanism that does what to what and goes where, and this mechanism always has the energy and drive to do these things. In the typical program these things are simply built in, just as the connections are built in. It is as though the programmer is omniscient as to what the program should notice and that it should notice. Of course this is the case for the typical mathematical, or even simulation, problem. But it need not be the case, and it should be noted that sensing, responding, and being in a state of need are already built in, even if trivialized, in order that the program run at all. They are built in in the same way that "memory" is built in. The analogy between the computer's memory and the human being's memory is a painful one for most people, since there obviously is an analogy (of appreciable but unknown looseness) and yet it is equally obviously wrong. The computer's memory is much better, much worse, and much different. But it certainly is a memory. If any human being had such a memory he would likely end up as an idiot savant (although he might have an outside chance of becoming a professor, let us say of history or Far Eastern languages to keep from getting too close to home), but we would certainly credit him with a memory. Similarly a computer, in the way it sticks to its over-all flow diagram might with justice be credited with looking (if only in front of its nose) and being driven to do such things as look.

A pattern recognition program always has the computer look (for a pattern that is input). Then the computer (needs to) performs operations upon, in order to measure, the pattern. Then it combines these measures, compares them with expected alternates, chooses among the alternates, and outputs its choice. Pattern recognition studies pattern measurement and decisions as to classification. It ignores questions about responses, needs, or internal connections (except for programs that attempt some modification of connections). When a pattern recognition program must draw its outputs, instead of outputting from among a predetermined code that the programmer has defined for both the program and himself, it is getting involved in problems of response. When it tries to transform from one set of measures (those that characterize patterns to be recognized) to a second different set of measures (those that characterize patterns to be drawn), and to develop these transformations as a function of its experiences, it is getting involved with problems of modification of connection that make input-output (within the central cognitive system) rather subtle. When it begins to ask when it should try to recognize, when it should try to respond, and why (which might be thought of as another set of conditional probabilities), it is developing a need and drive system that might well be of interest to the psychologist. Finally, there might be several organisms in the universe, so that each individual is embedded in an environment that is not only natural but social.

Similarly, the germ of values is almost certainly present in any program that computes success counts, or weightings, or evaluations. When a program makes successive modifications of some quantity as a function of its experiences as to the successes (need satisfaction) and failures of its own responses that were a function of this quantity in order to make a decision to change these responses, then the program is attributing a value to the function that leads to the response. If it is true that a program must generalize on its methods, in order to learn quickly and efficiently and powerfully, then it will have to generalize on these specific values. In fact these generalizations, as to the types of things that are successful, are probably the central place where learning must occur. This leads to two interesting consequences. First, general values, generalizations over ever wider domains, will be developed, and this value system will act as one of the organism's most important driving forces. But, second, this value system will inevitably be wrong. It will be wrong in a Procrustean manner as to specific instances from which the over-all generalization was made. And it will be wrong in a Hegelian manner when super-generalizations are attempted. That is, the specific details for which a generalization is designed will not fit the generalization exactly; and the need to generalize will lead to a tendency to generalize across domains that are not generalizable (but may occasionally synthesize). Thus we might expect a system of conflicting values to grow in a program that learned its bodily-hunger satisfying responses through experience with an external world that was largely natural, its libido-satisfying responses in a social world, and its ethical responses in a different social world. We might even raise the question: from what (provincial) point of view (or generality) is the compartmentalized program acting irrationally?

Summary

We have been trying to develop a suitably complex and powerful model for psychological processes. The use of computer simulations, which can handle many degrees of freedom, gives us some hope toward this end. The study of the discovery and learning of percepts and symbols gives some hope that it may be possible to avoid some of the detailed specification of the model, by asking the model to, in a certain sense, evolve and build itself as a function of its experiences with its environments. Perceptual learning is an unsolved problem, in both psychology and "artificial intelligence," and it is a relatively clear-cut problem. Thus, any progress one makes can be recognized, and itself serves as supporting evidence for the model. Perceptual learning is also a reasonable place to begin when one hopes to develop "higher" processes in a more complete system.

We have simulated various simple attempts toward such a model. The pattern recognition simulation encouraged us to try to generalize our first attempt. It was able to recognize a wide variety of patterns, in several sensory modalities, over a wide variety of non-linear distortions. It did this despite the need to discover at least some of its own methods and to learn about patterns only through experience with them. The symbol transformation program gives at least some indication of the possibility of using similar methods for problems where words and numbers must be manipulated. In fact, the symbol transformation program can be interpreted and used as a sensory pattern recognition program. From another point of view, a pattern recognition program that controls a second pattern recognition program that _outputs_ its operators, in the manner of drawing out a response, can be thought of as a translator from one (perceptual) language to another. Thus our simulation of a drawing-response mechanism under the control of the pattern recognition program is performing functions close to some of those necessary in language translation or question-answering.

Such simulation programs must have a good bit wired into them, or abstracted out of the situation, in order to simplify the problem down to workable size. But already present are germs of motivating, socializing, and value-instilling functions. More powerful simulations will almost certainly contain more powerful personality-related functions when they begin to approach the human being in their abilities to adapt, generalize, control themselves, and develop their own concepts, motives and purposes.

15 | JEROME KAGAN
Fels Research Institute

Discussion: Human Perception or Machine Perception-- The Problem of Cognition

It is rare for a paper in a pioneer area to combine excitement about a problem with provocative empirical data and also supply its own apology and critique. Professor Uhr is surely a triple-threat man. It is not difficult to take pot shots at essays and experiments in the area of simulation. An idea as fresh as this—especially one that requires new language and new techniques—is guilty until proven innocent. Since initial steps in simulation are necessarily halting and fragile, it takes neither brilliance nor bravado to point to deficiencies in any one investigation. Moreover, Professor Uhr is an able critic of his own work, and he does not evade or gloss over the problems in the simulation studies he reports in this paper. Nonetheless there are some fundamental questions raised by this report and the entire conference, namely the contemporary intent of computer simulation in general and of simulation of perception in particular. I emphasize the adjective "contemporary" because I do not question the eventual usefulness of computers—only their current strategy. There are at least four reasons for investing effort in simulation of perceptual and conceptual processes. The first two have been regarded as subordinate at this meeting. Simulation is fun, and it enables us to perfect more efficient translations of language and develop rapid ways of solving problems that humans do awkwardly or with difficulty. The last two intents have been regarded as more vital by this group. Computer programs force us to state our theories precisely and allow us to test complex hypotheses with elegance. Finally, it is hoped that such work will help us to understand how humans learn patterns by providing clues to the fundamental mechanisms of human perceptual and conceptual learning. I sense in Professor Uhr's paper and at this meeting a contamination of the last two intents. Professor Uhr begins his paper by stating that "the importance of computers does not lie in any specific type of model that they may suggest...rather computers present the unique opportunity to explore efficiently and effectively with any theory or model." However, unlike Dr. Colby (Chapter 9)—and here the contrast is important—the theory Professor Uhr prints into his program does not seem to be dictated by the data that exist on human perception. The model Dr. Uhr programs may be applicable for infrahuman visual systems but, as I will argue in a moment, does not seem consonant with what we know about the human process.

This paper embodies a critical contemporary issue in the philosophy of simulation work. That is to say, do we look to the computer for discoveries about mechanisms of human behavior or should it be viewed as an elegant test device for theories that are derived from empirical data? I sense both goals in Professor Uhr's paper. I have no quarrel with the latter intent but do have reservations about the former. Let me elaborate on this statement.

If simulation of pattern recognition is to discover laws of perceptual learning, we must first inquire about the possibility of fundamental differences in the information processing of these two species. We are not interested in which species is better at recognition of patterns, for I fear that the computer would win many rounds hands down. Rather, we seek to ask if the processing activities of these two kinds of animals are different. A whale and shark can both remain under water, but the mechanisms of respiration are markedly different. In animal genetics, we find many examples of phenocopies in which two forms appear alike for different reasons. The way Professor Uhr's program recognizes a pattern may be sufficiently unlike human recognition that the program, as it is presented here, can tell us little about this aspect of human learning. The display of similar error curves for machine and man as an argument for similarity of process may be misleading. Professor Uhr's program requires successive, albeit rapid, scanning of small units—an atomistic hairsplitting analysis of the figure. The human appears to be wired to do quite the opposite. The human's unit of input, especially when he becomes conceptual and has symbolic labels for inputs, tends to be a meaningful chunk which can be classified. Much of the research on perceptual and language development converges on the same conclusion; namely, children have a prepotent tendency to react to wholes, to categorize syncretically. Adults perceive what they can label. I would like to test the predictive power of the program on some empirical data we have acquired on 200 second-grade children. The child was presented with a nonsense design which he studied for five seconds. The design was removed for 15 seconds and then the child was presented with an array of designs, one of which was the standard and the remaining stimuli variants of the design. One of the variants involved changing a straight line to a curved line; one involved turning the figure upside down; one involved turning the figure 90 degrees to the right or left; one involved a decrease in size of the figure; and a final variant involved making a break in one of the lines. If I understand Professor Uhr's program correctly, the error most likely to be made by his program would be the last variant in which there was a broken line in the design. This error was least frequent among the children, whereas the most frequent error was one in which the total figure was reduced in size. I suggest this was due to the child labeling the whole figure with a meaningful symbol.

The stimuli in Figures 2 through 4 in Chapter 14 are suited for this particular program, for it is difficult to apply labels to the parts to be discriminated. They are, in Beach's words, "species specific tasks." One could easily make up a set of stimuli that would result in more rapid learning for humans. Tasks differ in their friendliness to varied species. The fact that there is no difference in the learning curves in Figure 3 between an "easy stimulus set for people" and a "hard stimulus set for the program" suggests that the evaluation "easy-hard" is made from the point of view of the program. Flying is easy for birds, difficult for humans; jumping furnishes the reverse ability profile. If one goal of simulation is to learn about human perception, then we must tailor the program to the general facts and thoughts in the area. It is obvious, therefore, that an enormous amount of empirical information is necessary before we can begin to profit from the power of our new toy.

I am in awe of Professor Uhr's efforts in this exciting area. My dissatisfaction is with his specific program for pattern recognition, not with his ultimate intent—an intent that I hope will soon be realized.

16 | WILLIAM KESSEN
Yale University

Discussion:
Strong and Weak Simulation --Mimic or Model

In the eleventh hour of the conference and as the twelfth discussant, it is unlikely that I can add anything of substantial novelty to our deliberations. And, because Professor Kagan has spoken in some detail about Professor Uhr's subtle and complex paper, I will take advantage of the role of the last day's discussant to raise briefly a general and troublesome problem.

I hope that not everyone shares my entropic development but, as the conference has gone on, I have become less certain about the place of computer simulation in personality study. We have heard, at one extreme, of Professor Tomkins' great eyeball-rolling, walking computer surrounded homily by all his little computerettes and, at what I take to be the other extreme, of Professor Uhr's admonition that the computer is a great piece of blank paper on which he who will may write. I confess to little sympathy for the first or duplicative view of the computer and I do not believe that Professor Tomkins meant it to be taken altogether seriously, but if we go to the other end of the range and see the computer as a wondrous complex device for transforming us all into error-free, hypothetic-deductive theorists, in what sense may it be said to simulate? Clearly we have again one of these disagreeable continua that get in the way of our human attempts to come up with unambiguous categorical answers. Let me suggest a formal analogy to the problem of simulation and ask you if it makes sense.

For any particular problem in the prediction of behavior (and Professor Uhr's paper, for one, is valuable in part because it starts with a particular circumscribed problem), we can state a set of inputs, hypothetical processes, and outputs for the human being. There walks Joe in his human dignity, talking, emoting, perceiving, affecting. Now, we have spent some time discussing whether we can in fact say a great deal about Joe, but for an understanding of the place of simulation, it seems to me that we must have some idea at least of the nature of the events to be simulated—Joe the simulandum.

But having our simulandum, what about our simulans? What about the shape of the computer-program-programmer complex? There seem to be three classes of answers to these questions.

As I suggested earlier, I do not think that we can demand what might be called the wider Turing test, in which the computer acts like Joe, looks like Joe, and strikes his forehead in astonishment to learn that we are surprised because he thinks he thinks.

Then there is the weakest form of computer simulation, where given some defensible representation of Joe's inputs, the computer comes up with some defensible representation of Joe's outputs. What occurs in between is (however complex and demanding on the builder) not examined for its relevance to human process. Apparently there are few such programs, programs where art imitates Hull, because the computerphile apparently gets his kicks from playing with process—from his attempt to reconstruct the anatomy of thought or, in the case of Professors Tomkins (Chapter 1) and Colby (Chapter 9), the anatomy of melancholy.

Thus, then, to the apparent larger intent of computer simulation—not to be God in all his creative artistry and not to be a more efficient S-R theorist but rather to handle S-R relations, to model Joe, and to do so with some success in modeling his conceptual innards too, to simulate process as well as behavior.

Now you can see why I said earlier that we are on a continuum that resists easy fractionation. How often should we break into the computer's work to see if it is doing the job the way Joe would? What will be the width of the band of permitted variation? Can we let the computer do better or faster than Joe the things it can do better and faster or does that mock our attempt to build a simulans?

I have avoided until now the question direct, the problem that resists debugging. How, with our current ignorance of human process _without_ the computer, shall we judge whether the computer has simulated man or not? This is another form of the Reitman question, and I am uneasy about its early solution. We know too little of man to imitate him.

In this regard, let me append two last dangling notes. We may, in our search for verification of our views of human process, be driven to a new introspectionism, an outcome I do not relish. Finally, I would like to express my enthusiasm for the weaker view of simulation—that the best current use of this momentous tool is to extend the theorist whether or not it mirrors man.

17

ROBERT P. ABELSON
Yale University

Computer Simulation of "Hot" Cognition

The fact that a session of a computer simulation symposium is titled "Cognition and Affect" is rather extraordinary. No more extraordinary, perhaps, than the goings-on during other sessions of the symposium, but consider the implications. One would think from reading the psychological literature that computer simulation of cognitive processes means the study of logical problem-solving behavior: proving theorems (Newell, Shaw, & Simon, 1958a), playing chess (Newell, Shaw, & Simon, 1958b), forming concepts (Hovland & Hunt, 1960), and so on. Though there is considerable variety in the various cognitive tasks that have come under study, there seems to have been no provision in the computer game for the study of cognition dealing with affect-laden objects—of "hot cognition" as opposed to the "cold cognition" of problem solving.

Meanwhile, Miller, Galanter, and Pribram (1960), in their book on Plans, have chided cognitive theorists for their sedentary models. They remind us that cognition has something to do with action. They develop their concept of Plans with computer programs as metaphor. The Plan is said to intervene between Image and Behavior. Yet curiously enough, in a loose moment these authors state that the human mind is 75% Image, 25% Plan. Hardly anything at all is said about the 75% Image. The Image is said to contain the evaluative function, and thus any relations between cognition and affect are tucked away in the 75% of the cognitive area that Miller, Galanter, and Pribram choose not to tackle.

For the psychologist (as opposed to the psychoanalyst), one major area conjoining affect and cognition is that of _attitudes._ Although computer simulators have ignored the attitude area, the last several years have seen a number of theoretical developments. Heider (1958) elaborated his earlier concept of cognitive balance, Festinger (1957) introduced cognitive dissonance, and Osgood and Tannenbaum (1955) presented incongruity. Rosenberg (1960) and others dealt experimentally with the relation between affect change and belief change. The single theme dominating these developments (and many others that could have been adduced) is that there is a tendency toward the establishment of consistency between affect and belief under conditions of confrontation with an inconsistency. This tendency has a number of implications for the study of cognitive processes, and it would certainly seem that these processes ought to be computer simulable. However, the level of specificity of previous developments is insufficient for this purpose, for assorted reasons I will take a few moments to indicate.

Heider has been more concerned with interpersonal perception than with cognitive processes in general. A more important difficulty is the uncongeniality of Gestaltist dynamic terms for the construction of a tight process model. It is hard to express this difficulty, but I can perhaps indicate the problem by saying that, for Heider, things flow instead of click.

Festinger's theory has been very provocative and has given rise to many experiments, but the fact must be faced that although labeled "cognitive dissonance theory," it is in essence not a cognitive theory, but a theory of action. That is to say, Festinger and his students are not really concerned with processes inside the head, but with the behavioral consequences of the presentation of dissonant situations. To the extent that cognitive variables are involved, they tend to turn on the concept of volition (Cohen, 1960), which is theoretically similar to Miller, Galanter, and Pribram's term intention. Festinger, in other words, is concerned with the Plan, rather than the Image. There is nothing wrong with this save that it doesn't help those of us interested in the Image.

When applied to the phenomenon of attitude change, both balance theory and dissonance theory suffer from a certain degree of gratuitousness. When it is asserted that an individual may resolve cognitive disharmony by changing his attitude toward some object X, the mystery remains as to how attitude change is effected. If attitude change were a simple operation, we should all go about changing our attitudes like topcoats to conform to the prevailing social weather. Clearly it is not always easy to change an attitude, no matter how cognitively harmonious the result, and models in this area must somehow deal with this problem.

Osgood and Tannenbaum's "principle of congruity" asserts a general rule by which the evaluations of different cognitive objects come into congruence with one another when the objects are associated. For example, if an esteemed colleague of mine has a kind word for the OAS terrorists, I come to think more highly of the terrorists and less highly of my colleague, says the congruity principle. Instead of letting attitude change dangle gratuitously, this principle goes to the other extreme and explicitly makes attitude change inexorable. It can be shown mathematically (Abelson, 1962) that these postulated changes tend in the long run to wash out highly polarized evaluations. With repeated applications of the principle to a variety of objects, the individual would find himself adrift in a sea of neutrality. Here again there is a problem of specifying resistances to attitude change.

The work of Rosenberg (1960, 1962) brings us closer to what is needed for a reasonably full model of hot cognition. Rosenberg and I struggled with many of the theoretical issues together, and the general theoretical posture I will take descends largely from our joint work (Abelson & Rosenberg, 1958; Rosenberg & Abelson, 1960).

Theoretical Position

The theoretical problem may be posed as follows: Is it possible to specify a realistic model for attitude change and resistance to change in sufficient process detail so that a computer could simulate it? The major focus here is on cognitive processes, but I propose to explore some limited relations between cognition and affect. I would not want to claim a general theory of cognition and affect. However, within the context of attitudes and attitude changes, one might hope to develop a simulation model which would do for hot cognition what others have done for cold cognition. One might even speak of attitudinal problem-solving, wherein the individual is confronted with a challenge to his belief system and the "problem" he must solve is, "What am I to believe now?"

It has become more or less usual to study the verbal production of subjects in thinking their way aloud through the solution of logical problems. In the same way one might study thinking aloud through the solutions, or attempted solutions, of psychological problems. Let me give a very mild example of the differences between these two types of problems...This is the last session of the conference. Some of you are no doubt engaged at this moment in mental calculations of the time you must leave here in order to catch the plane. This is a logical problem. Suppose, however, that you tentatively conclude you must leave before the end of the session. Now you are faced with the psychological problem of whether you should leave while someone is talking, or wait until he is done and then rush, or try to slip out unobtrusively, and so on. The cognitive process is clearly involved during and after this decision, but its calculus is not well understood. What theoretical account can be given, for example, that would explain in detail why the fellow says to himself as he leaves the room and is noticed by the speaker, "Well, he walked out on my paper in Chicago."

We are led to an interest in the cognitive details of rationalization, denial, and related processes. Of course psychoanalysts and psychiatrists have for years been listening to people think aloud about psychological problems. However, it is probably not unfair to say that manifest cognitive process has been of little or no interest in psychiatry. [With more attention being given lately to ego function, there are a few exceptions to this flat assertion. Certainly Colby's paper (Chapter 9) is an exception.] At any rate, I intend the term "rationalization" to have somewhat more general applicability and dignity than is usually accorded it. Similarly for the term "denial." I will take these processes seriously and examine them in their own right, rather than solely as indicators of, or defenses against, deeper latent processes.

With this brief setting of my theoretical interest, let me define some terminology for what is to follow. By a cognitive element will be meant any object or quality symbolically represented in thought. The elements of major interest are actors, attributes, states of affairs, and actions. Actions, however, are not considered as elements when divorced from their objects. An action-object pair is taken as an element, and we refer to it as a predicate. Thus the predicate "hires detectives" is an element in the system, whereas "hires" alone is not. An element not a predicate shall be called a concept.

A sentence or band is a sequential construction of two elements, the first of which is a concept and the second of which is a predicate; for example, "The wife hires detectives." To avoid the predicate-predicate sequence in a sentence such as, "Controlling prices damages initiative," a linguistic transformation must be imagined which converts the first predicate to a concept; thus, "Price-control damages initiative." Incidentally, the two-element concept-predicate form of expressing sentences seems to be more convenient for computer simulation purposes than the standard three-element concept-relation-concept form used by Heider, by Osgood, and previously by Rosenberg and myself. The two-part construction is also more in accord with the computer-oriented methods of linguistic analysis being pursued by Yngve (1962).

Longer sequences can be built up by regarding a sentence as itself a concept. Then a predicate may be suffixed to it to yield another sentence; e.g., "The wife hires detectives follows the husband." Or, conversely, the sentence may be first lengthened into a predicate and then a concept prefixed to it, as in "Kennedy wants price-control damages initiative." One notes a certain barbarism in these constructions. Indeed, the missing words "to," "who," or "which" are differentially meaningful, but at this point I only want to list what constructions are admissible in the system.

Sentences can be further lengthened to produce breathless super-sentences like "Barry Goldwater attacks Kennedy wants price-control damages initiative ruins economy."

The left-to-right ordering of these long strings is crucial. The causal agents appear to the left and the ultimate consequences appear to the right. The extended linear form of the super-sentences seems unnatural, but the simulation model, as we shall see, does not explicitly use this extended form; rather, it deals with two-element sentences packaged within two-element sentences, and so on. When a sentence is packaged as an element in a larger sentence, it acquires a summary name in the larger sentence, as, for example, the name "all this liberal stuff" in the sentence "I'm against all this liberal stuff," overheard from a Yale undergraduate.

More than one sentence may be summarized in an element. Indeed, a large set of sentences (listed vertically instead of horizontally) may reside in an element and, as it were, specify its meaning.

By a _belief_ I will mean any sentence recoverably stored within an element. A _belief system_ is then a set of belief-carrying elements which are themselves interrelated in a set of sentences. In a previous paper (Abelson, 1959), I used the term _belief dilemma_ to refer to a situation in which the individual is confronted with the apparent necessity of changing one or more beliefs. The present usage of the term "belief" is quite broad. In particular, it includes what might ordinarily be called facts or bits of knowledge, such as "Goats give milk." Even if facts were excluded, the usage would still be broader than is sometimes customary. Some present-day psychologists, such as Rokeach (1960), use belief to refer to the conviction or feeling of the reality of some being or phenomenon. The concern is with existence or non-existence. I see advantage (as does Colby) in the broader definition including "the conviction of the truth of propositions," and, in particular, sentences specifying means-end relationships or attributions of personal responsibility.

As for the term attitude, I would define it in the present context as a belief system invested with affect; or, perhaps, since a belief system can be quite extensive, as that portion of an affect-invested belief system relevant to a given element.

Now, what about affect? Most often, attitude theorists do not refer directly to affect, but rather to the evaluations of attitude objects. We shall use that term with the understanding that evaluation represents a cognitive summarization of affective consequences. Any element may have the capacity to arouse and release affect when present in thought. Consider a variety of elements: electronic music; Prince Boun Oum; urban redevelopment; Willie Mays; nuclear war; and the sentence-elements Carpenter's-successful-flight, or the foolish-thing-I-said-yesterday. This variety of elements can arouse interest, anger, pride, fear, joy, shame, distress, excitement. Some of them may arouse no affect, and some of them blends of more than one affect. What one means by the evaluation of an object, or the alternative usages "value of the object" or "attitude toward the object," is presumably the net positive or negative affect aroused by the object.

We now make the assumption that when a sentence is present in thought, the affect aroused by each of the two elements tends to become attached to the other element. For example, the sentence "Smith supports the White Citizens' Council" leads me to have negative feelings toward Smith. However, it is not reasonable to postulate that the process of affect transfer takes place all at once, immediately. Instead, we postulate a gradual transfer throughout the time period when the sentence is present in thought.

We may note certain theoretical difficulties if we attempt to deal with particular affects in the postulated transfer. The sentence "My wife loves salad" does not transfer my particular positive affects toward my wife onto the salad. They would be wasted on the salad. Presumably there is some question of the appropriateness of particular affects for particular objects. However, we might still say that there is a tendency for positive evaluation (of unspecified quality) to be transferred from the element "wife" to the element "salad." My long-standing negative evaluation of salad would work against this, of course, but that is an additional effect.

Some quantitative rule is necessary to specify the degree of evaluative transfer as a function of the evaluations of the two elements in the sentence. Something along the lines of Osgood and Tannenbaum's congruity principle seems reasonable. Thus, we assume that when elements A and B appear in thought in the sentence AB, the amount of change of evaluation of A is an inverse function of the extremity of evaluation of A and a direction function of the extremity of evaluation of B; and, conversely, for the change of evaluation of B. The direction of change of evaluation of element A is positive or negative according to whether the evaluation of element B is positive or negative. Here is a mechanism for evaluative change (or attitude change, in the operational sense of change of score on an evaluative scale). Evaluative change takes place whenever one or both elements in a cognized sentence have non-zero evaluations. Except for the case of direct affective experience with the object symbolized by an element, most of our image of the environment is cognitively mediated. Many attitude objects are quite remote from the realm of direct object experience; for example, Communism, Congress, fluoridated water, etc., etc. The explanation of racial prejudice in terms of contact with prevailing attitudes rather than contact with Negroes falls, of course, in the mediational category, too.

The hooker in this postulated mechanism of evaluative change is in the phrase "a sentence present in thought." What is intended is a mental analogue of the central processing unit of a computer, or the "communication cell" in the IPL programming language system. It is assumed that but one sentence at a time can occupy the center of thought (although many sentences may be temporarily held in "working storage"). It is that one sentence to which evaluative transfer applies at any given moment. Since evaluative transfer is gradual, a sentence must remain or recur in thought over a long time period for important evaluative change effects to occur. Here is where we part company with Osgood and Tannenbaum. In giving examples of incongruous assertions that presumably should lead to extensive evaluative changes, they offered sentences like "Eisenhower praises the Bulgarians." While it is true that they allowed for a reaction of incredulity to get subjects off the hook when confronted with extreme incongruity, the present view is that there is a great deal more to getting off the hook than mere incredulity, as we shall see. For any substantial evaluative change to accrue from, say, the assertion "Eisenhower praises the Bulgarians," one must suppose that the individual keeps mulling this over: "Eisenhower praises the Bulgarians"; "Eisenhower praises the Bulgarians"...But introspectively this is absurd. Many derivative thoughts flash very rapidly through consciousness rather than simply the one original sentence. "Who says he praises the Bulgarians?" "Has he gone soft in the brain?" "Is there some hidden virtue in the Bulgarians?" "Maybe it's a propaganda device," etc. Either this, or else dropping the whole subject from attention.

A cognized sentence with elements of opposite evaluative sign will be unstable, according to cognitive balance theory. Attempts will be made to alter the sentence so as to eliminate the imbalance. In present terms, imbalance represents a situation of potential affective transfer between a cognitive element arousing positive affect and an element arousing negative affect. This is the basic aversive situation, which the mechanisms of cognitive imbalance reduction can serve to avoid or mitigate. Our computer simulation model hypothesizes a set of detailed specifications for these mechanisms. In a previous publication (Rosenberg & Abelson, 1960) we have called these detailed mechanisms "microprocesses." In the language of Miller, Galanter, and Pribram, these microprocesses are Plans for changing Images.

Previous listings of mechanisms have included the following: stopping thinking or, more properly, removing the particular sentence from thought; denial, that is, denying the truth-value of the sentence; rationalization, the acceptance of the truth-value of the sentence, but somehow deflecting its evaluative implications; differentiation, the creation of two elements to replace one element; transcendence, a difficult higher-order mechanism; and bolstering, a side process of evaluative change which has the function of compensating for some of the damage done by the imbalance; finally, we should include evaluative change by default of resistance, whereby as a consequence of the failure of all other mechanisms, substantial evaluative transfer takes place between the two elements of the key sentence.

The Model

In this paper I will sketch out a model for one of these mechanisms, namely rationalization. I shall only say enough about the other mechanisms to indicate where they fit in the total model.

Figure 1 gives the gross flow chart for the total model. We start in the upper left-hand corner with #1, "Sentence enters thought." How it got there is another question, but let us suppose it is a representation of something just heard or read. Now the general idea is that the system cycles in a clockwise direction on the diagram, and, unless there is an exit in one of three ways at the right, there is a return to the starting point with either the original sentence or a new sentence in thought. On each cycle, there is evaluative transfer between the two elements of the sentence. This might as well be represented by a routine, #3, through which the process must pass each cycle. Prior to routine #3 is #2, "Is sentence explicable?" For a sentence to be

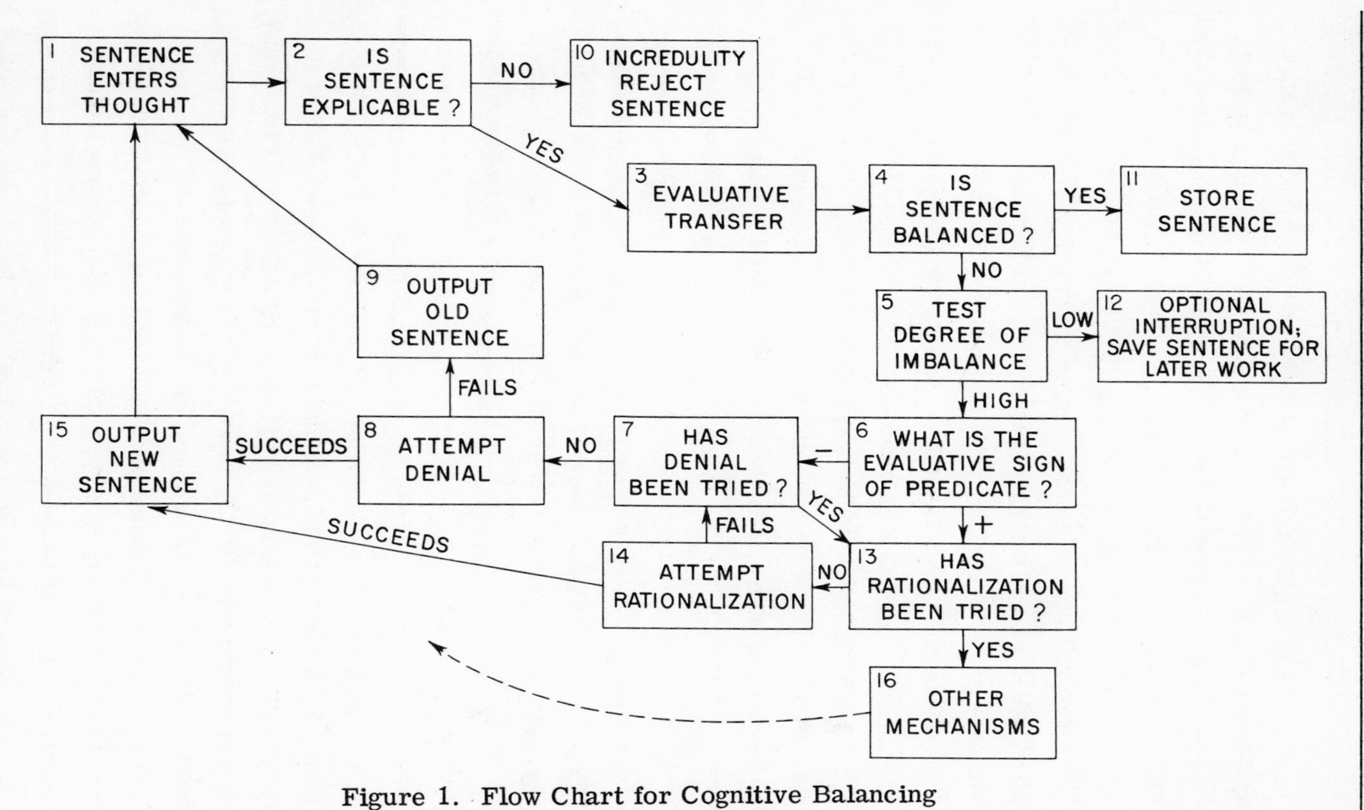

Figure 1. Flow Chart for Cognitive Balancing

inexplicable means that there is no context in which it makes sense, that there is nothing in memory which could provide an explication for it. The function of routine #2 is to substitute a meaningful sentence, if any, for any ambiguous sentence. If I were to assert, "There is a spy in this room," you would be forced to explicate this assertion by finding some context in which the word spy would be presently appropriate. If no explication is found, then there is a reaction of incredulity, #10. If the sentence is clarified, then the clarified sentence is sent through routine #3 to a balance test, #4.

If the sentence is balanced, then it ends up stored in memory via #11. If the sentence is not balanced, that is, if the evaluative signs of the two elements are opposite, then there is a test, #5, of the degree of imbalance. The degree of imbalance is a function of the extremity of evaluation of the two objects. Imbalance is greatest when the two evaluations are equally and highly extreme in opposite directions. Without getting tangled for now in a quantitative specification of this function, we may imagine that at any moment there is a quantitative threshold for degree of imbalance. If degree of imbalance exceeds the threshold, the test sends the process into the lower arm at #5. Otherwise, the process moves to #12 at the right. Parenthetically, I might remark that the threshold for imbalance is conceptualized as a variable, sensitive to such factors as the mood of the individual and the number of cycles through which the process has already passed.

First let us dispose of the low degree of imbalance alternative. If the sentence is not really disturbing, for example, "My friend got a parking ticket," then the individual may or may not spend further cognitive effort on it, but go on to something else instead. This is the meaning of the phrase "optional interruption." Or he may save the sentence in temporary storage and come back to it later for further thought or transfer to permanent memory. A further alternative, not explicitly listed in box #12, is that the individual may treat the sentence humorously, engaging in playful elaborations upon it. So long as the degree of imbalance is low, the thought process need not follow the route through #5 intended for more "serious" problems.

Routine #6 is a simple one which merely establishes whether the evaluative sign of the predicate is positive or negative; in other words, whether the action specified in the predicate presages good or bad consequences. If these consequences are good, the individual would presumably like to believe in them, and thus should prefer rationalization to denial. Conversely, if the consequences are bad, the individual ought to prefer denial to rationalization. Thus the test in #6 offers a plausible way to establish a hierarchical order between the mechanisms of rationalization and denial.

Examples may help. Remember that in order to get to #6, a sentence must be highly imbalanced. An imbalanced sentence with a negative predicate might be "The new president of my club (a splendid and admirable fellow) has completely ruined the club's financial standing." Introspectively one senses an initial impulse to say, "He didn't do it! "—that is, a preference for denial rather than a rationalization, "Well, he may have done it, but it wasn't his fault, you see, because of such-and-such."

An imbalanced sentence with a positive predicate is the hypothetical news item, "Southern Senators may abandon civil rights filibuster." Here the first impulse is to accept the sentence with a rationalization, such as "They know they can't win," rather than to deny it.

These first impulses need not necessarily eventuate in the success of the first mechanism. Let us trace through the possibilities, starting with the denial arm at #7. "Has denial been tried?" serves a branching function. During the first cycle around, the answer is No and we go to #8, "Attempt denial." If denial fails, we come through #9 back to #1 and the original sentence re-enters thought. For example, the individual may think, "Yes, our wonderful club president really ruined us. I still don't understand it, but..." And around we go again, with a further shot of evaluative transfer (the president now seeming somewhat less wonderful and the ruination of club finances now seeming somewhat less disastrous). The sentence is still unbalanced, though the degree of imbalance is somewhat lessened by the evaluative transfer and the process may slide off into #12. Assume, however, that the degree of imbalance is still high and we get around through #6 and #7. This time denial has already been tried, so the process goes to #14 which asks whether rationalization has been tried.

Now let us interrupt this chain of events and return to the denial attempt on the first cycle. Suppose instead that it succeeds. The individual may think, "The president actually helped the club's finances (and I can tell you why)." With this outcome, the process moves through #15 back to #1, and this time the new sentence, the negation of the original one, enters thought. *This* sentence results in evaluative transfer which tends to restore rather than wash out the original evaluations. This sentence is balanced and gets stored.

Returning again to a first-cycle situation, suppose that the evaluative sign of the predicate is positive, and rationalization is tried first. The process moves through #6 to #13 and then #14. Suppose the sentence is "Russia suggests United Nations control of East Berlin." Rationalization may well fail, in which case the process moves to #7, "Has denial been tried?" On the first cycle the answer is No, so that denial is attempted, and so on. On the other hand, if rationalization succeeds, a new sentence is formulated such as, "The Russian suggestion is a propaganda trick." This sentence then passes along the upper arm.

You may work through the one or two other possible chains at leisure. Routine #16, "Other mechanisms," is here used as a residual category, since no details will be specified. Our chief specific interest is in the details of #14, the rationalization routine.

Before moving on to that, let me broadcast some general words of caution about the model envisaged here. First of all, the scheme is a little too neat. Cognition, like all open processes, is interruptable. Something more demanding, or more interesting, or what-have-you, may intervene while the process is in mid-stream. To be specific, the individual might be engaged in a political debate or an office quarrel or a scholarly discussion, and the antagonist may persist in introducing new assertions to defend previous assertions. Therefore the cognitive arena may after ten minutes assume the dishevelment of a used convention hall, strewn with bits and scraps of half-digested sentences. Even without interruptions, even in quiet contemplation, the several process routines will develop by-products which will divert the process into channels difficult to capture in a deterministic model. If our cognitive hero had resolved the sentence about the Russian suggestion with the denial "Russia would violently oppose UN presence in East Berlin," he might then be stricken with the new sentence, "The Berlin situation is awful," and find himself ruminating on that one for awhile. The conceptual problems posed for the simulation model are not insurmountable, but it is hard to specify non-gratuitous processes to keep the system running autonomously beyond the input of a single sentence.

A second difficulty related to this first one is that in experimental manipulations designed to cram particular sentences into subjects' thought, there is no guarantee that what goes in is what was intended. Take a sentence like "My neighbor set afire my house." There are two distinct courses of concern to the individual here. One concerns the negative fact given within the predicate, which when transformed into a sentence becomes "My house has been set afire." The second concerns the entire original sentence, "My neighbor set afire to my house." If my neighbor is a dangerous paranoid, the second sentence is cognitively balanced, but the first is not. The issue of double import of sentences, in the senses of (1) consistency, and (2) hedonic gain or loss, has arisen in work I did jointly with Rosenberg (Rosenberg & Abelson, 1960) and subsequently in a separate study of Rosenberg's (Rosenberg, 1962). The question of operational priority between the two types has not been foreclosed in the model, but the intent is for both types to run through the flow chart.

A third caution about the general model has to do with the question of individual differences, so pointedly raised in the discussion following Dr. Reitman's paper (see the résumé in

Chapter 19). Referring to Figure 1, one might imagine at least four levels at which individuals might differ. They might all have the same processes and flow chart, but differ in the content of their belief systems; they might have essentially the same processes available, but differently hooked together; they might differ because some individuals lacked some of the processes (for instance, the explication of sentences is undoubtedly a function of intelligence, so that dullards might lack routine #2); lastly, and most ghastly, individuals might have different processes entirely, differently hooked together. I would like to believe that individuals differ primarily in belief content and secondarily in style, that is, the relative degree of development of different processes.

Let us turn now to Figure 2, which gets as specific as I will get about the model in this paper. This figure explicates the routines within #14, "Attempt rationalization." The notation used is as follows: the sentence entering the routine is denoted xY. Lower-cased letters refer to concepts, upper-cased letters to predicates. The letter z refers to a third element which is retrieved from storage to suit the purposes of the particular sub-routine. There are three sub-routines, named "Reinterpret final goal," "Accidental by-product," and "Find the prime mover."

In "Reinterpret final goal" the general idea is to generate an implication of the sentence predicate which reverses the evaluative sign of that predicate. For example, starting with the sentence "My simulation produced silly results," the predicate Y is "Produced silly results." The first box says "transform Y to y." That is, drop out "produced" from "silly results." Next, retrieve from memory sentences for which y is the concept and some third element Z is the predicate. This search operation generates candidates for the role of the Z-element one at a time. Each candidate for this role undergoes two tests. If either of these fails, a new candidate is generated. The first test requires that Z be evaluatively more polarized than the original predicate Y, and the second requires that a new sentence xZ be both explicable and balanced. If both tests succeed, then a new sentence is output. Specifically, in terms of our example, the generate Z routine may come up with "Silly results are non-publishable." Suppose that non-publishability is evaluatively more negative than silliness per se. The first test is passed. But the sentence xZ, "My simulation is non-publishable," is not balanced, since the concept is positive and the predicate negative. This then is rejected as a rationalization for "My simulation produced silly results" (though it perhaps also creates a new sentence for subsequent worry). Suppose next that the generator comes up with "Silly results enrich my understanding." If "enrichment of understanding" is more evaluatively positive than "silly results" is negative, then the first test is passed. Further, the sentence "My simulation enriches my understanding" is explicable and balanced. The box that says "Name xY as w" indicates a process by which the original sentence "My simulation produced silly results" is "condensed," as it were, into a single element, call it "That early-run failure." Finally, what is output is the sentence, "That early-run failure enriched my understanding."

In the "Accidental by-product" routine, the third element, the Z, is a predicate which interposes between x and Y and "explains" as accidental the issuance of bad Y from good x or good Y from bad x. For example, Z might be "Having program bugs," and the rationalization is, "My simulation had program

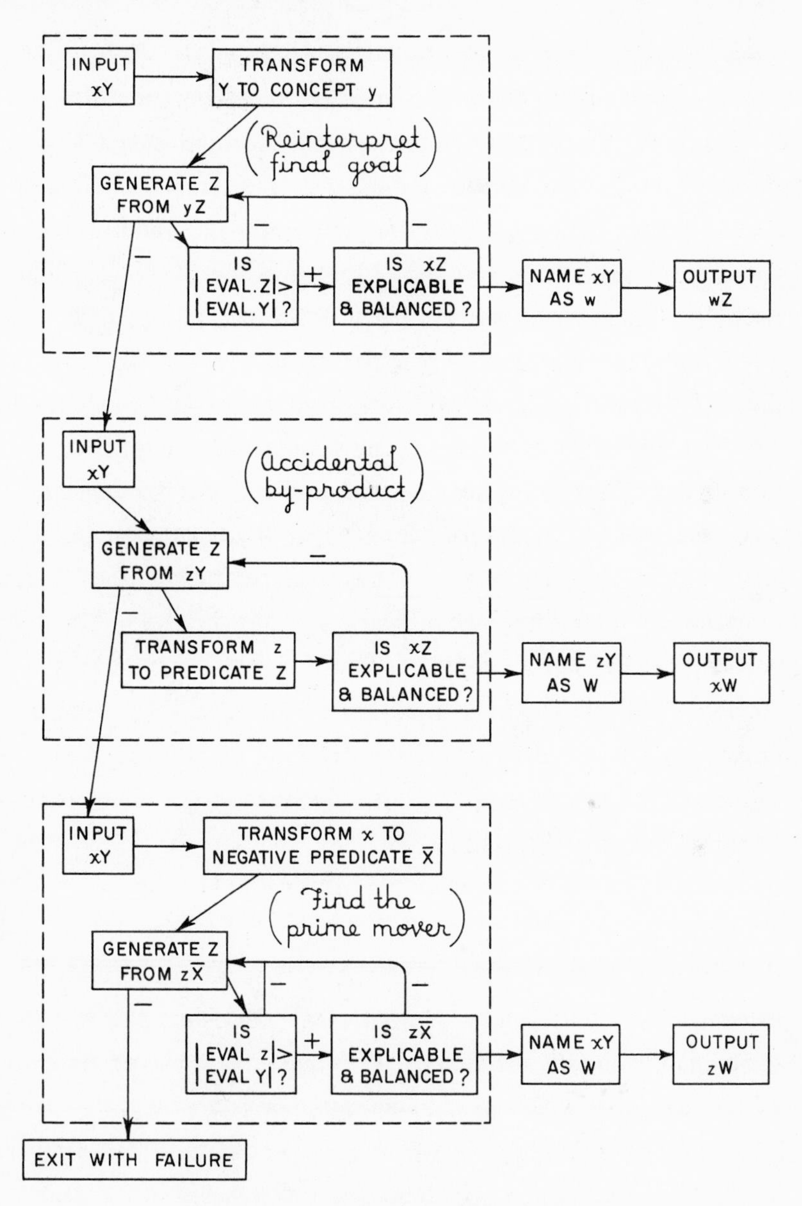

Figure 2. "Attempt Rationalization"

bugs which caused silly results." The renaming routine would put "Program bugs caused silly results" together as an element, let us call it "The usual trouble," so that the final product is "My simulation had the usual trouble."

The third routine, "Find the prime mover," puts the retrieved third element at the left of the sentence. This element might be "That crazy programmer." With the renaming of xY as "that early-run failure," the output sentence becomes "That crazy programmer caused that early-run failure."

These routines are now in the process of being programmed. A great many loose ends remain in the theoretical system, but I hope that I have given some idea of the lines along which it is possible to develop a model in this area.

18 | DAVID L. ROSENHAN
Educational Testing Service

Discussion: Affect and Attitude Structure in Simulating "Hot" Cognition

In listening to Abelson's paper, as indeed to several others, I was impressed by several things. First off, the modesty of his paper, like that of Reitman's, was striking. Gone were the claims that computer simulation might save psychology, or at least personality theory. Gone also were the global, literary terms which so abound in some areas of psychology, intuitively meaningful perhaps, but by no means amenable to the specificity of experimental endeavor.

I was also grateful for definitions in Abelson's paper—precise, perhaps debatable, but nevertheless clearly defining the territory upon which he stands. The theory terms which have cropped up most often in this conference are, I think, Cognition, Affect, and Consciousness. I, for one, do not quite know what Cognition means, and I gather from recent journal articles that I am not alone. I fail to fathom the limits of the term Cognition (particularly, I suppose, when people speak of unconscious

---

This paper was read while the author was affiliated with the Department of Psychology, University of Pennsylvania.

cognitions). The same is true for Affects and for Consciousness. What is the difference between an Affect and an evaluation? Are Affects Conscious? Etc., etc. I protest that I am not thinking small in this respect; that indeed, I could hardly hold a larger difference with Dr. Reitman's admonition (Chapter 4). Reasonably "tight" definitions are different things from thinking small, and Abelson's paper is interesting in part because of the care he took in defining his area of concern.

Abelson's distinction between rationalization and denial, and particularly to the circumstances which lead to a choice of one defense over the other, exemplifies virtues of moleculalarity and process specificity for which computers may be of assistance. If one is attracted to the concept of defenses in the first place, then the choice among defenses is a crucial and hitherto unspecified variable. It is significant that both Blum (Chapter 7) and Abelson, concerned with different processes but employing molecular models, have been able to make plausible theoretical forays into this area. Blum and his colleagues are already attacking this problem experimentally, and it is clear that Abelson's model is also amenable to experimental (noncomputer) verification. These are advantages not to be ignored, and I expect they arise in large part from the careful specificity of their models.

It should be clear by now that I possess a high positive evaluation of Abelson and a high positive evaluation of his theory. Thus, cognitive imbalance is below threshold and his paper, in its entirety, will be stored in memory via the route #3 to #4 to #11. This is perhaps acceptable to Abelson, but hardly leads to hot discussion. There are, nevertheless, several issues which trouble me about his theory.

Abelson defined belief as including "the conviction of the truth of propositions." In his model, conviction or certainty does not vary. In fact, however, certainty is variable: People are more certain about some things, less certain about others. Moreover, it is probably true that the degree to which a belief system is invested with affect (regardless of sign) determines in part the degree of certainty with which that belief is held. Finally, and by the same token, it is conceivable that the degree of certainty associated with a belief (and not merely the content of the belief) affects the intensity of feeling invested in belief. Thus, a deep conviction of the verity of a deity is, by itself, likely to generate powerful attitudes toward the deity.

A more disturbing aspect of the theory lies in the requirement that cognitive elements and sentences, and hence attitudes, must "appear in thought." That is, there must be awareness. This requirement makes it clear that the model can accommodate only those attitudes which are isolated or so encapsulated that they lie, as it were, apart from attitudinal networks or hierarchies, particularly those that are unconscious. Where, however, the attitude is embedded in, or perhaps the result of, other broader and more powerful attitudes, it is hard to predict what will happen. Take, for example, a negative attitude towards an employer which is embedded in a powerful and generalized negative attitude towards authority. Now the employer performs a generous and benign act. Does attitude toward the employer change? And if so, does the larger attitude towards authority also change, even if the subject was not aware of it? Or does it, because of its rootedness elsewhere, remain impervious to the new information, or only momentarily responsive, such that the alterations in attitude towards the employer are unstable? The requirement that one and only one sentence appear in thought at a given time, necessitated by the limitations of the computer, makes it difficult for the model to accommodate these possibilities.

Finally, there is throughout the theory an implicit equation of affects. All affects are held to operate on beliefs in the same manner. Thus the amount of evalutive change in sentence AB is said to be some function of the extremity of the evaluations of the elements (that is, the extremity of the affects associated with the individual beliefs). As Abelson has stated, we know very little about the operations of "hot cognitions"—and, for that matter, about "hot behavior." But at least insofar as anxiety is concerned, current evidence would suggest that it operates differently from other affects in that beyond certain (unspecified) moderate limits it exerts a marked inhibitory effect. Thus, small amounts of anxiety associated with a belief might operate in the manner which Abelson posits, but larger amounts would exert greater resistance to change than "equal quantities" of other affects. It would be necessary, therefore, to specify a more complex model for antagonistic attitudes, depending on the nature of the antagonism and of the associated affect.

In sum, most of what has been said above, if valid, can easily be incorporated into the model in time. This fact alone is tribute to the care which Abelson has taken in designing the structure of his theory.

PART IV

RÉSUMÉ

19

SAMUEL MESSICK
Educational Testing Service

Computer Models and Personality Theory

Webster defines "simulation" as "false resemblance, as through imitation," and "to simulate" is "to pretend, to feign, or to have the external characteristics" of some prototype. Yet a synonym listed for "simulate" is " to assume," which has somewhat different and more respectable connotations for scientific endeavor. Unfortunately, overtones of these common meanings of simulation blended with more technical and specialized usages in discussions at the present conference, to color and frequently confound specific issues raised by the formal presentations. Running throughout the conference was a constant interplay of confusion centering upon the meaning of the word "simulation" in the context of personality theorizing, upon the intentions of the simulators, and upon the precise delimitation of the

---

The preparation of this resume was partly supported by the Mental Health Training Grant Program, National Institute of Mental Health, United States Public Health Service, under Grant No. 2M-9453 to Educational Testing Service. The paper was completed while the author was a Fellow at the Center for Advanced Study in the Behavioral Sciences. The author wishes to thank Alvin Gouldner and Perry London for their helpful comments on the manuscript.

objects of simulation. In fact, so much more heat than light was shed upon these issues at some of the sessions that we were sorry the term "simulation" had been introduced at all. Yet the conference was so named and could hardly be changed after the fact. Besides, some of the argument may have had a substantive as well as a semantic base, so that an attempt at clarification seems warranted. The issue is joined: What is computer simulation of personality and what are its possible contributions to personality theory?

These questions will be addressed by examining computer simulation as language translation, as mimic, and as model and by discussing the context of simulation and the role of individual differences in computer formulations.

Uses of Computer Simulation in Psychology

Simulation as Language Translation

In the course of computer simulation, the necessity to translate verbal descriptions of process and action into the precise language of the computer program often provides the incentive for rigorous thinking in specifying the psychological properties under investigation. The specific mechanisms and sequences of steps necessary to write a workable computer program frequently require more detail than the available psychological conceptualizations can provide. This requirement serves as an impetus for empirical investigations to ascertain missing information and for rigorous theoretical analyses to specify consequent relationships (cf. Feldman, 1962). Thus, as Reitman (Chapter 4) and Uhr (Chapter 14) have emphasized, attempts at computer simulation serve an important function in the objectification of theories, in requiring the detailed representation of psychological processes in a rigorous language. Once formulated in these terms, the actual running of the program on a computer can provide information about further implications of the theory and about possible inconsistencies in it.

In underscoring the values of objectification obtained by translating verbal and mathematical models of psychological processes into computer terms, however, one should not overlook the possibility that the potential power of the computer for resolving complexity may thereby be kept at a relatively low level—namely, at the level of complexity embodied by the verbal and mathematical models being translated. Thus, although the objectification of existing theories by translating them into a rigorous language is a significant aim in itself, even greater contributions may accrue from attempts to formulate psychological theories directly in computer terms, thereby taking advantage of the massive increase in the complexity of interrelationships that can be assimilated.

Simulation as Mimic

One important application of computer simulation has involved the design of computers and programs to imitate a response pattern or the end product of an activity, without particular regard for the process by which the end product is achieved. Thus, in artificial intelligence systems the concern is primarily with the solution of a problem or the performance of an activity like chess-playing, with no necessary attempt to imitate the processes by which a human being solves the problem or plays chess. In fact, the speed and algorithmic capabilities of the computer are often deliberately capitalized upon for "intelligence amplification," generating problem solutions faster and more systematically than a human being possibly could. This type of programming differs from simulation in intent but often also bears some similarity, in that stimulus characteristics and their coding may be portrayed and human-like response patterns generated. These artificial intelligence systems, however, were not particularly germane to the present conference: The discussions of personality simulation emphasized the appropriate representation of processes as well as the imitation of end products.

Given the intention of representing human processes and response patterns in computer terms, how much of the human system must be captured in the simulation to achieve an adequate representation? In simulating a particular personality system or process, which human characteristics are salient and how many other characteristics should be incorporated? Should a computer simulation of affective and cognitive relationships be expected to tell jokes? Although it seems obvious that a computer simulating a neurotic personality need not lie on a couch to emit responses, should a simulation of pattern perception include somewhere in the computer-program complex a section that resembles a retina? The problems of delimiting the object of simulation and of specifying the salient characteristics in the corresponding human process are difficult to communicate, and sometimes different conceptions of the intent of particular simulations arose at the present conference. In these different expectations there appeared to be a bias for evaluating programs against the criterion of "strong" or extensive mimicry, and the attendant criticisms, being at different levels, were not always appropriate. These issues may be clarified by considering computer simulations as psychological models and by discussing the characteristics of models, their role and evaluation.

Simulation as Model

A computer program purporting to simulate certain psychological processes constitutes in a formal sense a model of that particular psychological domain (Lachman, 1960). The program comprises a separate representational system in which symbols are defined in correspondence to properties of psychological variables, relationships among these variables are specified, and rules of inference are usually incorporated. The role of such a model in theory construction is thus no different from that of a mathematical or verbal model: The psychological theory can be stated in terms of a presumed correspondence or isomorphism between certain properties, operations, and relations within the model and certain specified operations and relations in the empirical domain. Given rules of inference, which are usually included in the model in terms of computer operations and logic, consequences may be derived from the initial specifications and relations that are empirically testable. These consequences may be examined to ascertain the consistency of the model as a formal system, but the ultimate evaluation of the program as a psychological theory rests, as with mathematical and verbal models, upon the validity of the empirical consequences. That is, computer models of psychological processes are tested in the same manner as other models—in terms of their goodness-of-fit in describing empirical results and the validity of their derived consequences in predicting empirical relationships.

Thus, computer models are not *tested* by running them on the computer, as some observers apparently feel is the contention. Running the program on the computer serves an extremely important function, but not that of testing the model. Rather, the computer run permits the implications of the model to be determined and evaluated for consistency, and it does this with two major advantages over the calculation of consequences from mathematical models and the logical or psychological analysis of verbal models: First, the implications are derived with great rapidity; second, and more important, a massive increase is effected in the complexity of relationships that can be handled and in the resulting complexity (and hopefully the adequacy) of the consequent predictions. Thus, the experimenter could change the parameters or values on several different variables at once, more than could easily be coped with conceptually or mathematically, and, by pursuing the implications of these changes on the computer, he can frequently generate genuine novelty, in the sense that an unanticipated result is encountered.

In considering computer programs as models, it is well to keep in mind that the isomorphism specified between the model and the psychological domain is an isomorphism between aspects of the two systems. The correspondence need not involve all of the elements in the model (or indeed all of the properties of selected elements), nor need it include all of the properties of the empirical phenomenon. For example, in constructing a measurement theory an isomorphism may be drawn between some of the elements of a model (usually the real numbers) and some of the elements in the empirical domain (gradations of the attribute or property of the objects to be measured) and between some of the relations and operations defined on the real numbers and certain specified empirical operations and relations. Note that all attributes of the objects are not measured at once: It is irrelevant to criticize the measurement of the length of rods varying in thickness and composition by pointing out that their weight is not thereby assessed, and it is irrelevant to criticize a computer simulation of pattern perception by objecting that color perception is not also simulated. Note also that only some of the operations and relations defined on the model elements require empirical counterparts. For example, the ordinal measurement obtained by ranking the rods from longest to shortest utilizes only the "$>$" relation on the assigned numbers and not interval and ratio properties. Nevertheless, the real numbers and this relation form an acceptable basis for a model of ordinal measurement, even though many other properties of the numbers are not utilized. Similarly, the fact that computer languages and hardware have many obvious characteristics that fail to correspond to human qualities does not reflect upon the utilization in model-building of other properties for which a useful correspondence can be drawn. Thus, the delimiting of the isomorphism between simulated mechanisms and psychological processes does not imply a derogation of the simulation as a model, but instead may provide a means of rigorously specifying the object of simulation.

"Simulation" As Red Herring

Much of the disagreement voiced at the present conference was grounded in the semantics of the term "simulation" and in a confusion about the intent of specific models as opposed to general mimics. A seductive version of this blurring of intentions appeared, for example, in the objection that symbols manipulated in a simulation of personality may represent affective properties, but they were not in fact affects. This statement is certainly true, but to frame it as an objection misses the point that computer simulations serve as models and that the distinction drawn between the representation of an object and the object itself is intrinsic to the function of models as representational systems (see Borko, 1962). In many ways it is a tribute to computer models—with their potentialities for representing dynamic integration over time and for resolving an order of complexity approaching that of the processes simulated—that such objections are raised. It is unfortunate, however, that the concomitant utilization of physical hardware in computer simulation (and perhaps the enthusiastic claims of some adherents) has permitted at the present stage of development this befuddling fantasy of the literal embodiment of the object, when such an impression would be absurd to maintain for mathematical models or verbal representations.

The Context of Simulation

In the evaluation of a computer simulation as a model of psychological process, what should be, as Kessen asked in Chapter 16, the "width of the band of permitted variation"? Over what range and at what level does the program attempt to model human mechanisms? How often should we interrupt the computer's activity "to see if it is doing the job the way Joe would"? At a broad general level, should the computer look like Joe as well as act like Joe, and should it act like Joe in eating and reproducing as well as in problem-solving? At a more atomistic level, should we be concerned that vacuum tubes and transistors have many different properties from neurons? These questions may be resolved in terms of the previous discussion of simulations as models: The nature and extensiveness of the isomorphism attempted in the model-building provides a basis for delimiting the bandwidth of permitted deviation, and the intended isomorphism may be deliberately limited to only _some_ of the properties of a personality subsystem or associated processes. In these terms, then, to criticize, for example, a simulation of a _neurotic process_ because it does not simulate a _neurotic person_ may be to lament its incompleteness or to question its realism or relevance to therapy, but it is not a criticism of the simulation as a circumscribed model.

Individual Differences and Computer Models

The ubiquity of consistent individual differences in personality raises the question of how computer models in this field would handle reliable individual variations. Should a separate simulation be specified for each individual subject, or should a generalized average individual be summarized as the object of simulation? Since individuals display many similarities as well as consistent differences, there may well be fewer dimensions of individual variation than there are individuals, so that the first, idiographic approach may prove inefficient and redundant. On the other hand, the simulation of a generalized modal prototype, by conglomerating descriptions of the average properties of several individuals, may not represent anyone particularly well. A multidimensional approach to this second, more nomothetic view would be to ascertain relevant, reliable dimensions of individual differences in the domain of interest and to construct as many simulations as there are consistent differences, or to represent the dimensions of variation as variables in the simulation and generate individual cases by varying parameters (cf. Loehlin, Chapter 11). Immediate advantages accrue to each of these alternative strategies, and at this stage in the development of computer simulation, knowledge obtained from each approach should be welcome, although the long-term contributions of the strategies may turn out to differ considerably. A mixed strategy is also possible, as exemplified in Colby's paper (Chapter 9), wherein normative mechanisms were simulated along with individualized belief contents.

Abelson (Chapter 17) pointed out that some individuals may differ from others because they lack some of the usual processes, a contingency that could easily be handled in computer simulation by by-passing some of the sub-routines in a particular program. However, even if some individuals had entirely different processes, a general model could be formulated which included all of the relevant process dimensions, but permitted some individuals to have null values on certain specified dimensions. For example, suppose ten relevant dimensions had been isolated in a particular domain by studying various groups of people, none of whom displayed all ten characteristics. A general model of the domain might stipulate all ten variables but include the proviso that each individual case generated in the model have null values on some dimensions. Thus, individual A may reveal dimensions 1, 2, and 3, while individual B displays dimensions 4, 5, and 6, or 1, 5, 8, and 9, or some other combination. Such a formulation is consistent, for example, with the factor analytic model (cf. Cattell, 1957), but its utilization in computer simulation would not necessarily be similarly limited to a consideration of linear relationships.

Thus, individual variation does not pose a different or more peculiar problem for the computer simulation of personality than it does for personality theory in general. Many difficulties in simulation that arise in this connection are not specific to computer formulations per se, but should be viewed as part of the general problem of making normative statements about personality from the investigation of individual differences or from individual case studies.

Promise and Compromise

On the frontier of new developments—where there is so much novel information to accumulate, so much unfamiliar material to assimilate, and so many potentially valuable procedures to try out and evaluate—there is often an understandable, but possibly undercutting tendency to compromise between the uses of the past and the developments of the new. These compromise strategies offer tremendous potential pay-off per unit cost because they efficiently utilize available procedures and information in attempting to solve new problems and in initiating new structures. Reitman (Chapter 4) has illustrated the power of such an approach in his ingenious use of the general problem-solving model (and its years of developmental effort) to formulate a description of personality as a coalition of problem-solving systems, some mutually supporting and some competing. In the course of his systematic analysis, Reitman also underscored several points where the problem-solving formulation would need to be changed to reflect appropriate personality characteristics. Thus, careful attempts to apply available models and procedures in the development of new simulations may not only efficiently characterize large portions of the new domain, but they may also focus attention quickly upon points requiring modification.

A potential danger lurks in this approach, however, particularly if it is followed as a prescription for the field: The substantive domain of interest may become subtly diverted into the domain simulatable in terms of available models and techniques. Another aspect of this danger appears in the emphasis upon objectification of existing psychological theories, a significant aim in itself and a particularly attractive undertaking since considerable work has already been done by the psychological theorist, and dramatic demonstrations or extensions might be effected in the translation. But again, attention is thereby subtly diverted from the potentially more powerful enterprise of initiating computer models of psychological processes directly, with the possibility of capitalizing upon the complexity-handling capabilities of the computer to assemble models that capture more of the dynamic contingencies and multivariate diversity of personality than available mathematical and verbal theories can cope with (cf. Abelson, 1962).

In closing, a few heuristic uses of computer simulation should be mentioned to illustrate the scope of its potential application: For example, a computer simulation might provide an experimental subject for whom conditions could be manipulated that were too extreme, time-consuming, difficult, dangerous, or unethical to attempt with human subjects without a prior basis for expectations. This technique may prove especially useful, as Colby (Chapter 9) suggested, in comparing the limits and values of many therapeutic techniques within a time span that permits an application of the results during the course of a particular therapy, but without at the same time subjecting the human patient to the possibly adverse effects of prolonged experimentation. A computer simulation of personality may also, as Loehlin (Chapter 11) indicated, provide demonstrations for teaching personality theory and a tireless, re-testable client for use in training clinical techniques.

The computer, then, offers psychology an objective language for formulating and translating personality theories and provides an elegant and rapid device for deriving implications and evaluating their consistency. In addition to the rapidity of manipulation, the computer also allows a massive increase in the complexity of the relationships manipulated and in the multiplicity of influences affecting derived consequences or predictions. By permitting changes in several parameters at once and by subjecting specified variables to many interacting influences, the computer may also generate novelty or unanticipated results, the resolution of which could be quite instructive. Another potential, perhaps more tenuous contribution of computer simulation to personality theory lies in the possibility that computer programs might provide clues to the discovery of fundamental mechanisms of human functioning. Although such clues should be generalized cautiously and tested experimentally in the context of human behavior (Kagan, Chapter 15), the possibility of such discovery should not be discounted out of hand.

Following Kelly (Chapter 13) in kind, then, we suggest that

> A computer so stolid and stern
> Can simulate man to a turn.
> Though it lacks flesh and bones
> And erogenous zones,
> It can teach—but, oh, can man learn?

BIBLIOGRAPHY

Abelson, R. P. Mathematical models of the distribution of attitudes during controversy. Paper read at Educational Testing Service conference on Contributions to Mathematical Psychology, Princeton, N. J., April 1962.

Abelson, R. P. Modes of resolution of belief dilemmas. J. Conflict Resolution, 1959, 3, 343-352.

Abelson, R. P., & Rosenberg, M. J. Symbolic psycho-logic: a model of attitudinal cognition. Behav. Sci., 1958, 3, 1-13.

Allport, G. W. Pattern and growth in personality. New York: Holt, Rinehart & Winston, 1961.

Allport, G. W. Personality. New York: Holt, 1937.

Amarel, S. On the automatic formation of a program that represents a theory. Paper presented at conference on Self-Organizing Systems, 1962, in press.

Ashby, W. R. An introduction to cybernetics. New York: Wiley, 1956.

Atkinson, J. W., & Reitman, W. R. Performance as a function of motive strength and expectancy of goal-attainment. J. abnorm. soc. Psychol., 1956, 53, 361-366.

Attneave, F. Transfer of experience with a class-schema to identification-learning of patterns and shapes. J. exp. Psychol., 1957, 54, 81-88.

Blum, G. S. The Blacky Pictures: a technique for the exploration of personality dynamics. New York: Psychological Corporation, 1950.

Blum, G S. Defense preferences in four countries. J. Proj. Tech., 1956, 20, 33-41.

Blum, G. S. A model of the mind. New York: Wiley, 1961.

Blum, G. S. Psychoanalytic behavior theory: a conceptual framework for research. In H. P. David and J. C. Brengelmann (Eds.), Perspectives in personality research. New York: Springer, 1960.

Borgatta, E. Sidesteps toward a nonspecial theory. Psychol. Rev., 1954, 61, 343-352.

Borko, H. Computer applications in the behavioral sciences. Englewood Cliffs, N. J.: Prentice-Hall, 1962.

Broadbent, D. E. Attention and the perception of speech. Scientific American, 1962, 206, 143-151.

Broadbent, D. E. Perception and communication. New York: Pergamon Press, 1958.

Buck, D., & Shoulders, K. An approach to micro-miniature printed systems. Paper read at Eastern Joint Computer Conference, Philadelphia, Pa., 1958.

Buck, R. C. On the logic of general behavior systems theory. In H. Feigl and M. Scriven (Eds.), Minnesota Studies in the Philosophy of Science, Vol. I. Minneapolis: Univer. Minnesota Press, 1956. Pp. 223-238.

Burks, A. W. Computation, behavior and structure in fixed and growing automata. Behav. Sci., 1961, 6, 5-22.

Cattell, R. B. Personality and motivation structure and measurement. Yonkers-on-Hudson, N. Y.: World Book, 1957.

Chapanis, A. Men, machines, and models. Amer. Psychologist, 1961, 16, 113-131.

Cohen, A. R. Attitudinal consequences of induced discrepancies between cognitions and behavior. Public Opin. Quart., 1960, 24, 297-318.

Dalton, M. Men who manage. New York: Wiley, 1959.

Deutsch, J. A. A theory of shape recognition. Brit. J. Psychol., 1955, 46, 30-37.

Dill, W. R., Hilton, T. L., and Reitman, W. R. The new managers. Englewood Cliffs, N. J.: Prentice-Hall, 1962.

Doyle, W. Recognition of sloppy, hand-printed characters. Proc. Western Joint Comput. Conf., 1960, 133-142.

Dunham, B. The formalization of scientific languages. Part I: The Work of Woodger and Hull. IBM J., 1957, 1, 341-348.

Erikson, E. H. Childhood and society. New York: Norton, 1950.

Farley, B. G., & Clark, W A. Simulation of self-organizing systems by digital computer. IRE Trans. Information Theory, 1954, 4, 76-84.

Feigenbaum, E. A. The simulation of verbal learning behavior. Proc. Western Joint Comput. Conf., 1961, 121-129.

Feldman, J. Computer simulation of cognitive processes. In H. Borko (Ed.), Computer applications in the behavioral sciences. Englewood Cliffs, N. J.: Prentice-Hall, 1962.

Festinger, L. A theory of cognitive dissonance. Evanston: Row, Peterson, 1957.

Fitts, P. M., & Leonard, J. A. Stimulus correlates of visual pattern recognition—a probability approach. Final Report, Contract Nonr-495(02). Columbus: The Ohio State University Research Foundation, 1957.

Gelernter, H. Realization of a geometry theorem proving machine. Proc. Int. Conf. Information Processing. Paris: UNESCO, 1960. Pp. 273-282.

George, F. H., & Handlon, J. H. Toward a general theory of behavior. Methodos, 1955, 7, 25-44.

George, F. H., & Handlon, J. H. A language for perceptual analysis. Psychol. Rev., 1957, 64, 14-25.

Grimsdale, R. L., Sumner, F. H., Tunis, C. J., & Kilburn, T. A system for the automatic recognition of patterns. Proc. IEE, 1959, Part B, 106, 210-221.

Guilford, J. P. Personality. New York: McGraw-Hill, 1959.

Hake, H. W. Contributions of psychology to the study of pattern vision. WADC Tech. Report 57-621, 1957.

Hall, C. S., & Lindzey, G. Theories of personality. New York: Wiley, 1957.

Harlow, H. F. Mice, monkeys, men, and motives. Psychol. Rev., 1953, 60, 23-32.

Harlow, H. F , & Zimmerman, R. R. Affectional responses in the infant monkey. Science, 1959, 130, 421-432.

Hartmann, H. Ego psychology and the problem of adaptation. New York: International Universities Press, 1958.

Hebb, D. O. Drives and the CNS (conceptual nervous system). Psychol. Rev., 1955, 62, 243-254.

Hebb, D. O. Organization of behavior. New York: Wiley, 1949.

Heider, F. Psychology of interpersonal relations. New York: Wiley, 1958.

Hilgard, E. R. Introduction to psychology. (3rd ed.) New York: Harcourt, Brace, & World, 1962.

Hoffman, H. S. The analogue: a new kind of teaching device. Amer. Psychologist, 1962, in press.

Howland, C. I., & Hunt, E. B. Computer simulation of concept attainment. Behav. Sci., 1960, 5, 265-267.

Hubel, D. H., & Wiesel, T. N. Receptive fields of single neurons in the cat's striate cortex. J. Physiol., 1959, 148, 574-591.

Kelly, G. A. The psychology of personal constructs. New York: Norton, 1955.

Kendler, T. S. Concept formation. Annu. Rev. Psychol., 1961, 12, 447-472.

Klein, G. S., & Krech, D. The problem of personality and its theory. J. Pers., 1951, 20, 2-23.

Lachman, R. The model in theory construction. Psychol. Rev., 1960, 67, 113-129.

Leeper, R. W., & Madison, P. Toward understanding human personalities. New York: Appleton-Century-Crofts, 1959.

Lindsay, R. K. Toward the development of a machine which comprehends. Austin: Univer. Texas, 1961. (Mimeo.)

Lorenz, K. Z. King Solomon's ring. New York: Crowell, 1952.

Lowes, J. L. The road to Xanadu: a study in the ways of the imagination. Boston: Houghton Mifflin, 1927.

Lundin, R. W. Personality. New York: Macmillan, 1961.

McKeachie, W. J. Problems and perils in controlled research in teaching. In E. R. Steinberg (Ed.), Needed Research in the Teaching of English, 1962. (Proceedings of a conference held at Carnegie Institute of Technology, May 5-7, 1962.)

Miller, G. A. The magical number seven, plus or minus two: some limits on our capacity for processing information. Psychol. Rev., 1956, 63, 81-97.

Miller, G. A., Galanter, E., & Pribram, K. H. Plans and the structure of behavior. New York: Holt, 1960.

Miller, J. G. Toward a general theory for the behavioral sciences. Amer. Psychologist, 1955, 10, 513-531.

Milner, P. M. Sensory transmission mechanisms. Canad. J. Psychol., 1958, 12, 149-158.

Murray, H. A. Explorations in personality. New York: Oxford Univer. Press, 1938.

Newell, A. A guide to GPS-2-2 program. Pittsburgh: Carnegie Institute of Technology, 1962. (A dittoed report.)

Newell, A. (Ed.). Information processing language-V manual. Englewood Cliffs, N. J.: Prentice-Hall, 1961.

Newell, A., Shaw, J. C., & Simon, H A. Elements of a theory of human problem solving. Psychol. Rev., 1958, 65, 151-166. (a)

Newell, A., Shaw, J. C., & Simon, H. A. Chess-playing programs and the problem of complexity. IBM J. Res. Develpm., 1958, 2, 320-335. (b)

Newell, A., Shaw, J. C., & Simon, H. A. Report on a general problem-solving program. Proc. Int. Conf. Information Processing. Paris: UNESCO, 1960. Pp. 256-264.

Newell, A., & Simon, H. A. Computer simulation of human thinking. Science, 1961, 134, 2011-2017.

Osgood, C. E. Method and theory in experimental psychology. New York: Oxford Univer. Press, 1953.

Osgood, C. E. & Tannenbaum, P. H. The Principle of congruity in the prediction of attitude change. Psychol. Rev., 1955, 62, 42-55.

Peirce, C. S. Collected Papers. Cambridge: Harvard Univer. Press, 1931-1958.

Piaget, J. The origins of intelligence in children. New York: International Universities Press, 1952.

Rapaport, D. The structure of psychoanalytic theory: a systematizing attempt. In S. Koch (Ed.), Psychology: a study of a science. Vol. III. New York: McGraw-Hill, 1959.

Reitman, W. R. Programming intelligent problem solvers. IRE Trans. Human Factors Electronics, 1961, 2, 27-33.

Reitman, W. R. Some Soviet studies of thinking, problem solving, and related areas. In R. A. Bauer (Ed.), Some views of Soviet psychology. Washington, D C.: American Psychological Association, 1962, in press. (a)

Reitman, W. R. Systems engineering in interdisciplinary curricula—the program at Carnegie Institute of Technology. IRE Trans. Education, 1962, 119-121. (b)

Rochester, N., Holland, J. H., Haibt, L. H., & Duda, W. L. Tests on a cell assembly theory of the action of the brain, using a large digital computer. IRE Trans. Information Theory, 1956, 2, 80-93.

Rogers, C. R. A theory of therapy, personality, and interpersonal relationships, as developed in the client-centered framework. In S. Koch (Ed.), Psychology: a study of a science. Vol. III. New York: McGraw-Hill, 1959.

Rokeach, M. The open and closed mind. New York: Basic Books, 1960.

Rosenberg, M. J. Cognitive reorganization in response to the hypnotic reversal of attitudinal affect. J. Pers., 1960, 28, 39-63.

Rosenberg, M. J. Some content determinants of tolerance for attitudinal inconsistency. J. abnorm. soc. Psychol., 1962, in press.

Rosenberg, M. J., & Abelson, R. P. An analysis of cognitive balancing. In M. J. Rosenberg, C. I. Hovland, et al., Attitude organization and change. New Haven: Yale Univer. Press, 1960.

Rosenblatt, F. Perception simulation experiments. Proc. IRE, 1960, 48, 301-309.

Rosenblatt, F. The perceptron: a probabilistic model for information storage and organization in the brain. Psychol. Rev., 1958, 65, 386-408.

Sechrest, L., & Strowig, W. Teaching machines and the individual learner. Educ. Theory, 1962, 157-169.

Selfridge, O. G. Pandemonium: a paradigm for learning. In Mechanization of thought processes. London: HMSO, 1959. Pp. 511-535.

Selfridge, O. G. & Neisser, U. Pattern recognition by machines. Scientific American, 1960, 203, 60-68.

Sherman, H. A quasi-topological method for the recognition of line patterns. Proc. Int. Conf. Information Processing. Paris: UNESCO, 1960. Pp. 232-238.

Simon, H. A. Administrative behavior. New York: Macmillan, 1947, 2nd ed., 1957.

Simon, H. A. The architecture of complexity. Proc. Amer. Phil. Soc., 1962, in press.

Sterne, L. The life and opinions of Tristram Shandy, Gentleman. New York: Fawcett Publications, Premier Books, 1962.

Stevens, Mary E. Abstract shape recognition by machine. Proc. Eastern Joint Comput. Conf., 1961, 332-351. (a)

Stevens, Mary E. A survey of automatic reading techniques. NES Report, Washington: National Bureau of Standards, 1961. (b)

Taylor, W. K. Automatic control by visual signals. In Mechanization of thought processes. London: HMSO, 1959. Pp. 841-856.

Tucker, L. R. The extensions of factor analysis to three-dimensional matrices. Paper read at Educational Testing Service Conference on Contributions to Mathematical Psychology, Princeton, N. J., April 1962.

Uhr, L. Intelligence in computers: the psychology of perception in people and in machines. Behav. Sci., 1960, 5, 177-182.

Uhr, L. Pattern recognition computers as models for form perception. Psychol. Bull., 1962, in press.

Uhr, L., & Vossler, C. A pattern recognition program that generates, evaluates, and adjusts its own operators. Proc. Western Joint Comput. Conf., 1961, 19, 555-569.

Uhr, L., & Vossler, C. The search to recognize. ONR-NBS Symposium on Character Recognition, 1962, in press.

Uhr, L., Vossler, C. & Uleman, J. Pattern recognition over distortions, by human subjects and by a computer simulation of a model for human form perception. J. exp. Psychol., 1962, 63, 227-234.

Unger, S. H. Pattern detection and recognition. Proc. IRE, 1959, 47, 1737-1752.

Uttley, A. M. The design of conditional probability computers. Information and Control, 1959, 2, 1-24.

Vanderplas, J. M., & Garvin, E. A. Complexity, association value, and practice as factors in shape recognition following paired-associates training. J. exp. Psychol., 1959, 57, 155-163.

Vossler, C., & Uhr, L. A computer simulation of pattern perception and concept formation. Bionics Symposium, 1962, in press. (a)

Vossler, C., & Uhr, L. Computer simulations of a perceptual learning model for sensory pattern recognition, concept formation, and symbol transformation. Paper presented at International Federation of Information Processing Societies, Munich, 1962. [To be published by Butterworth, London.] (b)

Weitzenhoffer, A. M., & Hilgard, E. R. Stanford Hypnotic Susceptibility Scale, Forms A and B. Palo Alto: Consulting Psychologists Press, 1959.

Whinston, A. Price coordination in decentralized systems. Unpublished doctoral dissertation, Carnegie Institute of Technology, 1962.

White, B. W. Studies in perception. In H. Borko (Ed.), Computer applications in the behavioral sciences. Englewood Cliffs, N. J.: Prentice-Hall, 1962.

White, R W. Motivation reconsidered: the concept of competence. Psychol. Rev., 1959, 66, 297-333.

Wiener, N. Cybernetics. (2nd ed.) New York: Wiley, 1961.

Wiesner, J. B. Communication sciences in a university environment. IBM J. Res. Develpm., 1958, 2, 268-275.

Wolpe, J. Psychotherapy by reciprocal inhibition. Stanford, Calif.: Stanford Univer. Press, 1958

Yngve, V H. Computer programs for translation. Scientific American, 1962, 206, 68-87.

Zipf, G. K. Human behavior and the principle of least effort. Cambridge, Mass.: Addison-Wesley, 1949.